Totch

Totch

A life in the Everglades

Loren G. "Totch" Brown

with a foreword by
Peter Matthiessen

University Press of Florida
Gainesville   Tallahassee   Tampa   Boca Raton
Pensacola   Orlando   Miami   Jacksonville

98   97   96   95   94   6   5

Library of Congress Cataloging in Publication Data

Brown, Loren G. Totch
  Totch: a life in the Everglades / Loren G. "Totch" Brown: with
  a foreword by Peter Matthiessen.
    p.   cm.
  ISBN 0-8130-1227-9.—ISBN 0-8130-1228-7 (pbk.)
  1. Everglades (Fla.)—Social life and customs.   2. Brown, Loren G.
  Totch   3. Everglades (Fla.)—Biography.   I. Title.
  F317.E9B76   1993
  975.9'39—dc20   93-4529

The University Press of Florida is the scholarly publishing agency for the State
University System of Florida, comprised of Florida A&M University, Florida Atlantic
University, Florida International University, Florida State University, University of
Central Florida, University of Florida, University of North Florida, University of
South Florida, and University of West Florida.

University Press of Florida
15 Northwest 15th Street
Gainesville, FL 32611

Contents

Foreword by Peter Matthiessen   vii
Preface   ix
Maps   2, 3

1 / Layout of the country . . . pioneers and outlaws . . . 1880 to
   1915   1

2 / Everglades City, a one-man town . . . 1920 to 1926   16

3 / Miami and Possum Key . . . the Depression . . . pickled
   grasshoppers and swamp angels   29

4 / Coon-trapping and fire-hunting . . . life at Camp Huston   40

5 / Liquor Still Bay . . . making 'shine . . . Prohibition bugs   53

6 / The old Watson place . . . shooting the bull . . .
   Uncle Doc and Big Boy   64

7 / Life at Chatham Bend . . . my first boat . . . how to catch a boar
   gator   75

8 / School days on Chokoloskee   82

9 / A man at fourteen . . . the squall of the panther . . .
   fifty long miles in a rowboat   89

10 / Showdown at Jewfish Creek . . . a dolphin and her baby   102

11 / Dying on the full moon . . . the Queen of the Everglades . . .
   a terrible fire   107

12 / World War II . . . remembering the River Rhine   119

13 / Stone-crabbing with Dollar Bill   128

14 / A new kind of fishing . . . pompanoing with the Queen . . .
   adventures in the *Fraulein*   136

15 / Lost in the Everglades   152

16 / The Seminoles in their Everglades   157

17 / Hunting for gators . . . the white ghost . . .Hurricane
    Donna   165

18 / Hell and high water   175

19 / Stranded in the Okefenokee Swamp   179

20 / The habits of alligators . . . the Hamilton Lakes . . . hide-and-
    go-seek with Little Eddie   187

21 / Making a movie . . . charter-boating with celebrities . . .
    my second heart attack   196

22 / Pot-hauling and passwords   206

23 / Crooks and problems . . . a trip to Colombia . . .
    learning the game   217

24 / The *Gambler* and the *Joker* . . . a perfect haul . . .
    Operation Everglades   229

Appendix 1 / What's happening to the Everglades?   239

Appendix 2 / The life and times of Grandfather McKinney   249

Appendix 3 / Captain Totch's recipe for Chokoloskee
                Chowder   267

Appendix 4 / Citation for a Bronze Star   269

Foreword
by Peter Matthiessen

Totch Brown's lively memoirs of vanished days in the Ten Thousand Islands—the last real frontier in Florida—are invaluable as well as entertaining. A wonderful background to his stories are the picturesque, wry reminiscences of his grandfather Charles G. McKinney that appear as an appendix to this volume. Mr. McKinney, born before the Civil War, provides much of the atmosphere of early frontier days in remote southwest Florida that were drawing to a close with the construction of the roadway across the Everglades known as the Tamiami Trail and that came to an end in 1947 with the transfer of this great, wild region, which includes the Ten Thousand Islands, to the Everglades National Park. (Even today the park remains the largest roadless area in the United States, but the Indian people who once lived freely in the Shark River headwaters and hammocks are now confined to narrow enclaves along the Trail, and the bear and panther and other creatures so common in McKinney's day and still met with in Totch Brown's boyhood are now all but gone.)

Totch himself was lucky enough to spend much of his youth in what is now the park, hunting and fishing and trapping with father and brother along the Huston and Chatham rivers and later exploring farther south to the mouth of Shark River and around Cape Sable all the way eastward to the Keys. In the Depression years, his father, John J. Brown, eked out the family's existence with moonshine stills constructed here and there along the rivers. Totch would later augment his own income as a commercial fisherman by hunting alligators, a livelihood he continued illegally within park boundaries for many years after the park came in. Later still, he would join in the marijuana smuggling that was rampant for many years along this labyrinthine coast, until eventually he ran a large pot-hauling operation back and forth across the Caribbean from Colombia. Thus he has lived much of his life along the edges of the law.

What is fascinating about *Totch: A Life in the Everglades* and about Totch himself (who has this in common with many men, past and present, along this coast) is the combination of a sometimes law-less life with law-abiding and civic-minded principles. As Sergeant Loren Brown, he was a decorated World War II hero, and he has always been and remains today a good husband and father, respected in his community as a fine fisherman and hunter and a generous neighbor.

In many research trips to Chokoloskee Bay and the Ten Thousand Islands, I have often camped at places mentioned in this vivid book, including the site of the original (1880) Brown farm at Everglade (now owned and occupied by Outward Bound) and the Watson place on Chatham River, where Totch himself lived in the early thirties. I owe Totch Brown (and many of his relatives and neighbors, including his late brother Bert) a considerable debt of thanks for his generous help in research for my own work. One has only to read a few pages of his fresh, colorful, and unabashed autobiography to know that Totch Brown, in depicting his own life, has created an invaluable record of the Everglades country and its people.

Preface

From scratching out a living as an alligator-hunter and commercial fisherman to smuggling marijuana from Colombia to the hidden waters of Florida's Ten Thousand Islands: that's just the beginning and end of this story. The most interesting part, to my opinion, comes in between: the frontier style of life I lived in the untamed Everglades. The Islands, a part of the Glades, are located along Florida's southwest Gulf coast, a "country" like no other place in the United States.

That way of living—free but hard—started for my family in 1880, when my paternal great-grandfather, John J. Brown, settled here on Florida's last frontier. Soon after, my maternal grandfather, Charles G. McKinney, came to the frontier and started a forty-year career as midwife, dentist, storekeeper, and sage.

Along with the pioneers came a desperado named Ed J. Watson in the 1890s, who claimed he'd killed the woman outlaw Belle Starr in Oklahoma, and was on the run from her lover, Jesse James. Whether he did or he didn't, he bloodied the water around the Islands, making believers out of many who didn't live to tell it. Outlaws like Watson were followed by lesser lawbreakers—plume-hunters, bank robbers, and when Prohibition came along in the 1920s, moonshiners and rumrunners.

For nearly a century it was a challenging and rewarding way of life. But as time rocked on, changes in the Everglades made it hard to earn a living fishing or hunting—so hard that by the 1970s many good family men got around to feeling that to survive, they'd just have to break the law themselves, or leave the country.

That's when the Glades and the Islands became a marijuana smuggler's paradise, and when my own way of life changed completely. Instead of stone crab or mackerel, I loaded my seventy-two-foot shrimp boat in Colombia with all the pot she'd float with, and drove 'er home across the Caribbean. Until then I'd thought hunting alligators up to fourteen foot, with some of 'em coming at me head-on, was scary enough, but the fright that came with pot-hauling would scare a full-grown tomcat out of all nine of his lives. Along with the frights, though, came experiences so exciting they'd make a sick man well.

All the same, hauling marijuana wasn't really my way of life. It was a means of survival when the chips were down. But the life I lived in the Everglades as a gator-hunter and commercial fisherman is an altogether different story. It was a way of surviving against odds as heavy as they come, in a country my forefathers made their own—a way of life that is probably gone forever.

While life in the Everglades was no picnic, the privilege of living a free life that close to nature was worth all the hardships that came with it: coping with alligators, panthers, and rattlesnakes on muddy lands filled with poison ivy, spiders, and mosquitoes so thick you could rake 'em off your brow by the handful. In 1934, when I was fourteen, times got so hard I quit school and started working full-time. By the time I was thirteen I had my own small motorboat for hunting (one of the few around). As a teenager I fought my way through the Great Depression hunting raccoons and alligators. By age seventeen I owned a commercial fishing boat and was captain of my own crew. Commercial fishing was both exciting and hard, sweating out eighteen-hour workdays and storms at sea.

Then came World War II, and I became a combat infantryman, fighting my way through the Battle of the Bulge. Only this time, instead of fighting the elements for survival, it was man-to-man combat fighting for my life. When I came back from overseas, my homeland soon became the Everglades National Park and my way of life became a fight all over again, having to outrun the park rangers and the Coast Guard on the high seas.

With a life like that, I felt the only way to do it right was for me to tell it in my own style, slang and grammer included. So as my memory goes back and

> While my writing is on the flow,
> I'm going to write as though
> I'm still in the Everglades
>   as hard as I can go—
> Not only writing history
> But reliving it for you.
>
> *Totch Brown*

1 / Layout of the country . . . pioneers and outlaws . . . 1880 to 1915

"The country" is made up of a group of mangrove keys known as the Ten Thousand Islands, laying along Florida's southwest coast. A narrow strip maybe five miles wide of low mangrove mainland separates the Islands from the western Everglades. Both the Islands and the Glades are too low to live on except for about forty small oyster-shell island mounds probably built by the Calusa Indians or some other early settlers, the books say before Christ. The mounds are two to twenty feet above sea level, ranging in size from fifty feet across to 150 acres, with Chokoloskee (pronounced Chuck-a-luskee) being the largest.

Chokoloskee Island and Everglades City are located eighty miles west of Miami just off the Tamiami Trail (U.S. 41) on State Road 29, the western gateway to the Everglades National Park. Until 1956, when a four-mile causeway was built out from Everglades City, the only way to reach the island was by boat.

In Chokoloskee's early years the only way to trade or communicate with the outside world was by sailboat to Key West. The first settlers had but few choices on how to go about making a living. In the winter months they hunted for raccoons and pretty much the year around for alligators.

There were plenty of fish, especially mullet, and for shipping out they were salted, no ice. Loggerhead turtles were kept alive on the deck of the boat. Large clams were more than plentiful and so were oysters (a little salt water kept them alive). Grandfather McKinney wrote that the Key West pet market paid up to $1.25 each for red-birds, and a good price for swallow-tailed kite eggs (used for what, I can't imagine).

Vegetables played a big part in survival in those pioneer days. The shell islands in this country are not exactly mounds, as they're often called, but more like a hilly field or a ridge, with enough soil on top of the shell in places to grow most anything. Sugarcane grew like wild, and after being made into syrup, it was shipped out by the barrel—

1

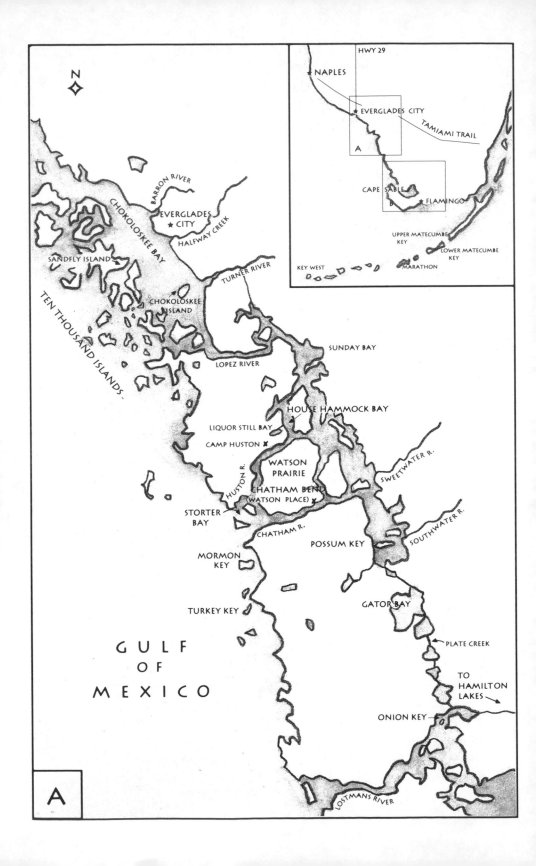

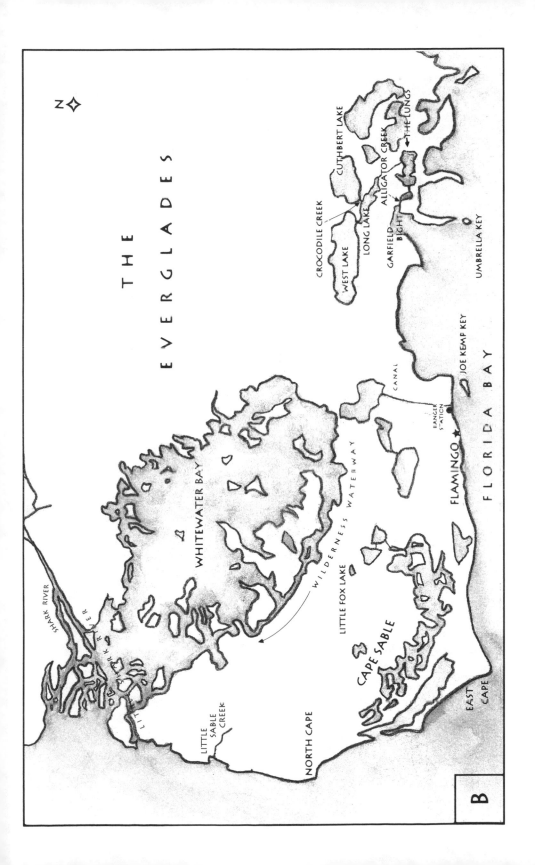

Chokoloskee Island in 1965. Courtesy of Evelyn Graham.

also the cane itself, for chewing. The stores weren't full of candy bars and the kids' pockets weren't full of quarters; a piece of sweet cane to chew on went pretty good.

The Islands were rich in fruit—guavas, sugar apples, sweet and sour oranges, limes, grapefruit, papaya, plenty of avocado pears— and there was always a good market for them. After reaching Key West much of the produce was shipped to New York by way of steam ships.

In trading, firewood probably played one of the biggest roles (remember, back then heating wasn't push-button like it is today). There's a good firewood in this country called buttonwood, similar to oak or hickory; it sold at three dollars a cord (128 cubic feet). The old-timers cut several cords a day with an ax and handsaw. Today it might be hard to find a man physically able to cut enough button-wood for a good campfire.

Getting food from the land was no problem, especially for the hunters. The waters were running over with fish, and the Glades and Islands were filled with wildlife, from deer to saltwater birds, that

Buttonwood trees, often used for firewood.

made great eating. There were usually a few cows around, but really more for milk than for meat.

Living in those pioneer days took strong men and women—many people would never have made it, not even in my time. Most of the houses were more like shacks, built out of anything from tin to palmetto fans and set up on buttonwood posts cut from the swamp, with wooden shutters or a sheet of tin or canvas for windows. The only lights were kerosene and carbide miner's lamps, for the home as well as for hunting and fishing at night. All cooking was done on a wood or kerosene stove or over an open fire.

There was no such thing as a bathroom or bathtub back then or for a long time after. For bathing, most of us used a galvanized tin washtub and a couple of buckets of rainwater caught from the roof; the women and children bathed first. The toilet was an outhouse in the back if you were lucky; otherwise, a log in the bushes to hunker

Ted Smallwood's store and post office became a museum in 1992. (Courtesy of Ted Smallwood's Store.)

down on. (I knew some people who once used a log from a poisonous tree called the manchineel—worse than poison ivy. You can guess what happened when they hunkered down on that.) Toilet paper was a rare thing, hardly ever for sale on the island. The story goes that sometime in the 1930s, a tourist stopped by Ted Smallwood's store to buy some toilet paper (my Uncle Harry Brown called it "bathroom stationery"). "No stock," Ted told the tourist. "Get yourself a mangrove root with barnacles on it. That's what we use around here."

My roots have been growing in this country for more than a hundred years. My grandfathers—C. Mel Brown and Charles G. McKinney—were among the first white people ever to try living on the shell-mound islands and the nearby wetlands of the western Glades, a country that for centuries was the hunting ground of the Calusa Indians and then the Seminoles.

Chokoloskee means "old home" in the Seminole language. When Grandfather McKinney settled on Chokoloskee, the largest of the shell islands, there were only two families living there: Adolphus

The headwaters of the Turner, leaving the mangroves and entering the Everglades.

Santini's and his brother's. Four miles north in Chokoloskee Bay (which is two miles wide by ten miles long), Grandfather Brown lived on the north bank of the Barron River (site of today's Everglades City). The Storter family, related to mine by marriage, lived nearby on the south bank. Just across the bay from the island was the home of a real old-timer, Captain Richard Bushrod Turner, veteran of the U.S. Army. Late in 1857, when the off-and-on war with the Seminoles was coming to an end, Turner and a Captain John Parkhill came to Chokoloskee with a seventy-five-man force of Florida Volunteers to hunt the Seminole leader Billy Bowlegs. Turner claimed to know the Everglades even better than Billy and talked Parkhill into hiring him as a guide. He led the Volunteers upriver through saw grass and cypress country—straight into a Seminole ambush. The Volunteers drove off the Indians, but Parkhill was killed on the spot. Years later, in the 1870s, Turner came back and built himself a home

Grandma McKinney in old age,
standing in the doorway of the
house Grandpa McKinney built
by hand.

on a large shell mound near the mouth of the same river he'd led the
Volunteers up—the Turner River, on today's maps. My mother, Alice
Jane McKinney, was born in this area in 1892.

Grandpa McKinney never went much for fishing or hunting but
seemed to get his kicks from trying to prosper. He started a post office
in High Springs, Florida, before coming here, and in 1891 he started
another one on Chokoloskee Island, along with the church and
school. In 1906 he began writing a weekly column, Will Rogers style,
for the *American Eagle* of Estero, Florida, and continued it just short
of twenty years. Eventually he came to be known as the Sage of
Chokoloskee. In 1971 the *Miami Herald* reviewed his columns and

Tintype of Grandpa
McKinney in his youth.

said, "McKinney's Writing Worth Reading Today." Here are some
samples, starting with what he wrote in 1912 when my parents-to-be
got married:

> Well, something has happened here that never did happen
> before. J.J. Brown, a kid that was raised here in the Ten
> Thousand Islands, takes Miss Alice McKinney off with him
> and says they was going to get married; we have not heard
> what they did about it. Of course, they would have to go to
> Marco [a nearby larger island] or somewhere as we have no
> official human [on Chokoloskee] and the preacher has done
> and gone.

✳   ✳   ✳

Mother (left) and Estelle's
Aunt Eire Noble Demere.

The *Ruth* (a schooner) is loading now and will leave Chokoloskee pretty near dead or at least nearer dead than usual
[because fishing and hunting were bad].

*   *   *

Fish are not very plentiful but children are doing fairly well.

*   *   *

We call this God's country because He could not give it to
anybody.

*   *   *

We had an eye carpenter [doctor] with us but most of us can
see well enough, in fact some can see too good because they
can see the faults of others and not their own.

When Grandpa was about to turn seventy-nine, the *Eagle* asked him
to sketch out the story of his life. He did just that—short, sweet,
straight to the point. (See the appendix at the back of this book for

the whole story.) I was only six years old when he died of heart failure on the dock at Everglades City in October 1926, just after the great hurricane of that year. Grandma Mckinney survived him for twenty-three years, living to be ninety-one.

About the time Grandpa first came to this country in the 1880s, feathers on women's hats were in style and there was a big demand for egret plumes. In Grandpa's little autobiography he wrote of only one hunt, for plume birds (and alligators). He went with Gregorio Lopez, his first neighbor to show up on the island. He came over from Spain and in 1890 settled on what became known as Lopez River, just south of Turner River. Grandpa wrote:

> We had just finished skinning fifteen or twenty alligators, and had dropped the carcasses in the water alongside the boat. Mr. Lopez told me to go and get some water to make coffee. The gators were thickly drifted against the boat, and I told him . . . I did not think the water very desirable for coffee. He said, "Push them out of the way." So I pushed the 'gators out of the way a little so I could get the bucket down between them. I got a bucket of clear water and we had some very good coffee. I thought if he could stand it I could also.
>
> We ate our lunch and went to the birds' nests a few hundred yards away and began to shoot the mother birds and kill them from their young; then the crows would . . . take the eggs and the young birds and carry them away to eat them. It looked too hard for me. I decided I did not think it was doing God's service, and I never went on that kind of a hunt any more.

There weren't many with a big, tender heart like Grandpa's. In his day there were outlaws and cutthroats in this country who'd shoot a man down just as quick as they'd knock down an egret, especially if he came between them and the plume birds. (They say one outlaw, John Ashley, got thirty five dollars an ounce for plumes—same as the price of gold back then.)

*　　*　　*

In 1901, when Florida passed laws to protect plume birds, the Audubon Society hired four men to be bird wardens, for thirty-five dollars a month. One was Guy M. Bradley; Dad said he was about as tough as they come.

In July 1905, Bradley ran into big trouble at a rookery called Oyster Keys, near Flamingo, seventy miles south of Chokoloskee. Bradley caught some plume-hunters red-handed—Walter Smith and his two sons. When Bradley tried to arrest one of the boys, an argument started that wound up with Smith killing Bradley in what Smith claimed was self-defense. Smith gave himself up and was put in jail on Key West. Five months later, the grand jury said they couldn't find enough evidence to charge him and he was let go.

Over the next ten years, three more bird wardens were murdered in the Glades. But you didn't have to be a warden to get bumped off in the Everglades. Back then we had killers right here on Chokoloskee that probably could have stood up to Billy the Kid. One in particular was Ed J. Watson. We've all heard of Jesse James, Doc Holliday and other famous outlaws from the West. But not many seem to have heard of Ed Watson. I guess Watson was kind of like Grandpa McKinney. Even though they were both famous in their own way, they were so hidden back in the Everglades they both lost out on their fame.

Most of what I know about Watson comes from the old-timers who knew him well, including members of my family and Henry Thompson and "Tant" Jenkins. When they were in their teens, they ran Watson's sailboat for him down to Key West. They say that around 1890, when Watson was on the run from Oklahoma—*maybe* after killing the infamous woman outlaw Belle Starr—he killed a man somewhere in south Florida. He ran still farther, winding up at Halfway Creek in Chokoloskee Bay; there he worked in the cane patch for Grandpa Brown. Soon after, he bought land up Chatham River from the widow of the owner, a man who'd been killed at the mouth of the river in a gunfight. Later Watson built himself a nice two-story home there (known both as the Watson Place and as Chatham Bend). That home played a big part in my boyhood and early manhood. Chatham Bend had thirty-five acres of good farmland on it and Watson was a good farmer. He raised a lot of

vegetables and sugarcane and shipped 'em to Key West in the sailboat he bought from Grandpa Brown's brother William. Everything
went along smooth for Watson for a while except for one incident at
Key West. He got in a scrape there with the same Adolphus Santini
who'd settled on Chokoloskee back before Grandpa McKinney, and
like to have knifed him to death—only somehow Santini recovered.

Then Watson tangled with a man named Tucker and his nephew
living on Lostmans Beach. Watson seemed to think the land they
lived on belonged to *him*, and he told 'em to get off. They refused,
and a few days later they were found dead on the beach. His bay-area
neighbors were angry enough over that to kill Watson, but he ran
again, this time up the mainland, and someplace in central Florida he
walked into a camp with two men in it. When he walked out, *they*
were dead too. Then he went back to his place on Chatham Bend.
The neighbors stayed out of his way but kept a darn close eye on him.

Over the next few years, other rough characters joined Watson at
Chatham Bend, including Leslie Cox, Dutchy Melbourne, and a man
named Waller. In October 1910, about the time a great hurricane
struck, Melbourne and Waller, along with a woman named Hannah
Smith who worked for Watson, were seen floating in Chatham River,
dead, with chains and weights tied to them, but not enough to keep
the bodies under water.

That done it—now the neighbors had had *more* than enough.
They were waiting for Watson when he showed up on the island with
his usual two guns, and they told him to give 'em up. Watson wasn't
any closer to giving up his guns than they were to turning their backs
on him, especially with his double-barrel in his hand. Instead,
Watson claimed that Leslie Cox, one of his buddies at Chatham
Bend, had done the three killings down there, plus others, and
Watson offered to bring him in. Because the neighbors figured Cox
was also a killer, they were glad to have Watson go after him. Before
leaving, he bought some shotgun shells at Ted Smallwood's.

A few days later, Watson came back in his motorboat, alone. The
neighbors could hear him coming, and by the time he tied up at
Smallwood's dock, they were standing there with guns ready. (My
mother, then a girl of seventeen, was on the beach nearby and saw
everything that happened.) Watson stepped up on the dock with a

hat in one hand, his double-barrel in the other, and a .38 revolver on his hip. He said Cox had refused flat-out to come to Chokoloskee with him, so he'd "had" to kill him; Cox had fallen in the river and sunk to the bottom. "Here's his hat," Watson added. "*It* floated."

The neighbors wouldn't go for the hat story and told Watson to give himself up. He raised his shotgun as though he meant to give up, but instead turned the gun on the crowd and pulled both triggers. But the ammunition failed to fire—the shotgun just "snapped." Watson then reached for his .38, but before he could draw, Henry Short put a bullet into him. Then everybody else opened up, and Watson went down loaded with lead.

It turned out his ammunition had been soggy. (The 1910 hurricane had just passed through, with all its rain and flooding; moisture usually damaged ammunition back then, especially shotgun shells made of paper.) Leslie Cox was never seen again. Either Watson had killed him as he said, or Cox had managed to slip away.

One of Watson's sons, Lucius, lived around Chokoloskee much of his life. Lucius was a personal friend of mine; his best friend was my brother Peg. We called Lucius "Colonel." He and I fished and hunted together. I never heard Colonel mention his dad and never knew a better man.

Things quieted down then for a while. But along about 1915, another round of killing broke out. That year, four drifters who'd fished in the bay from time to time—Hugh Alderman, a man named Tucker, and two half brothers, Leland and Frank Rice—robbed the First National Bank of Homestead, over in southeast Florida. (Criminals seemed to run in Alderman's family: Horace Alderman—called the Gulf Stream Pirate—was hanged at Fort Lauderdale in 1929 for gunning down two Coast Guardsmen and a Secret Service agent. The Coast Guard had arrested him for rum-running across the Gulf Stream, but Alderman talked 'em into letting him go back onto his boat for his belongings. He came out with his .38 a-throwin' lead. Before they could stop him, he'd put the three men on the ground.)

After the robbery at Homestead, Hugh Alderman and his buddies made their way south across the Everglades to their hid-away boat at the train trestle near Jewfish Creek, the first waterway leaving the mainland. Meanwhile, the citizens had formed a posse, found Alderman's boat and put it out of running order, and were waiting there when Alderman and his men walked up. A shoot-out began and two men in the posse were killed, two others were wounded, and the gang of robbers got away.

The robbers then poled their boat down to Key Largo and talked a fisherman into taking them to Chokoloskee Bay, a hundred or more miles north. Afraid to go directly to Chokoloskee Island, they hid out in the mangrove swamp nearby. Later, when Leland Rice and Tucker tried swimming to Chokoloskee, Tucker drowned. Rice made it to the island but was killed soon after—shot in the back by two men hoping for a reward from the bank. Sometime later, Leland's half brother, Frank, was shot trying to leave the island in a boat. Frank recovered, but he and Hugh Alderman were finally captured and sentenced to long terms in prison.

After the Homestead incident violent crime began to slow down considerable, but by no means did it come to a complete stop. The rumrunners, moonshiners, and a few others kept it going on for sometime. For a neighborhood with less than 100 people in it year-round, there was plenty of excitement

2 / Everglades City, a one-man town . . . 1920 to 1926

About the time I was born, in 1920, Dad set himself up a tannery on Chokoloskee Island. He made beautiful throw rugs out of panther, bobcat, and bear skins. He left their heads and claws on, making them really stand out. He also made alligator pocketbooks, belts, and other items. Dad soon got the idea he could do better mounting them, especially fish. But there wasn't much call in the bay area for the mounts, at least not yet. Dad soon figured out a way around that: he moved us to a place where there was plenty of demand for what he had to offer.

In 1922 our family moved eighty miles north of Chokoloskee to Fort Myers. I was only two; my oldest brother, Bert, was ten; my sister Laberta was seven; and brother Melvin (nicknamed Peg) was five. Dad set up a taxidermy shop and tannery. Mother had a job as secretary for an attorney. Just about then, a man named Barron G. Collier, who'd made millions in streetcar advertising, began to "develop" Everglades City, across the bay from Chokoloskee—and that convinced Dad to move us back there in 1924 and start a fish business. Just two years before, there'd been no city, only a small village named Everglade on the banks of the little Storter River, running from the bay back into the Glades.

In 1921 and 1922, Collier bought about a million acres around Naples and east of it, including the land to build Everglades City. He also promised the state legislature to build a good part of the proposed Tamiami Trail—a seventy-six-mile stretch across the Everglades, from one side of Florida to the other, through what was then called Lee County. That promise, plus his owning all those acres, got the legislature to change the county name to Collier, with the yet-to-be-built Everglades City as the county seat.

When he first got started on the "city" (on the site of old Everglade), the only land high enough above water to live on was a few

Aerial photo of Everglades City taken on April 26, 1928, the day the Tamiami Trail was opened in Collier County. In the background you can see the marsh the town was built on. (Courtesy of the Everglades City Council.)

spots along the riverbank. The rest was marsh and mangrove low-land—except for several acres of natural highland on the north side of the river mouth, on the edge of the Bay, where Grandpa Brown had been living since 1883. Half a mile upriver on the south side was another high spot. When Collier came, George W. Storter, Jr., was living there in the large boardinghouse he'd just built; he was the village postmaster and also owned the trading post. Storter's place really took Collier's eye. At that time, Storter had it open to the public and was offering rooms and meals like any hotel. The hunting and fishing you could do from there was something special. The fish were so thick you practically had to hide yourself to bait your hook. It was nothing to catch a hundred pounds of large snook or tarpon in one evening from a rowboat. There was also duck-hunting, with guides to take the tourists out—and plenty of quail, turkey, deer, pan-thers, and black bear just east a few miles in the Glades.

Collier made his first trip to the future city in his steam yacht, the *Baroness*. He probably stayed at Storter's in the wintertime (mos-quito off-season), saw the abundance of game, birds, and fish, and the thought came to his mind that he could turn this mangrove low-land into a sportsman's paradise—and a gold mine for Barron G. Collier.

Collier first bought out *everyone* in Everglade, including Storter. He then changed the name of the Storter place to the Rod and Gun Club; it's still there doing business today. Then he brought in a twelve-inch suction dredge and pumped in bay and river bottom to make a landfill on the east bank of what was now the Barron River; there he built a city in the mangroves. It took several years to do it all.

A mile upriver from the Rod and Gun Club, west of the present bridge, Collier built Port DuPont, a kind of supply depot. He had sev-eral large freight boats that ran up to Fort Myers for building supplies. The supplies were for three different big construction jobs: first, the Collier County stretch of the Tamiami Trail; second, forty miles of grade from Immokalee south to Everglades City for a roadway and railroad; and third, Everglades City itself.

The Trail must have been what gave him the idea of building the city to begin with; he could see it would pass within three miles of the place. When Collier got through building, he had himself a one-man town if there ever was one. Most everything in it belonged to him: drugstore, grocery, bakery, dry goods, hardware, laundry, movie the-ater, hotel, and liquor store (after Prohibition Repeal in 1933). Even the five-bed Juliet C. Collier Hospital, named for his wife, belonged to him; he paid the doctor by the month. His workers were paid part in cash, the balance in scrip (redeemable at Collier's stores). One business and one building that didn't belong to Collier, though, was my Dad's wholesale fish business and fish market—I really don't know how Dad got around him with that.

My boyhood memories were confirmed when I found an article written in 1975 by Col. Frank F. Tenney, Jr., then director of photog-raphy for the Collier County Historical Society. Tenney wrote: "Ever-glades City in 1928 was a company town pure and simple, operating

The Everglades Inn, built by Barron Collier, in the '30s (*above*) and the early '60s (*below*). (Courtesy of the Everglades City Council.)

very much like a pre–World War II military base. . . . In Everglades a whistle blew to get the people up, it blew again when it was time to go to work or school. At noon it blew again and everything closed down for an hour. At 12:55 it blew to start people back to their jobs and again at 1:00 p.m. to start work. At 5:55 p.m. it again sounded to get ready to go home, then at 6:00 p.m. to end the day's work."

Collier also put in a free electric streetcar. It ran from up near Port DuPont to "downtown," near the Rod and Gun Club. Most all the work hands rode the streetcar to their jobs and the children rode it to school. One time when I was eight, Peg talked me into playing hooky. He knew how to jump off the moving streetcar without getting hurt, but I got skinned from end to end.

The new and larger Rod and Gun Club did an unbelievable business, thanks mainly to a man named Claus Senghaas, better known as Snooky. He really knew how to make the people enjoy their stay. Snooky handled all the charter fishing arrangement, and at one time he had forty boats working from the club's guide dock.

Collier's plan turned out very successful—for a while. The railroad came in from Immokalee in 1928 and the Tamiami Trail was completed at pretty-nigh the same time. Even though the Florida land boom had collapsed by then and the Great Depression came along soon after, Everglades City done pretty good for the next twenty-five years. But in the late 1950s another place in Collier County, thirty-eight miles to the north—Naples, with its high, sandy land and beautiful beaches (and less mosquitoes)—began to win the people over, especially retired rich ones. By 1961, Naples had grown so big that the county seat and the bank were moved there. That was the beginning of the end for Everglades City. Today, though it's no longer a one-man town, Everglades City is still a quiet little place to live and for outsiders to winter in.

*   *   *

When we moved back to Everglades City from Fort Myers in 1924, I was four. This time we stopped at Grandpa and Grandma Brown's place at the river mouth. Grandpa's dad, my great-grandfather, had moved from Halfway Creek nearby to this place in 1883. Here Great-

The Storter home became the Rod and Gun Club, here shown in the early '30s.

grandfather and his three sons built a big home on a shell mound near the riverbank. Grandpa fell heir to the old place. He married Eliza Ann Stephens (later known as Aunt Toogie) and they raised their family there. In 1892 my father, John J. Brown, was born, the oldest of eight children.

Grandpa had a second house in the back that we moved into. It had no running water; instead we caught rain water from the roof and ran it into a cistern.

In 1914, eight years before Collier came on the scene, Grandpa Brown had sold half his property to a tourist from Indiana named George Bruner. Mr. Bruner built a nice home—one of the first winter homes in the area. The man who became Bruner's caretaker, Loren McCoy, was an old friend of my mother and dad, and when I was born they gave me his first name. I even wound up with his nickname. Mrs. McCoy called Loren "Tots" or "Tosh" (spelled Toch), and people started calling me the same. Well, I didn't quite like the sound of that. One day when someone called me Tosh, I said, "My name is Toch." They said, "Then put another 't' in it." I did, and I've been "Totch" ever since.

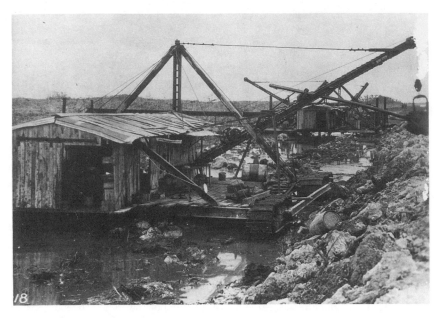

The Tamiami Trail connecting Tampa and Miami was built in 1927. *Above:* Three dredges at work on the eastern part of the Trail. *Below:* Hauling dynamite across the bogs of the Big Cypress Swamp, through which neither man nor beast may walk. (Courtesy of the Everglades City Council.)

I can just faintly recall Grandpa Brown. I remember him as a perfectly built man. He was a man of his word and liked by everyone. He
was a professional boat-builder, and until he retired in 1926, he built
most of the boats in the area. Dad came by boat-building natural:
records show that Grandpa Brown's grandfather was a boat-builder
in New York during the Civil War and may have owned a shipyard.

Grandma Brown (Aunt Toogie) always had a beautiful garden,
and she was an outstanding cook. She had a big wood stove with a
large oven and was always baking pies and making candies—some to
sell—while also spreading a big meal on Sunday with everyone
invited, especially the preacher. Aunt Toogie was very well-known
and as well-thought-of as Grandpa Brown, particularly in the Pente-
costal Church of God on the island.

After getting us all moved in at Grandpa's, Mother got a job doing
secretary work for the Collier Company, and Dad started building
boats under a big shed. I remember Dad cutting out natural-crook
timbers (large limbs or roots cut from a tree in natural shapes) for
rounded sections of the boat. It took a skilled hand and plenty of
work to cut out the timbers with an adz, an ax, and other hand tools.
I doubt there's a dozen people left in Florida today with that much
skill and energy. All this work kept him busy, but he still took out
time to make a little wooden gun for me. It shot some kind of pellet
and was painted black like a real gun.

Dad could do most anything there was to be done in this Everglades country, and he always made sure he done it right. I am not
bragging on my father, only stating the facts as I saw 'em. He was a
professional boat-builder, finish carpenter, house-builder and furni-
ture-maker, and a motor-mechanic. He was also a good mason and
did most of the cement work in this area. He never went much for
commercial fishing, but he loved to hunt—and was he ever a perfect
shot with a rifle and with a revolver from the hip, like Billy the Kid.
He wasn't just accurate, he was also lightning-fast. His brother
Clarence—my Uncle Doc—told me that one time he and a friend of
his went across the river with their dog, and the dog treed a panther.
The boys hurried home, got their guns, and yelled for Dad to come
along too. Meanwhile the dog kept the panther treed. When they got
there Doc fired first, but it wasn't a fatal shot, and the panther dove

Grandpa and Grandma Brown with Uncle Doc's baby.

from the top of the tree right at the dog. While the panther was still in its dive, Dad put a .38 bullet through its heart. He was seventeen at the time. Grandpa Brown recorded the event in his daily ledger: "Nov 8 1909—Johnnie killed his First Panther 6 ft. 4 in. long."

Dad told me that one day he was walking his baby brother Harry (nicknamed Dollar Bill) under a black mangrove tree near the dock, and something kept touching his hat. (Dad always wore a Stetson.) It turned out to be a big bobcat walking along an overhanging limb. As Dad walked under the limb, the cat would paw at his hat. He said the cat wasn't ferocious, he was just playing.

There was probably no musical instrument Dad couldn't play, from a saxophone to a Jew's harp, and he wrote some jim-dandy songs about good times and bad in the Glades, including one called "Miami Waltz." In his younger days Dad loved to play tricks on his friends. When his buddy Bill Gandees got married, he put a ladder up to the newlyweds' window in the middle of the night and played a saxophone solo that darn-nigh blew Bill and his bride out of bed.

Dad nicknamed most everyone on the island. He called another friend, Nelson Noble, "the Mayor of Chokoloskee," and it stuck with him the rest of his life.

Dad knew the Mayor was scared of panthers and large alligators, especially in the dark. One night, when Noble was out fishing for mullet, with one end of his net tied to the shoreline (where panthers sometimes prowled), Dad slipped around, got ahold of the net, and started pulling on it just a little bit while he bellowed like a boar alligator and squalled like a panther. The Mayor got so scared he cut the net in two, left his launch tied to the bushes, and rowed home in his fish skiff.

∗ ∗ ∗

The only way into or out of Grandpa Brown's was by boat—there was never a road to the place and today there still isn't, even though there's been a motel nearby for years. For us to get to Everglades City, we had to row our skiff across the river—about 200 yards wide—and then walk a half-mile into town. Across the river from us, Collier had pumped in enough landfill to set up a good-size dairy farm, with a

Grandma Brown with her daughters and one of her sons. *Left to right:* Aunt Annie, Grandma, Uncle Harry (Dollar Bill), Aunt Ethel, and Aunt Bessie.

road into the city. But to get onto Collier's road, we had to go through Collier's cow pasture. The problem there was the biggest bull I've ever seen. That ol' bull—imported from England and named Barron, of course—kept us kids scared half to death.

To get even with the old bull, my brother Peg and I rigged up a three-quarter-inch pipe, mounted it like a little cannon, and aimed it across the river at Barron's butt. We put a twelve-gauge shotgun shell in the pipe, with me holding a pointy file on the primer and Peg hitting the file with a hammer the minute the bull came into range—and off it went! I can't remember how good a shot we were, but I'm sure we blistered ol' Barron's behind more'n once.

Peg was a couple years older than me and he usually took Mother and others across the river in the rowboat to work. One morning I was out on the head of the dock when I saw Peg coming across the river toward me. He was rowing looking *forward* (what we called "shoving" the boat), heading for the beach. Just as he got there, I saw a big alligator stick its head up over the back of the skiff. I hollered and Peg jumped out onto the beach just in time. Dad came running with his rifle and killed the gator. It was eleven feet two inches long and had a big fishhook in its tail.

This was my first experience with a gator trying to attack anyone in a boat. The odd part is that there was no one in the water and nothing going on there to attract the gator. While alligators don't usually act that way, large ones are very dangerous, especially around children and small animals, like dogs and pigs. They usually catch little animals near the water's edge. If a child is playing on a riverbank near the water (or is in the water, all alone), the gator is likely to go for the child, thinking it's a small animal—unless there's someone or something around to scare it off.

A lifetime of experience with alligators tells me that the average gator will not attack a grown human—but don't ever risk it! Never try cornering one, because I know for a fact there are some large gators that wouldn't hesitate to take on a man. I have seen various animals—panthers, bobcats, bears—go a little crazy at times or get so hungry they attacked people no matter what. Most likely, if a gator is going to attack, it will have its head out of the water and you'll see it coming; it is not likely to swim underwater to its prey and then pop up. If your child is playing in or near the water in alligator country, keep a good lookout.

✳   ✳   ✳

I started school when I was five, but about the only thing I remember of my first year there is coloring my Santa Claus green. My teacher, Mrs. Blackburn, found I was totally color-blind. To me, red rosebush looks all one color—whatever color that is I wouldn't know. The only color I can really see is a bright yellow, like yellow elders. When I went over to Chokoloskee in the fall to see my McKinney grandparents, all the elders were in bloom, and to me the island was really beautiful.

The entire student body of the Everglades school in 1925. I'm in the front row, sixth from the left.

When I was six, a few months after the hurricane of 1926, we moved upriver to where the Everglades Seafood Market is located today. Us kids sure hated to give up that old river. We had so much fun swimming and playing along the bank. But I accepted what I couldn't change and it was good-bye ol' river.

3 / Miami and Possum Key . . . the Depression
/ . . . pickled grasshoppers and swamp angels

When we moved upriver into Everglades City, Dad started right in building us a new house. Here we had running water and electricity for the first time in the bay area, which must have meant a lot to Mother and Dad, especially Mother.

Dad soon built a fish house, with a walk-in icebox to keep fish in for a few days at a time, and went into business with the Crossland Fish Company. The fish he sold were mostly mullet. Every couple of days Dad made a trip in his "run boat" down to Lostmans River or Chatham Bend to pick up fish from the "lay boats," which iced the day's catch temporarily.

One night we were gassing up the run boat, using a kerosene lantern for a light, when someone put the lantern too close to the nozzle of the gas hose. The gasoline caught fire. But the oddest thing was that there was no explosion—just one big puff of flame, then out it went. Since that time I've figured out why we didn't get blown up: because the tank was full. If a container is lit when it's full to the top with gasoline, nothing happens. You can put anything over the hole and it'll go out—no explosion. But, it's got to be a *full* tank!

Ice came in 300-pound blocks and was chipped up by hand, usually with a four-prong ice pick made of heavy steel and a handle about four feet long. Dad kept his pick as sharp as a razor. One evening three fishermen—'Fonso Lopez (Gregorio's son), Rob Thompson, and Harry McGill—were drinking at our fish house, and Harry and Rob got in an argument. Harry threw a punch at Rob and broke his nose. The next minute Rob threw Dad's ice pick at Harry. I was watching that scrap and saw Harry pull in his stomach just as the pick whizzed by his belt buckle and stuck in the wall across the room. This was in bootleggin' days, when there was usually plenty of whiskey around because of the rum-running from the Bahamas to the Ten Thousand Islands and on through Everglades City. The whiskey was brought up the river at midnight, after the city lights were turned off, then smuggled by truck (unbeknowing to Barron G. Collier) to the trains the Atlantic Coast Line was running into Everglades City. Along the way it was repacked into tomato crates.

An FBI agent named Hutto was sent into Everglades City to stop the rum-running, but right off the bat he happened up at the wrong place. One night at the old dairy across from Grandpa Brown's place, Hutto jumped up on the running board of a loaded truck to arrest the driver. The driver reached through the window, grabbed Hutto's own gun, and shot him dead on the spot, so the state attorney said. At the trial, the state proved who done the driving that night, and they sure in hell wanted to hang him, but for some reason the jury refused to find the driver guilty even of manslaughter, let alone murder. So the rum-running, the hijacking, and the shooting scrapes kept on going, until Repeal ended it all in 1933.

The rumrunners from the Bahamas, the bank robbers, and the moonshiners making corn liquor in the Glades must've had a ball. Once they made it to their hideouts in the tricky mass of winding mangroves, even they themselves stayed lost half the time. But they weren't so lost that a lawman or two didn't come looking for 'em—and never made it back out.

*   *   *

Once we'd moved into our new home in Everglades City, everything began to come our way. In February 1929 my baby sister, Audrey, was born there; she was the last of the children. But in a couple of years, because of the land boom fading out and the Depression coming on, things began to slow down to almost nothing. Catching mullet in nets by the hundreds of pounds (often by the thousands) was the main way of making a living in the bay area. Beginning in 1929, though, the selling price of mullet went down to one cent a pound, with a limit on how many the fish companies would buy from you. It just simply got to where you couldn't make a living mullet-fishing. Most families were getting by, barely, on what little they could get from the land.

In the fall of 1929, Dad called it quits for Everglades City. He traded and sold out everything, lock, stock, and barrel. In exchange, he got a coffee shop in Miami near the Miami River, and a top-notch cabin cruiser, *The City of Naples,* large enough to live on. (The cruiser had been built for rum-running but had never been used. The federal agents had pointed their finger at the owner and warned him that if the cruiser ever tried to make a run with booze aboard, she'd be towed to port by the Coast Guard.)

We loaded up the cruiser and headed out—all but Bert: he'd just given up high school for a job with the U.S. Coast and Geodetic Survey, with living quarters furnished on a government yacht, a chance he just couldn't turn down in times like that. Reaching Miami, we tied up our boat in the river. While Mother and Dad were on shore running the coffee shop, us kids—Laberta, Peg, and myself—took turns staying aboard and looking after baby Audrey. Mother hated to leave us alone on that boat, I know; but in the Depression, people put up with just about anything to survive.

∗   ∗   ∗

Day by day, things just kept getting worse and worse in Miami. The coffee shop didn't break even. After a few months Dad sold it and the cruiser to Joe Johnson, a friend of his in Coconut Grove, just south of Miami. In that deal, Dad got a twenty-two-foot open launch, the *Nelly,* with a twelve-horsepower Universal motor, plus cash enough for at least a pot of grits or two.

The Johnsons had a son named Carl and a daughter named Ruby. Our two families became very close; there were times we pooled our food money and ate together. Mrs. Johnson had a way of cooking coarse grits that made 'em taste so good; it seems she cooked 'em for hours, same as the Seminoles do (they call it *sofkee*). If we had any lard or cooking oil, we had fried fish, usually snapper; if no lard, then it was boiled fish. One of our main meals was grits and boiled grunts (a kind of snapper).

Carl Johnson was a smart one—he really knew his way around. Us kids tried a lot of different things to make a dime. One was catching hermit crabs and selling them to tourists for fish bait (we built a little fire and heated the back end of the shells and the crabs came crawling out). Next we tried catching big land crabs—that was probably our most fun. Times were so hard, people even took to eating those.

Dad took part of the cash he got from his deal with Joe Johnson to make a commercial fishing trip in the *Nelly*. But, with our bad luck, on our way back in with what few fish we'd caught, we ran out of gas. Dad stretched up a sail and late that evening we made it into port. Only the fish went sour, and we wound up having to sell them for almost nothing.

That done it for Miami and Coconut Grove. Bert drove over from Everglades City in a Model A Ford truck and moved us back to Chokoloskee. Dad came in the *Nelly,* motoring around through Florida Bay.

✳   ✳   ✳

Back in Chokoloskee, we moved into one side of Grandma McKinney's big house. Grandpa Mckinney had died in 1926, and she had put a partition down the middle and rented one side and lived in the other. Times were now really hard on Chokoloskee. People were doing things you wouldn't believe to make a dime. Grandma had a contract with the government to send them pickled grasshoppers (for what purpose, I'll never know). The contract had started years before; in one of his newspaper columns Grandpa had written: "Mrs. McKinney is filling another contract for 10,000 grasshoppers. The school children catches them for her and it has a tendency to keep them out of mischief." Grandma pickled the hoppers in formalde-hyde. Eventually full-grown men and women were knocking down the hoppers right alongside us kids, "for a little bit of nothing"; in the Depression, that usually meant something to eat. There was some relief work going on, but very little; the WPA, the CCC, and all the rest didn't start until 1933 and thereafter.

By now we were down to nothing on earth but the little open launch, ol' *Nelly.* Dad decided to take us to the woods so we could live off the land, leaving behind what civilization there was. Laberta stayed with Grandma McKinney until early 1931, when she and Waddy Thompson were married and went to live in Immokalee. Peg also stayed with Grandma and went to school until he joined us the following winter for the coon-hunting season.

My older sister, Laberta, and her first child, Vivian, in the early '30s.

Before we left for the woods, Dad painted a few old tarpaulins with melted wax to make them waterproof. We took along a shotgun and what shells we could afford to buy, a few old traps, a good mosquito net or two, and some of Grandma McKinney's quilts for bedding. (She made 'em by the dozen; that was her hobby after Grandpa died.)

Dad had a few carpenter tools and always a good ax and a hatchet. Mother had a couple of galvanized tin washtubs (also used for bathing), a big cast-iron tub (the "boil pot") to boil clothes clean, a washboard (we called it a rub board), and a long clothesline. And she had her old Dutch oven—a smaller cast-iron pot with short legs and a heavy lid with ridges on top to hold hot coals.

We also took a few fishing lines and hooks, but to catch the large amounts of fish we were going to need, we counted more on the cast net that Dad was patiently making by hand. We planned to get fresh meat from the land, like saltwater birds, mainly white ibis (we call 'em curlew—although they're not really curlew—or Chokoloskee chicken) and other kinds of heron, along with ducks, deer, turkey, rabbits, turtles, and fish.

Dad knew the biggest problem would be drinking water. He picked up a few fifty-five-gallon wooden barrels, a few four-and-a-half-gallon demijohns with straw matting around 'em that Puerto Rican rum came in, and a couple of water buckets. He put them all in a big skiff, filled them with rainwater, and towed the big skiff and a small hunting skiff behind our launch. Our staples were a little white bacon (salt pork), dried lima beans, black-eyed peas, grits, rice, flour in twelve-pound bags, pure lard for cooking oil, and some canned foods like corned beef and tripe. For salt, we beat up the coarse salt used for gator curing hides, and we did without pepper. That was about it: no desserts.

One morning in early 1930 after several days' getting ready, Mom, Dad, baby sister Audrey, and I pulled out in ol' *Nelly* on our way to Possum Key, fifteen miles south of Chokoloskee and about eight miles inland from the coast. It's a good piece of high land, and one of the flatter-type mounds. The Indians who built it really knew their stuff. They picked out a nice harbor pass, plenty deep at any stage of tide, out of the north wind and good for the summer breeze, and not far to go for fresh water. Just across the bay a couple of miles to the east there's a little river called South Water and another called Sweet Water; in the rainy season, on falling tide, rainwater drains down into 'em from the Glades.

We used the big skiff to go after fresh water. If we couldn't get it from the rivers, we could from the cistern at the old Watson Place at Chatham Bend, five miles away, or from one at Lopez River, ten miles away. If bad came to worse, we had to go all the way to Chokoloskee.

Ol' *Nelly* was slow, but we made it to Possum Key before dark. I was ten years old, and I can well remember how excited I was when we pulled up to the campsite—our new home, with a beautiful poinciana tree right near the water. The mound-builders had piled up the shell right down to the water's edge; you could just step out of your boat onto high shell land.

Dad first built a good buttonwood fire so there'd be plenty of hot coals for cooking come suppertime. Then we got everything unloaded. The water took the longest; it had to be carried in buckets from one barrel in the boat to another on land. After that, we had

Possum Key, where we first camped in the woods during the Depression.

supper. The best biscuits I ever ate was here at this camp. Mother made 'em in the Dutch oven with little bits of cracklin' (fried salt-pork rind) mixed in. (We used the oil fried out of the pork for cooking; the leftover rind was something like the pork skins that's sold for snacks today.)

Right near the camp was a small key full of Spanish moss, about the only place in the Islands where this kind of moss grows. (In those days, Spanish moss was sold and used for upholstery.) Dad and I went out to the key and gathered a boatload of it. Then, back at camp, we cleared off a little out-of-the-way place and made the moss up into beds. After that we cut a few buttonwood poles and stretched our mosquito nets.

Next morning, everyone was scratching—covered with bites from red bugs (often called chiggers). They'd come out of that moss like a swarm of bees, a-diggin' into our skin like doodlebugs. We had kerosene for the lanterns and Dad gave us a little bowl of that to rub on the bite. It done the trick. There's something about red bugs I've never been able to figure out. Anytime you start a new camp, you're bound to get 'em. Some camps are much worse than others, but after a few days the bugs all leave you alone. The odd part is, if you get company, the bugs'll eat *them* up every time; and if you go to someone else's camp, they'll get on you, but not as bad as on a total newcomer. Red bugs can be kept off some by putting repellent around your sleeves, pants legs, and neck.

After coffee and a sponge bath with kerosene, we all went to work setting up camp. First we had to clean up after the raccoons; they were always a problem, digging around in the groceries at night and smart enough to open most anything. I cut buttonwood poles for our lean-to (several poles drove down and several placed crossways to lay the tarps on), plus a few more inside to hang our skeeter bars (nets) on. I also made little buttonwood tables for Mother to put her pots and pans on.

We stretched the clothesline off to the side and out of the way because if you ran into it at night you could just about break your neck. But still, the line had to be out in the open some, to get sun and wind on the clothes. For more than half of the year, most any place you may be in the backcountry of the Everglades, the water is fresh enough to wash clothes in.

After setting up camp we all took off in one of the skiffs (baby Audrey included) on an overnight alligator hunt. (We couldn't afford to use the launch. We had to save it to go into Chokoloskee to sell our gator hides and get supplies.) We went up to Gator Bay and camped at the mouth of Gator Bay Creek. It got its name, Dad said, from a wild alligator no one could kill.

This trip was my first time for "bay tea," which comes from a tree in the Everglades we call sweet bay. You strip the green, tender leaves off the limb and bring them to a boil for a pretty good tea. (I believe the same bay leaves, dried, are used in cooking.)

My second surprise was to see Mother scrubbing her teeth. She peeled the bark from a little tender twig about a quarter-inch in diameter, then twisted the end till it was stranded like a brush. She made one for me, too. In a pinch it worked good.

On the second night, Dad and I left Mother and Audrey at the camp in Gator Bay and hunted for gators through Plate Creek up to Onion Key. (Old man Lopez named these places. He said he lost a plate in Plate Creek and ate his last onion on a little round shell island he named Onion Key.) We didn't do much good hunting, but we did kill one eight-footer.

*　　*　　*

Back home on Possum Key, we cleared off a field and planted it with vegetables. Dad's favorite was black-eyed peas and those shell islands would really grow 'em—and you didn't have to spray any insecticide, because there weren't any bugs out there that bothered plants.

One afternoon, just as we got back to camp from Chokoloskee and were stepping out of the boat, we saw a big bobcat running across the field. Old Man Mathis, a friend from Fort Myers, had dropped by while we were gone and was sitting under the poinciana tree with his single-barrel shotgun at his side. Dad asked, "Is this gun loaded?" Mathis said, "Yeah, got an ounce ball in it." With the bobcat running in long, high jumps, Dad put that ounce ball in the center of the cat's eye. As usual, he tanned the hide later.

While we were living at Possum Key, something was going on there I didn't know anything about until time came for us to move on. Dad had set up a still nearby, and he was making moonshine and selling it to the natives of the area. Remember, in the Depression you did what you had to do.

*　　*　　*

I've been asked many times how we manage to live in this country with the mosquitoes. As the old-timers say, "It's one helluva dose." But if you know how, you can make it a bit easier for yourself. Once you get to the point that you *expect* 'em to be there, it's no longer a surprise, and somehow that seems to help. Mosquitoes—or swamp angels, as Grandpa McKinney called them—are usually at their worst just after rainy season starts in May, and that can happen overnight. Then for the next few months, they're really bad. The reason is, their eggs have been laid and it takes moisture to hatch 'em. Once the water in the Glades and in the little mangrove ponds starts rising and reaches the eggs, look out, 'cause here they come.

The worst times are at daybreak, just before black dark, and at big moon-up. Try to avoid moving around at daybreak and between sun-down and dark. Moonlit nights are much worse. Mosquitoes are also bad in drizzly, overcast weather.

Back then we didn't have any mosquito repellent. There was only one way to get out of the skeeters and that was to get under your skeeter net. However, there were ways that helped. First, you got to where they didn't bother you as bad as they did a newcomer. Second, if you know you are stuck with mosquitoes, and you make up your mind that you are going to stay and endure them, you've won the biggest part of the battle. Third, a lot depends on what you have to do or want to do "in the mosquitoes." For instance, playing cards wouldn't be any fun. But the skeeters probably wouldn't seem too bad if you were counting up a batch of found money, or maybe making love to your new bride. I'm sure they would bother you much worse if you were sportfishing than if you were commercial-fishing (something you had to do), and they probably wouldn't bother you at all if you were digging up a pot of gold.

We had several different remedies for fighting 'em off around the camp. The more open a camp is, the less shade and brush there is for the skeeters to hide in. They like dark, shady spots and will go for black every time. They don't seem able to stand the bright, hot sun very much.

If you're wearing dark clothes, especially black, they'll swarm you, and if your clothing is wet and tight, they can get to you much better. Always wear white or light-colored clothes, rather thick and very loose, with long sleeves. If you know you're going into a lot of mos-quitoes, it's a good idea to take your shirt off and have someone rub or spray repellent on your back and maybe your shirt, too, before you put it back on.

Mosquitoes come to scent, especially frying fish. Just-coming-dark is a bad time. If you can avoid cooking and causing strong scents at dusk and daybreak, it'll be a big help. Mosquitoes don't travel around that much unless given a reason.

A smudge pot helps, and a good one can be made by cutting the top out of a five-gallon gas can and putting about six inches of shell in the bottom. In this country there's a black mangrove tree. After it's dead for a number of years, the sap part of the tree becomes crumbly. Put some on top of the shell in your smudge pot, light it, and you'll get a good smoke that helps run skeeters off. Once they're gone, don't walk in the woods nearby unless you have to. If you do, you'll bring back a whole new bunch of skeeters every time.

4 / Coon-trapping and fire-hunting . . . life at Camp Huston

In the fall of 1930, we moved on from Possum Key to the Huston River area, an excellent hunting ground for raccoons. The word was out that even with prices falling the way they were, coons were going to be worth hunting this season, at forty to sixty cents a skin. Dad had just barely made enough money throught the summer with gator-hunting and cutting boat timbers, and a little moonshining on the side, to buy enough traps to start the season. Once again we loaded up ol' *Nelly* and headed out.

Before setting up camp on Huston River, we went into Choko-loskee and picked up what traps and supplies we could afford. Peg came along with us this time. He was going on fourteen, and Dad figured he was experienced and man enough now to tend the trap line on his own while Dad hunted gators and cut boat timbers.

The Huston River is ten or twelve miles south of Chokoloskee, just north of Chatham River. On the north bank, inland about three miles from the Gulf, there's a Calusa Indian mound called Camp Huston. The ground is high for mangrove country, three feet above sea level. Like most mounds it was covered with ash, stopper berry, pigeon plum, wild fig, gumbo-limbo, dogwood, and other trees that shed a lot of leaves, making a good, soft topsoil. (But there were no fruit trees of any kind except a few wild papayas—we call 'em "he paw-paws." They have a much smaller fruit than the tame papaya, nothing like as good, but edible.)

When Dad first pointed out our new camp-to-be on Huston River, it didn't look so exciting. No one had lived or camped there for years, and it didn't even have a landing, let alone a house or a shack. It was covered with underbrush something terrible, especially a vine we call "cat's claw" or "pull-back." This vine has thorns on it like the claws of a cat, and if you get too close, it kinda pulls you into it.

After we cleared the land and set up camp, things began to look a lot brighter. When Mother's little garden started blooming, every-thing else began to bloom right along with it. We built a little-better

A mangrove tree. Note the oysters growing on the roots. (Photo by Oscar Thompson.)

camp this time than we had at Possum Key, but still only had a lean-to over our skeeter bars and bedrolls.

By now it was October, and the northeast breeze was beginning to blow down the river, taking most of the skeeters with it and turning the weather cool and peaceful. The campfire was beginning to feel good again, especially in the late hours of the night, when we came in from hunting all wet and cold.

There were two reasons why we set up camp at Huston River. At first the only reason I knew was to hunt raccoons that winter. But one day I saw in the launch a piece of Dad's moonshine still. I knew right then there was something going on around Huston besides coon-hunting.

Once camp was set up, we started putting out our traps—a little early, to stake claim on the nearby hunting grounds—but we didn't bait the traps until the cold weather came. Raccoons live and range throughout this entire country, in the mangrove swamplands as well as the prairie grasslands. In cold weather, when the small crabs and fiddlers that coons feed on go down deep in the riverbank mud, the coons come to the shoreline looking for fish and small oysters. That's when we trapped 'em. I had a handful of traps myself. Being only ten-and-a-half, I put mine out pretty close to camp.

The traps were set about a hundred yards apart along the banks of the river and the bays. We built little pens about two feet in diameter out of mangrove roots. The roots were tall and close enough together the coon couldn't get to the bait in the middle of the pen without first going through the little doorway the trap was set in. There were a few wise old coons you simply couldn't catch that way. Every night they turned the trap over; sometimes they tripped it and sometimes they even drug it off to one side, or as Peg used to say, "They throwed my trap." After a few nights like that, we tied the bait up a little higher than they could reach and set the trap in a little hole right under it. Sometimes we could outsmart a wise one that way and catch him by his back feet, and when we did, you could bet your bottom dollar we had a dandy: a big boar raccoon.

At the start of the season, we usually found a few raccoon kittens in the traps. If only one leg was broken, we cut it off and let the kitten go. I'm sure at least some survived, for we caught several later that had healed up. If two legs of a kitten were broken, though, I was forced to kill it with a club made from a mangrove root. There's no way I could be that cruel today.

At Camp Huston luck started to come our way. By the time winter came and the hunting season got going, Peg had made enough money to buy what traps we needed and was doing as good at catching coons as any full-grown man. I helped him out on the trap line until the hard work of setting the traps was over. Then we started a little fire-hunting at night.

Fire-hunting started long before there were any kind of headlights. Hunters built a small fire in a pan mounted on a pole with another shiny pan behind it, upright, for a reflector. The pole was carried across one shoulder so the fire was in back of his own eyes, putting them in line with the eyes of the animal he was after. Even though hunters today have electric headlights, the term "fire-hunting" still goes.

Raccoons, as well as some other animals that roam around at night, have a reflector in the back of their eyes, and when a light of any kind (even so dim maybe you can't see it yourself) shines into them, the reflector intensifies it, enabling the animal to "see in the dark." When the hunter's headlight shines into the eyes of the animal, they reflect back very bright and can be seen for a long distance. Even in a wooded area a fire-hunter can pick up the eyes of an animal you'd never see in the daytime. Fire-hunting played a big part in making a living in this country from earliest times, same as it did in the years I was camping in the Huston and Chatham Bend areas.

When Peg and I first started fire-hunting, we went together in one skiff, rowing along the shoreline. We put a piece of rubber hose and some oil in the oarlocks to cut down the noise—some of the older raccoons were very scary and wise. We had a carbide hunting light to shine on their eyes, and a reflector made from one of Mother's baking-powder cans. We shot 'em with a twelve-gauge shotgun using bird shot (fine shot, no. 5, which doesn't damage the pelts).

We drew straws to see who got the first shot. First or last, it didn't do *me* much good, for two reasons. First, just starting out as a hunter, I sometimes shot at the wrong target. The eyes of a whippoorwill shine back just like a coon's, and Peg sure got a kick out of watching me shoot at 'em. To make it more interesting (to Peg), I usually missed and the "coon's" eyes flew off into open space. (Peg knew what I was shooting at but wouldn't tell me—for the kicks it gave him.) The second reason is that I wasn't much of a shot back then, so when I aimed at an honest-to-goodness raccoon, most times I only wounded it. Then Peg got another laugh, watching me run after that coon and try to kill it with a mangrove root.

Coons have a way of communicating by whistling. Some of the old-timers could imitate that whistle and call 'em that way. Eventually I got pretty good at it myself, but later on when my wife, Estelle, went along with me, she wasn't about to let me shoot any raccoon that came when I called it. Through the years I've had several for pets, and today I still have places on the shoreline near home where I go in my outboard and call the coons and feed 'em fish.

There were times out there in the late hours of the night, with a cold north wind a-howling, when we couldn't hardly hold onto that old cold shotgun to fire it. Usually our britches were wet up to our butts, and we had no waders or even a pair of shoes on. In fact, we were more barefooted than the coons we were after; they at least had a little fur on 'em.

There are a few birds in this country that feed at night, such as the night heron we called squawk (from the sound they make when they start to fly off). Occasionally, when a couple of us hunters met out there we built a little fire in the mangroves and had a squawk roast. We killed and split the bird in half, put it on a stick near the fire, and turned it around now and then. If we didn't have a bird to eat, we roasted a little slab of salt pork. While cooking the pork, we stuck it in the river occasionally to get the salt out (it worked even though the water was salty itself). For bread we mixed up a little flour and water into a good, tough dough and kind of twirled it around a stick, holding it near the fire and letting the oil from the saltpork drip on it. Believe me or not—roast squawk or white bacon with a twirl of dough on a mangrove root had it all over a Big Mac.

*   *   *

When it came to skinning the coons and tacking their hides up to dry, Dad always helped. We skinned 'em on a little shell beach and threw the carcasses in the river. With gators, buzzards, and sharks eating on 'em, they just seemed to fade away.

Most every time we started skinning, my little baby sister Audrey came down to the beach saying, "Daddy, want coon foot." A coon's back feet are kinda long, round, and soft, and when one is caught in a trap, the bone is usually broken and flops around in the skinner's way, so he generally cuts the foot off, skin and all. There wasn't much else for Audrey to play with out there, so whenever she came down to the beach, Dad had a coon foot waiting for her.

We washed the skins in the river and then popped them dry, like cracking a cow whip. The pelts were cured by drying in the sun. We nailed together one-by-four boards to make a ladder of coon frames the width of an average hide. The hides were stretched out tight and lightly tacked onto the frames with small nails, with the skin side of the pelt exposed to the sun. After about two days' drying, the hides could be stacked away 'til selling time.

Selling the hides brought me the first real money I'd ever made, and was it ever hard-earned. The hides were sold several different ways. Sometimes the dealers hired a guide to take them around to the hunting camps. Their favorite guide was Dan House, who was married to my Aunt Willie (McKinney). He was raised around House Hammock Bay, a few miles inland from Camp Huston, and he really knew the country. Other times, we went to the dealers ourselves—they came to Chokoloskee and Everglades City about twice a month. Some old-timers on the island bought hides every day—Ted Smallwood at his trading post, for one. They didn't pay as much as the dealers, but what they did pay looked mighty good to us at times. Then there were three dealers from around Fort Myers we called the Crook Brothers; they'd start out trying to get our hides for about ten cents apiece, but if we held out, they'd pay us fifty cents.

*   *   *

At Camp Huston I got my first shotgun. A dealer from Miami figured out a slick way to outdo some of the other dealers: he brought down some Eastern Arms shotguns (much less expensive than the old brands, like Winchester, Savage, and Ivor-Johnson) and let us have them at cost, six dollars each. I paid for mine with my own coon-hide money. I was only eleven, and that 12-gauge knocked me flat on my back the first time I fired it. But you can bet your life I got up from there and fired 'er again.

The salt water was very hard on our guns. Mother gave us the oil paper from her cooking lard to grease them with (the lard held up longer than regular oil) and coffee cans to keep our shells in. The lid lapped over the top, making it watertight in the rain. Shotgun shells were made out of paper, and if they got wet they'd swell and wouldn't fit in the chamber of the gun. Then we would peel off a thin layer of the paper, but, sometimes the moisture had already gotten through the paper and damaged the powder, so the gun would "snap" or misfire.

About the time I started fire-hunting on my own, we woke up one morning and saw big panther tracks all over our camp. When time came to go hunting that night, I was too scared to go out there alone. Dad was worn out from his own work, and Peg, of course, just laughed at me. Like always, it fell on Mother to go with me a few nights, until I "overed" my fright. She must have been terrible cramped-up in that little wet hunting skiff of mine, but she never let on. I often think of how caring and loving she was for all of us. I wonder how many mothers would be willing to go through the misery she did, living on the bare ground out in the rainy weather and mosquitoes. One thing she always made sure of was that I had some kind of dry clothing to take with me when I went out hunting, even if it wasn't anything but a dry corn sack to help keep me warm, plus a little something to eat—usually a piece of hoe johnny, a big, thick pancake. If you add a little oil to the dough, it's cooked dry in a cast-iron fry pan. If no oil is added, then you put oil in the pan for frying. The name hoe johnny comes from "Johnny Reb." During the Civil War the Rebs baked their bread in their trench tool, which back then they called a hoe.

During our stay at Huston River we had no stove. Mother had to cook on the campfire. Back then it never crossed my mind how hard it must've been on her, to have to squat and kneel down around a hot fire to do the cooking, sometimes in the rain and most always in the mosquitoes.

She usually fried or stewed our meat. The breastbone, back, and wings of the white curlew, with the red liver thrown in, was especially good stewed. The liver of a white ibis also makes a larrupin' good gravy, but there's no better taste than the breast and legs of a young brown one, fried. Now and then Mother baked a few of the big mallards in her Dutch oven with sweet potatoes and homemade Clabber Girl baking-powder biscuits.

Occasionally, when Dad and Peg were out hunting, Mother, Audrey, and I rowed out to fish near camp, with a little picnic lunch. We used fiddler crabs for bait, and it was never hard to catch whatever fish we needed. I cleaned 'em and Mother usually had 'em frying in her big iron skillet by the time Dad and Peg came rowing home.

We had plenty of fish and vegetables to eat, but for fresh meat we relied mainly on saltwater birds, like duck, curlew, and squawk. The only problem was that at certain times of the year there weren't too many choice birds around. I know this may sound rough, but if we got hungry enough, we'd go to the roost at night, blind the birds with the hunting light, and knock 'em down with a long pole (to save shotgun shells). In the summer months, no problem: there were plenty of feeding birds on the shoreline and out in the prairies on the Islands. In the winter months, the birds fly over a particular spot on the shoreline on their way to roost at the head of the rivers near the Glades. They usually started a little before sundown. To keep them from seeing us, we hid our hunting skiff under the overhanging limbs along the water's edge. Shooting birds on a flyover took double the shells for most of us, but not for Dad—he brought his down with one shot.

There used to be a lot of mallard ducks in this country the year 'round (though we called 'em "summer ducks"). For most of the day they fed in the marshes on the Islands, but beginning about four o'clock in the afternoon, they started for the mainland. If the tide was low and the oyster bars were out of water, the ducks stopped on their way and fed on 'em 'til sundown. Some of the bars had a small mangrove key on 'em, just right for a duck blind: the ducks lit within fifty feet of us.

Once we'd managed to kill one for a decoy, we had it made. We stuck a forked stick down in the oyster bar and put the duck's head in the fork. The live ones never knew the difference, until we opened fire. Because shells were so scarce, we'd wait until two and sometimes three ducks lined up together and then kill all three with one shot. Dad made some decoys out of gumbo-limbo trees that were so perfect we shot the heads off some of 'em thinking they were the real thing.

While we were out getting wildlife to eat, there was never any law or anyone to bother us in any way. Occasionally, an Audubon Society bird warden stopped by, but only for a friendly visit. They understood that we didn't disturb the rookeries and that we only took what birds we needed to eat.

By this time Dad had finished the cast net he'd started making in his spare time back at Possum Key. Making one by hand takes many weeks of tedious work; I remember Dad working on his every night after supper. The twine for the net was threaded on a net needle made from a red mangrove root. To get the size mesh he wanted, Dad wrapped the twine around a little board. It was going on three months before he got the net finished.

We fished at night in the big skiff. Peg and I rowed the boat while Dad threw the net. The fish, especially mullet, gather around the oyster beds at night. We usually caught a few mangrove snapper, along with sheepshead, brim, trout, redfish, channel bass, and occasionally a snook; but our main catch was mullet. Some of those we salted for coon bait.

✳   ✳   ✳

You might think from the way we go after the saltwater birds, wild animals, and especially mullet (what some people call a bait fish) that we'd eat most anything that moves in the Everglades. But that doesn't seem to be the case. For some reason, the natives at home shy away from certain foods that people outside my homeland seem to like so much: shark, octopus, conch, ray, skate, catfish, coon, opossum, even snake. To my mind, all of these animals are just as clean and good to eat as hog (if not cleaner), but most of us just don't go for it. Probably not more than half of us eat turtle, not many eat wild hog, and hardly none eat manatee (unless we're drunk or starving to death). We do like deer and rabbit, but not bear.

My family never ate any gator or coon meat. I am sure there is nothing wrong with eating gator meat—it looks mighty good and clean to me. Pobably because we hunted them so much for their hides, we never acquired a taste for the meat.

We're very choosy about our fish, but I think that's also in our heads. For instance, when there was plenty to choose from, we had pompano (one of the most expensive fish there is) and snook (one of the tastiest), and we wouldn't even touch a sheepshead or a little black drum. But as fish got less plentiful, we began to eat the "no-no's." Today the no-no's are just as good as the best. It's all in the mind, not in the taste.

The fish we eat most down here is mullet, but there's a reason for that: they were and still are handy and very plentiful. To my notion, a mullet caught in the right place at the right time of year is the best fish to eat that swims—but not if it's caught in fresh water and muddy bottom. The difference there is like the difference between a steak from a scrub-fed cow in the Glades and a U.S. prime cut from a corn-fed steer out of Texas.

Of the birds, curlew takes the cake. In the Depression we ate some herons now and then, especially the night and Louisiana heron, and a few other small ones, but not the big gray heron, the wood stork, or the gannet. We were prejudiced against the larger birds, probably because our parents and grandparents didn't eat them either.

*   *   *

At Camp Huston we didn't have much for light, except for one old kerosene lantern we called a flambeau—so dim you couldn't see your hand in front of you on a dark night. But we did have the old standby for camping and hunting: carbide, a binary compound of carbon. (When water touches carbide, it foams and lets off a gas that burns like propane.) The carbide light I used was a small, one-piece type that could be worn on the head, but it was so heavy it gave you a headache, especially with the fumes from the burning carbide and it wasn't a strong light. Many times, though, that's all we had to hunt with, and at least it beat a fire pan.

That year at Huston we had a red mangrove for a Christmas tree. The decoration was only a dim old carbide light with some of Dad's white twine from his cast net laid around it and maybe a lightning bug or two. I'll never forget the one present that came under that tree for me. Mother and Dad managed to get me a little pocketknife. In the Depression that was a big present for a ten-year-old, and one that would come in handy for living and hunting in the woods. But right after Christmas, when we were out trying to kill a mess of birds to eat, Dad shot a night heron, and while we were picking it up, somehow I dropped my brand-new knife overboard. We tried our best to find it but finally had to give up. Mother was along, and I believe it made her cry. The knife was lost on an oyster bar in House Hammock Pass, so I named it Knife Bar. That point of land is on a main route and I never pass it without thinking about the present I lost that meant so much to me, and the red mangrove Christmas tree it was under.

✳   ✳   ✳

Daddy nicknamed Audrey "Frog"—maybe because frogs (and coon feet) were about all she had out there to play with. She was his pick of the children and he was never too busy to take out a lot of time with her. I remember him gathering little Christmas berries and coco plums and picking little cherry tomatoes from the garden especially for her. And somehow he always managed to buy her a little penny candy whenever we went in for supplies. Dad would give the little birds and animals different names, just for her amusement. We had a lot of catbirds at Camp Huston, and one he named Whee Wha. We could always hear it in the late afternoon.

To me, the two most interesting birds are the hoot owl and the whippoorwill. The hoot owl is a very odd-looking creature, about the size of a small chicken, with large eyes—and I do believe he can turn his head completely around twice. The sound a hoot-owl makes is really nice to hear, especially when several are hooting to one another. But the scream they let out in the middle of the night would be enough to shake up a saber-toothed tiger, if there was one left. Not many creatures in these woods can shake you up like that.

The whippoorwill, on the other hand, makes the most attractive call of the wild. It is most always heard at just-coming-dark. Like owls, whippoorwills are nighttime feeders. Their eyes shine bright and will fool a greenhorn hunter, especially when the bird is four foot from the ground like a deer or up in a tree like a raccoon. But the whippoorwill seldom moves, which is a giveaway to a pro hunter.

* * *

We stayed at Camp Huston about a year, until the summer of 1931. I don't ever remember a campsite I liked as much as that one. When we first went there we were really on the bottom. But by the spring of 1931, the end of hunting season—with Peg trapping with Dad and doing a little fire-hunting on his own, and Dad killing gators and cutting timbers, and my little bit thrown in—we were beginning to crawl out of the hole. In fact, under the circumstances—with the Depression on—we were doing okay.

I was now only eleven years old, but I was being taught the ways of the land by Dad and Peg. I was learning fast how to make my own way. I probably didn't realize how hard it was for us just to get by. To me, moving from the little city of Everglades and going out in the woods camping and hunting was like a long vacation.

It meant a whole lot to me to lay out my own raccoon hides to sell to a dealer. So did handing over my own greenbacks to pay for my guns and ammunition and C.O.D. packages from Sears, Roebuck and Montgomery Ward (old Ted Smallwood called 'em "Come On Down" packages). For some reason, the folks at Sears paid good for just a few hides at a time, so kids like me usually came out fine with them; and in turn, I then had a little money to order things from their catalog. In fact, other than the staple foods and the few odds and ends we got at Chokoloskee, most everything we bought came from the mail-order houses. Their catalogs also served an important purpose in the outhouses at some campgrounds. (At Huston, all we had was a log.)

With summer coming on and the coon-hunting and trapping ended, all that was left for a living was to hunt gators and make moonshine whiskey. That's just what Dad was fixing to do now, same as at Possum Key, only on a larger scale at Camp Huston. Unbeknowing to me and to many others (Dad was always one to keep his mouth shut), he was setting up a large liquor still in a little bay with a creek running into it, in the south end of House Hammock Bay.

A little before this time, the law had busted a still on Mormon Key, near the mouth of the Huston River. Because of this, Dad was playing it safe. In this country there are only about forty shell mounds with ground high enough to operate a still on. Dad's problem was that too many people knew where all the mounds were. But he got around that with a Calusa Indian trick: first he picked out a place where no one would have any reason to go fishing or hunting—a shallow mud bay with lots of mangrove and buttonwood trees for cover. Then he collected shells from the oyster bars in Huston River and *built his own mound by hand.*

Oyster bars have both live oysters and dead shell on them, and both make good fill. But it's a hard job to handle by hand. Dad used the big skiff to bring in the oyster shells. For the mound-building he used only a shovel, a wheelbarrow he made himself, and a five-gallon gas can with the top cut out. There was no worry about being spotted from the air. We hardly ever saw an airplane.

Some sixty years later, the little place where we lived and Dad did his moonshining is still called Liquor Still Bay, just as the campsite I loved so well is still called Camp Huston. If somehow I could call time back, like I see in the movies, and if I could choose a place to relive the best year of my boyhood, without a doubt I'd stretch my skeeter bar on Camp Huston.

5 / Liquor Still Bay . . . making 'shine . . .
/ Prohibition bugs

In the summer of 1931 we broke camp at Huston and moved on a couple of miles to Liquor Still Bay. At this camp, we never left a boat at the landing; Dad said if we did, we might as well get out there and start flagging down the revenuers. Instead, he built a perfect little hid-away dock about two foot wide by fifty foot long. It started just back from the water's edge in the mangroves, wound around through the big mangrove trees he didn't want to cut down, and over the roots and mud out to the shell mound he'd been building while we were all living at Camp Huston. He laid out that dock so cunning: for a walk board from the boat to the dock he had a long two-by-twelve plank; when it wasn't needed, it was put out of sight and no one passing by could see anything.

Then he built a little skiff, small and light enough to drag out of the way when it wasn't in use; he could even drag it aboard our launch and carry it along with him. Dad named the little boat *Hockey Pot*, because it wasn't much bigger than a chamber pot (which Grandpa McKinney called a "thunder mug").

When we first moved to Liquor Still Bay, we had to pretty well stay put most of the day to keep from being seen. To cut wood and hunt for fresh meat, we usually went out a little early or pretty late, when no one was apt to be around; to fish with the cast net, we went out only at night.

Having to stay so close-in that summer, and everybody working so hard, made life a lot less exciting than at Camp Huston. By now, though, we were able to afford a little gas for the launch, and about every other week, generally in the late afternoon, we towed the big skiff, loaded with empty barrels, to the old Lopez River place for fresh water from the cistern. Like all of us, I looked forward to that trip—not only to get out of camp and take a ride, but also 'cause I couldn't wait to climb the tamarind tree there (which is still standing today). While Dad and Peg were filling the barrels, I climbed the tree and threw the tamarinds down to Mother. Back at camp she made

The water cistern at the old Lopez place.

tamarind-ade. Even with no ice and shy on sugar, that warm ol' drink tasted mighty good.

One day, a little three-foot gator showed up at the foot of the dock. Sometimes gators will dig caves under the riverbank, as this one did. When they do, it's their home for the season. Dad and I enjoyed feeding and playing tricks on the little fellow. He stayed with us until the water turned too salty; then he took off into the Glades to hibernate through the dry season.

*   *   *

After we'd been living here for a while, sleeping on the ground, Dad built us a little tar-paper shack. It wasn't screened in or shuttered 'til later. But least we had a roof over our heads, and when it rained, we no longer had to get out of our bedrolls, stash away the bedding to keep it dry, and sit it out among the swamp angels.

Meantime, we kept on bringing in more shell for the mound. We usually went out a little before sundown, after what few fishing guides there were from the Rod and Gun Club at Everglades City had gone home for the day. One time I gathered up a bunch of mangrove bobs (seeds) and planted them on the oyster bed in front of the camp. Today it's a little mangrove key about 100 feet across.

There was certainly nothing easy about making that shell mound by hand. The ground we piled the shell on was nothing but mud, from totally wet to partly dry, as determined by the rainy season. We eventually piled up enough to raise the mound to just above tide-water.

When the live oysters in the shells began to die, the stink and the flies were terrible. Dad spread lime around to help take care of that. But first he had to make the lime: he set fire to a big bunch of buttonwood logs, piled oyster shells on the fire, and then covered the shells with more wood. It took a lot of doing, but we eventually ended up with a pretty nice camp.

✳   ✳   ✳

The kind of whiskey Dad made—'shine, or bush lightning, or corn liquor, as others called it (and still do)—was distilled by boiling beer, or "buck." The buck was made from grain (usually corn), sugar, and water. The corn came in 100-pound burlap bags and the sugar in 100-pound cotton bags; in the Depression, the cloth in these bags was upgraded so it could be made into clothing. (The sacks with pretty flowers on 'em that chicken feed came in were especially good for girls' dresses; we called 'em flower sacks.) As for the corn sacks, many times when the mosquitoes were thick I pulled a sack over my head, another over my feet, and one or two over my stomach and then curled up for a nap on the ground or in the bottom of my skiff. The hair on the burlap helped keep the swamp angels off.

The buck was normally "set up" (mixed) in 55-gallon barrels: half a sack each of sugar and corn to the barrel, which then was filled with water. Not long after, if the weather was warm like summertime, the buck began to "work," or ferment. After ten days or so it was ready to be distilled. If for some reason more time was needed, Dad just added a little sugar, and the buck continued fermenting.

When Dad started out he couldn't afford barrels to set his first batch of buck in. Instead he borrowed my brother Bert's eighteen-foot fishing skiff, drug it out of the water into camp, leveled it up, poured it full of corn and sugar, and topped it off with fresh water we boated in from the Lopez cistern. Soon he had himself a boat full of buck. But, like always in 'shine-making, there came a little problem: the buck ate the paint off of the skiff and Dad had to take about a week to sand and repaint it. After a while he was able to buy 55-gallon oak barrels from Sears, Roebuck.

Dad's 250-gallon boiler was made out of copper. The cone-shaped top narrowed down to fit a three-quarter-inch coil of copper tubing, which was kept cool by running it through a barrel of water. Once the buck starts to boil, the steam is forced down the cool tubing and is condensed, or distilled, to 'shine. Alcohol boils before water, and the first liquid that comes out is the strongest: over 100 proof. The 'shine comes out slow—from a good drip to sometimes just a little more than a drip—and colorless, like vodka.

When first made, it's called fresh-run 'shine and has a slight aroma and a fiery taste. The "fire" can be put out by aging it in a charred-oak barrel with oak chips thrown in to color it. For a quick sale, sometimes Dad added a touch of syrup. He made the syrup by carefully heating sugar in a cast-iron fry pan until it melted and the liquid turned rather dark—a perfect color for what looked like aged-in-the-wood whiskey.

∗   ∗   ∗

About the time we got the corn liquor to flowing good, we ran into another problem, a terrible one this time. There's a tiny bug, about as big around as a toothpick, that cuts a hole into wood like a termite. The difference is, these bugs like whiskey. Dad named them Prohibition bugs. One morning we found several barrels leaking. The bugs had been working for some time, of course, but they were so small they weren't noticed. We whittled out little plugs to stop up the holes. This worked for a while, but the bugs soon outdone us.

Dad was a pro with cement and decided to set the buck in cement-lined vats instead of the oak barrels. But to make cement we had to

Dad's still at Liquor Still Bay, 1930.

go to the coastline for sand. This meant a trip for all of us to the beaches, which of course sounded good to me.

While we were out on the beach at Rabbit Key, we gathered clams and stone crabs. Dad must have picked a new or full moon to make the trip, when spring tides go real low and high, because the tide was so low we were able to walk all over the Rabbit Key sandbar digging clams. They were about the size of the palm of your hand and were lying just under the sandy mud surface.

Until the late 1940s there were plenty of clams. (In the early days, they were dug by hand commercially—it was nothing for a man to dig thirty bushels a day.) But something unknown killed off all the clams in southwest Florida and, at the same time, all the bull conchs, sponges, and most of the stone crabs. (It wasn't red tide because no fish were killed.) The only thing that came back was the crabs.

Dad showed me how to "keyhole" clams. When they bury themselves in the mud or sand, they leave a small hole above, about as wide as a pencil, called the keyhole. After you find this hole, just dig down a few inches and get the clam. Another way is to "feel"

Clam and conch shells left by the Calusa Indians on Mormon Key. The Calusas knocked holes in the conch shells, then knocked out the meat.

underwater with your heels. You walk around that way until your heel strikes a hard place in the bottom, then dig. The clams will live for several days if kept cool and moist.

After catching what stone crabs we could and all the clams we wanted, we loaded up the skiff with sand. With the tide now real high, we could lay the boat right alongside the dry sand and just shovel it in.

Back in camp, we had clam chowder and a great feast on stone-crab claws. Fresh clams right out of the salt water have a real seafood taste, maybe a bit on the strong side, but not for grown-ups, especially me. (For my personal recipe, see appendix 3.)

Next we unloaded the sand, mixed up the cement, and started making the vats. Then, another surprise: the buck ate up the cement—actually destroyed the lining! Dad tried plastering the vats with cement again and again, but it didn't do any good. Then he decided to go with plaster of Paris. He thought for sure that would work, but after a setting or two, it fell apart. Then Dad decided he was going back using oak barrels and he was gonna fix them damn Prohibition bugs—and he did. He plastered every danged inch of the outside of the barrels with cement. I can still see the smile on his face as he walked away. Once the barrels were covered, the bugs gave up on 'em, went into a big buttonwood tree, and whittled it to sawdust.

Soon afterward, Dad charred some little twenty-gallon oak kegs, filled them with whiskey, and hid them to age in the woods away from camp. Then we found out the bugs had tracked down those kegs and were drunk again. I don't know how much whiskey was lost or how many bugs got snowed under, but I do know Dad finally damn well sobered 'em up. He sealed the entire keg with plaster—bottom, top, and all—and made a little X over the bunghole. When the time came to get the 'shine out, he broke the plaster at the X, pulled the plug, and siphoned the 'shine out with Mother's syringe hose.

Solving this problem took a lot of time, but by fall that year we had outdone the Prohibition bugs and had the corn liquor flowing like rain across the Everglades.

* * *

When we could take some time off, Dad, Peg, and I went up a little creek in House Hammock Bay to the old House family place. At the end of the creek, the Houses had dug a ditch about half a mile through the mangroves to a shell mound they lived and farmed on.

Mangrove deer feed on both the mangroves and on the mounds. As we walked up the side of the ditch, we saw plenty of fresh tracks of a big buck, but we didn't spot him.

We spent the night in an old shack that was still standing there Dad showed us a hole in the door screen. He said Henry Short—the man who put the first bullet into Ed Watson on the dock at Chokoloskee, back in 1910—shot a panther one evening right through the screen. An old-timer had told Dad there was a shell ridge out in the mangrove swamp between Huston River and House Hammock—a very odd place for one to be and hard to get to. Seeing a lot of deer sign at House Hammock, we figured for sure the deer ranged back and forth from that ridge to here.

One morning later on at Camp Huston, Uncle Doc (Dad's brother Clarence) and his two older boys, James and Albert, stopped by on their way to hunt deer. When Dad mentioned the sign we'd seen at House Hammock, Uncle Doc says, "Let's go get 'em!" Then Dad says, "Instead of the hammock, let's try that third ridge the old-timer told me about. I think we'll do better there."

We paddled south down the river about half a mile to the nearest point of land to the ridge. We spread out right and left along the river-bank within hollering distance of each other and then went north-west. We each had a gun, not only for hunting but for signaling as well. I had my little 12-gauge single-shot thrown across my shoulder, and my eyes were peeled like a banana. Dad and Uncle Doc took the sides so us kids wouldn't get lost.

When hunting in the thick mangrove country, we usually use a shotgun. The woods and brush are so thick you don't generally get but a glimpse of the animal, like maybe you see a deer jump about twice and that's it. (Seeing or shooting one moving like that is called "jumping a deer.") For quick shooting at close range the shotgun with buckshot is much more effective than a rifle and is also a good signal—its muzzle blast carries a long ways. When in distress we fired two close shots, took a short pause, and then fired another shot. That signal was never mistaken by us natives.

Late in the afternoon, Uncle Doc fired his ol' L.C. Smith double-barrel shotgun: he'd found the third shell ridge. It turned out to be probably seventy-five yards wide by two or three hundred yards long, and three or four foot high above the mud it sat on. The ground was real rich, with the biggest mastic tree on it I've ever seen (the mastic looks like a tamarind and its resin makes varnish). We didn't see any deer but, like we thought, they sure had torn that place up, and Uncle Doc's eyes got as big as rough lemons. The deer had beat down a trail going toward House Hammock that you wouldn't believe. When Dad saw it, he says, "Let's set a gun on this trail."

Setting a gun is very, very dangerous and naturally against the law, and it wasn't done but very little in this country. It's too easy to walk into one in the woods. (One old-timer here, before my time, walked into his own gun and shot himself in the stomach.) To set a gun, a wire or dark cord is stretched taut across the trail. The gun, aimed about shoulder-high, is tied down with something solid behind the stock. A short post, sawed off flat on top, is driven down near the gun, with a foot-long stick nailed on top by one nail—to pivot and act as a lever. The wire is tied to one end of the lever and the other end lays against the trigger. When the taut wire is bumped, the trigger is pulled and the gun fires. It's so easy to trip that wire—that's why you should never set a gun.

Dad was quite positive no one would come near the ridge, so he decided to take the one chance. He set the gun with a cord he had in his pocket, and we were soon on our way back to the boat. Forty-five or fifty minutes later, just as we were stepping into the boat, someone thought he heard a gunshot, only not for sure. Instead of going back to see if the set gun had really fired, we decided to wait 'til morning. Dad left camp about daybreak and was back by nine that morning with a big deer. Where the buckshot went in was already getting sour, so the gun we thought we'd heard the evening before had to have been ours.

✳   ✳   ✳

We stayed at Liquor Still Camp through the summer and fall of 1931 and into part of that winter. Peg and I set raccoon traps in a trail we'd cut through the mangrove swamp to Camp Huston and a few in the little bay and creek; we didn't do any good to speak of, but the swamp angels did—they came damn close to eatin' us up. Because Dad was afraid someone might see us if we trapped in the river, and that could lead 'em to the still, we didn't do it, even though Old Man Lopez did. But that was all right—he was a good friend and we could count on him to keep his mouth just as shut about the still as Dad did.

Mr. Lopez had an old sloop that he anchored right near the mouth of Liquor Still Creek and camped on for the winter. He also had a small motorboat to tend his traps with and for going into Chokoloskee for supplies. His little runabout had a one-cylinder motor, probably two or three horsepower, with a flywheel that weighed a hundred pounds or more and fired about one time a minute. You could hear it pop-popping for miles. Every morning, just like clock-work, the ol' pop-popper came a-poppin' down the river, stopping at each trap.

One day, we didn't hear the pop-pops and Dad got a bit con-cerned. The next day we still didn't hear anything and Dad said we'd better check on the old man. We went out to his sloop and found him burning up with fever. Dad soon found out why. Some of the coons Mr. Lopez had trapped must have been covered with ticks because in the old man's ears there was three of the biggest ones I've ever seen. Dad got the ticks out and made Mr. Lopez some hot tea. He seemed to feel better, and sure enough, next morning at daybreak we heard the pop-pop again.

The old man's son, 'Fonso, sold most of Dad's 'shine for him. Dad and I used to leave jugs of it by a black mangrove tree in Turner River for 'Fonso to pick up. We usually went there at night and always left a note tied to one of the jugs telling him when to expect the next pickup. 'Fonso never failed to leave the empties and any supplies Dad had ordered in the note.

One time Dad stayed at camp by himself while Mother and us kids dropped off the jugs and waited at Grandma's for delivery of a Sears package. (Sometimes we had to wait several days.) One night while we were gone, he was sitting alone at a table out in the open near the fire, reading by a dim carbide light, when all of a sudden a panther jumped completely over the table!

Dad figured he was sitting so still while reading, not moving a muscle, that the cat hadn't even seen him at first. But when Dad made a sudden move, to roll a Prince Albert cigarette, it startled the cat into making a jump. The tracks where he landed—after a jump of more than twenty feet—were there for a long time.

*   *   *

After getting the Liquor Still camp set up good, Dad moved us on again in 1932; this time we went south about six miles to Chatham River. Uncle Doc had gotten the claim on the old Watson place, which the desperado Ed Watson had built twenty-five years earlier at

Chatham Bend, about twelve miles south of Chokoloskee and four miles inland from the Gulf. Doc gave us the use of half of the eight-room, two-story house.

We loaded up ol' *Nelly* and headed out again, but this time we didn't completely break camp. We only took what we had to have and left enough for Dad to come back occasionally and run off the 'shine.

6 / The old Watson place . . . shooting the bull . . . Uncle Doc and Big Boy

The old Watson place was pretty well run-down when we got there, but it still looked good to us and was plenty big enough for both families: Uncle Doc, his wife, Hilda, and their four kids; and the five of us—Mother and Dad, Peg, Audrey, and me (brother Bert was on his own, and sister Laberta had just married).

Watson had set his home overlooking the Chatham river, on one of the few shell mounds that the Calusas built above hurricane water. The two beautiful poinciana trees in front were placed just right, one off each corner near the riverbank, and they're still standing today. The house had a long screened-in porch facing the river, and a nice front room with several bedrooms upstairs. The big kitchen and dining room were in the back, with a large back porch. The old wood stove was large enough for both Mother and Aunt Hilda to cook on at the same time.

Before doing much cooking, though, they scrubbed every inch of the house, which meant I had to tote a lot of water from Watson's big cistern (it was guttered down from the roof). Back then the wash water from clothes washing was used to scrub the floors too, and Aunt Hilda and Mother kept theirs spotless. One of the walls at the Watson place was stained with blood from all the killing Watson done before he was done in. (At least that's what we were told when we moved in; I now believe that blood was actually from a man that lost both arms in a cane grinder.) Whatever it was, we couldn't scrub it off. Dad patched up the old screens, then painted them with cylinder oil to keep out the little bitty sand flies. The oil closed up the holes in the screen just enough to keep 'em from crawling through.

I helped Mother and Aunt Hilda set up their wash pot. Back then, all laundry was done outdoors in a boil pot with plenty of Octagon bar soap but no chlorine bleach (there wasn't any such thing at Chatham Bend). After the clothes were boiled, they were scrubbed on a rub board, wrung out by hand, and rinsed from tub to tub. By the time they were hung out to dry on a clothesline, the biggest part

Coconut palms at
Chatham Bend,
around 1937. This
photo was taken by
my dad.

of a day was gone, and some of those clothes still had to be ironed,
with a flatiron heated on the old wood stove.

After getting our home halfway together and starting a garden, we
went to work on the sugarcane patch. It was quite a job. There was
old cane there from Watson's time, but it had just about grown out.
We cleared off several acres, all by hand, and replanted the cane.
Next we went to House Hammock and dug up new sprouts, or

The Watson place at Chatham Bend, 1938.

suckers, from around the old banana trees and replanted 'em at our place. (A tree only buds one time and is cut down; new sprouts come up around the stump.) The hammock was covered with the same tropical fruit trees they all have, especially the ones we call "horse bananas" (very good fried and rolled in sugar, but not too good to eat outright). There were four different kinds of bananas there: ladyfingers, apples, dwarfs, and horse bananas.

We also cleaned out around the old fruit trees—guavas, sugar apples, key limes to put on the fish, sour oranges for pies (Dad's favorite), and plenty of alligator pears (avocados). Along the riverbank were the tallest and most beautiful curved coconut trees I've ever seen.

After getting the field work under way, we went to work on the old cane-grinder, or mill, and the syrup kettle (a large iron pot shaped like a soup bowl, measuring five or six foot across). The kettle was left at the mill when Watson was killed, and it's still there today. Most people would've just built a fire under it and laid a piece of tin up to keep the wind off, but not Dad. Using some of Watson's firebrick, he built a furnace around the kettle and a cement block for the mill to sit on.

The mill had two rollers, like an old-fashioned clothes wringer, and the cane was fed in between 'em. When the cane came out the other side, it was flat and all the juice had been mashed out into a barrel. In Watson's day, most mills were powered by man or mule, but he powered his mill with a one-cylinder, one-spark-plug motor, and it was still there when we moved in. Being a mechanic, Dad soon had it running like a clock, but the governor was broke. One of Doc's boys, James, had to control the motor by putting the spark-plug wire on and off (so Dad nicknamed him the Governor).

While the cane we'd planted was coming along to harvest time, Dad built a perfect little farm wagon with old-time spoke wheels, for bringing it in from the field. It was a dandy, complete with yoke, tongue, the works. He made the U-shaped yoke out of a big, tough vine that grows in the Glades, and it worked fine.

We had a pretty little yearling bull that we fed cane juice till he was as fat as a pig. To all of us the bull was more of a pet than anything else—but what we needed for the wagon was an ox. So we went out to Mormon Key and talked an old cattleman into coming in and castrating the little bull. I hated to see my pet done that way, but he didn't seem to mind; what he did mind was pulling the wagon. But finally we got him broke enough to start him to work come harvest time, a few weeks down the road.

Then right out of the blue yonder, a couple of state agriculture men came down and dumped a terrible problem on us. A new Florida law said you had to dip your cattle for ticks; they'd built a vat at Chokoloskee and forty cows were being dipped there every two weeks. The men told Dad we had to take in our ox and our one old milk cow and have 'em dipped right along with the rest. This could have been done, but it would've been a hard job. It just simply wasn't worth the trouble. It ended up that we did take the milk cow in but chanced keeping the ox.

Just before time to harvest the cane, I was staying with Grandma McKinney at Chokoloskee, waiting for a Sears package, and three men hired me to guide 'em to Chatham Bend. When we got there, they went direct to the field and killed our ox! Dad got out his .45 revolver and I really thought he was going to clean house; but we somehow talked him out of it. Those state men butchered my pet in just a few minutes, threw the carcass on the front porch, and took off.

That ox was down there fifteen miles from nowhere and probably didn't have a tick on him, for I kept him as slick as a peeled onion. He wasn't doing anyone on earth any harm, but that didn't matter to them. Today, looking back on it, I still think it was stupid and unfair.

Because deer carried the same ticks, Florida actually hired professional hunters by the dozens (my Uncle Mick was one of 'em) to go out and kill 'em. The hunters brought in the deer's ears to prove how many they'd killed. I believe the records show the total as just short of 9,000; some of the old hunters claimed there were twice that. But when the stupid politicians got around to ordering deer killed in the Big Cypress country that the government hadn't yet took back from the Seminoles, the Indians said no! The same tick that was on the cows was on every animal in the Glades, they said, including snakes—and the state backed off. It took the Everglades Indians to teach those buzzards a lesson. But they probably knew from the start they were wrong: it was just another way to sponge on the State Treasury.

We had no ice at Chatham Bend, and there we were with the carcass of a full-grown ox on our hands. He was the fattest, with chunks of tallow in him as big as grapefruits. We salted, dried, smoked, canned, jarred, and cooked on that meat for days. We didn't have many cans on hand and it took over a week to get more from Sears, so we couldn't do much canning. Instead, Mother and Aunt Hilda melted all the tallow, and as they cooked the meat, they put it in large containers and covered it with hot tallow. That way it kept for several days. Dad, of course, tanned the hide and made leather, but I never saw a piece of it that I didn't think of my onetime pet.

Getting the cane out of the field without an ox to help us was one helluva job. Some of it we carried out in bundles on our shoulders, the rest in the wagon that we had to push and pull ourselves. It took all hands to do it—Mother, Aunt Hilda, and all—but somehow we managed.

Grinding the cane took one of us to feed the cane into the mill, with James "governing" Watson's old motor; others to stack the cane handy; still others to tend the fire under the kettle; and anyone who could be spared to carry the juice from the mill to the kettle. The juice was boiled down into syrup. (Because the juice is so hot, it's hard to

Our old syrup kettle. The Chatham River is in the background.

tell when to quit boiling it. If it's cooked too long, it becomes thick like candy; or if the fire's too hot, the juice "burns" and leaves a scorched taste in the syrup.) What we didn't need ourselves we sold.

✳   ✳   ✳

At Chatham Bend we put out some *work*. The kind of labor we done, sweat rolled off our brows in drops as big as horse dobs. It took a man-size breakfast to give us the energy for it—not like today, just a little glass of orange juice with a cup of coffee and a piece of light-bread toast. By daybreak we had a hot buttonwood fire going in the stove and Mother had several pans of soda biscuits in the oven, along with a pot of grits and a slab of white bacon. There was always a bottle of good homemade cane syrup to go on those hot biscuits and a little bit of lime to put on the bacon to cut the fat.

Many times, though, we didn't have bacon or eggs and had to settle for fresh tomato gravy. First you fry pork chops; to the fat left over from that, add plenty of onions and black pepper. Fry out the onions and pepper a bit first, add a little water (but not much), put in your sliced tomatoes, then cook for twenty minutes. A few pork chops—or salt pork, which is my choice—is good cooked in with the gravy.

At midday we didn't have lunch, we had our dinner, and it was a full-grown meal. The same in the evening for "supper" (what you call dinner), which usually included a big pot of dried lima beans. They were soaked overnight and then cooked for about two hours with white bacon for seasoning; you didn't put the bacon in at first (or the beans wouldn't ever soften). A bowl of those beans with plenty of raw onions and black pepper would stick to your gut for a while. Add a side of mullet with a little Key lime squeezed over it, and you really had something to chew on. There was always fresh vegetables (especially sweet potatoes and field peas), rice or grits, fried fish, some kind of leftover game, or maybe some corned beef or tripe from the can. Whatever it was, it stayed with you long enough to help you put out a good day's work.

To my thinking, the best meat nature provided us with was the curlew. We could usually find a few feeding birds along the riverbank or on a flyover, going to roost, but not enough for all the time. Our main and faithful hunting ground was just around the bend on Watson Prairie, a grass plain two miles long by a mile wide, where we could usually get wild meat of some kind. Not only curlew but deer as well, and plenty of ducks, especially the big mallards that were so good baked in the old wood stove. We knew the main spots on the

In later years, cutting swamp cabbage (hearts of palm) to eat.

prairie where the birds fed, so we'd put up a blind with tree limbs, prop up a couple of dead birds for decoys, and really mop up. Across the river was another prairie with a large cabbage hammock where we got our swamp cabbage, or hearts of palm. The black bears that hang around there get their cabbage a little different from the way we did. They climb the tree and take hold of the heart with their front paws and rip away at the tree with their back claws until the heart and the bear both hit the ground. If you see the tops of a few cabbage trees missing, you can be sure a bear's been around—and may even still be there!

We kept most of the prairies, especially Watson Prairie, burned off to bring in more game. Burning brought new, tender sprouts and young, green grass for the mangrove deer, which averaged much larger than the deer in the mainland cypress country back in the Glades. Burning also kept the ponds from getting choked with mangroves and saw grass, especially along the southwest border of the Glades. Every bird in the country, along with small animals and gators, thrived on the little ponds—especially in drying-up season, when all the small fish, crabs, crawdads, snails, and whatever were forced into them. It was a big kick for us kids to set fire to the wetland prairies. With a little breeze and the mud wet like it was then, they burned like wildfire. A few days later, they looked as green as the White House lawn—you could have landed a plane on them.

The more we burned, the more game there was. But if we *didn't* burn a place, the saw grass and the mangroves took over and soon there'd be no game. So when the rangers stopped all burning in the Everglades National Park around 1950, the prairies that had been overrun with game became, before my very eyes, a swamp that even a Glades rabbit would be forced to turn down. The wildlife is there no more. Thank God ol' Mother Nature does start a few fires on her own, but she's a-needin' help, and bad. Would you believe it, the rangers would do their damnedest to put her fires out too. Now that it's about too late, they are doing some controlled burning. Somebody must have finally saw the light, but the light wasn't bright enough.

In 1955, long after the park was closed to hunting, I snuck up to one of the marshes where we used to go for deer. The saw grass had grown higher than my head, and there was not a deer track to be seen on the marsh. I was so damn aggravated I stuck a match to it! About three weeks later, I slipped back and killed two deer there in less than an hour. At least the deer had some tender green grass to feed on for a while and I had another taste of wild meat.

Every time we would set fire to Watson Prairie, the biggest old buck I ever saw showed up there afterward for a few weeks and then moved on. Uncle Doc got started trying to kill that old buck, which we named Big Boy, but the buck outsmarted him every time. Still, Uncle Doc kept coming so close to getting Big Boy that he just couldn't give up.

One day he was on the edge of the prairie, well hid in the mangroves, when he spotted Big Boy far, far away on the other side. Sometimes you can wave something white that's about the size of a deer's tail and a deer will come to it, maybe thinking it's another deer's tail flashing. Doc charmed Big Boy that way with his handkerchief and got him to come from the far side of the prairie almost all the way to him. But just before the buck came into range, someone started up the motor in a charter boat on the river. The noise scared Big Boy, he cut and run, and Doc lost out again. After his hours of coaxing he was just all the more determined. He said that ol' buck loping across the prairie in the afternoon sunlight was the prettiest thing he'd ever seen.

Doc finally got to the point where he couldn't hardly work or sleep for trying to outsmart that buck. One rainy evening, usually a good feeding time for deer, we were all working in the cane field when all of a sudden Doc threw down his hoe, looked at the overcast sky, and said with a gleam in his eye, "I'm gonna kill that ol' buck this evening." It wasn't long before we heard his motorboat heading up the river for Watson Prairie.

He didn't make it back until just dark, but when he did, he had half of what he'd gone after. Doc had killed Big Boy on the far side of the prairie back out in the mangroves. But that old buck was so big he could only carry his front quarters. He'd left the hams hanging up in a tree. We set up most of the night while Doc told us how he'd outsmarted Big Boy.

Next morning, bright and early, we went after the rest of the deer.

We thought by then a panther might be there claiming the hunk of meat, so we all carried our guns, planning on a big kill. But the meat was just like Doc said he'd left it.

Uncle Doc was proud of his kill and he should have been, for as I said, it was the largest deer I've ever seen. Today, though, bucks like that are few and far between, and I'm not so glad now Doc killed ol' Big Boy.

7 / Life at Chatham Bend . . . my first boat . . . how to catch a boar gator

By the fall of 1932 we had the old Watson place pretty near shipshape and were much better off financially. We had enough syrup put away in one-gallon cans to sell through the winter, but we still had to keep grinding out cane juice for Dad to make 'shine with, because cane juice won't keep.

Coonskins and other pelts were holding their own, pricewise. Gator hides seven foot or larger stayed at about $1.50 per hide. Today, of course, a permit is required to hunt gator, and the hides are $4.50 a foot, plus $6 a pound for the meat. (There was no market for the meat back in the thirties.) Dad was making out fine at the still at Liquor Still Bay. We had plenty of traps and good guns and lights for fire-hunting. By this time we could well afford gas and Dad decided to rig up a small motorboat, or kicker, for Peg to tend traps in.

The little one-cylinder water-cooled motors weren't real dependable: they'd take you out but seldom brought you back. So Dad started looking for a better one. The Sears catalog offered a little one-horsepower, lightweight, air-cooled motor. It wasn't much bigger than an old-time coffeepot, but Dad finally got up enough nerve to order one.

Meanwhile he built a little twelve-foot skiff for the motor, and you should've seen the smile on Peg's face the day he motored off—instead of rowing—to tend his traps. The little motor was so small it didn't seem possible for it to shove that boat at all, but it really tore up the water. Dad named it the *Little Wonder,* and we'd all sing, "It's a wonder what makes this thing go."

But one day Peg came poling the *Little Wonder* back in. She wouldn't make another pop. Dad ground the valves and the motor ran like a clock for a few weeks, until one day here come Peg poling back again. Finally, Dad figured out the problem: he'd been using leaded gas, like we had always used on our water-cooled motors. So this time, after he overhauled the *Little Wonder,* he used nothing but white (unleaded) gas. From that day on, no problem.

The *Little Wonder* soon gave other people ideas. 'Fonso Lopez rigged up a boat with a six-horsepower motor that could outrun everybody's. But he had a problem: his son Virgil, who was about my age and such a wild one that Dad nicknamed him Tarzan. (The men on the island called Virgil's buddies "the Apes." They'd say, "Look out—here comes Tarzan and the Apes!") 'Fonso just couldn't keep Virgil from stealing his boat and running away. The worst of the problem was that 'Fonso couldn't find a boat fast enough to catch him in.

Growing up, Virgil and I were close friends, and several times he came down to Chatham Bend in 'Fonso's boat. One trip he hung around a little too long, and when 'Fonso slipped up on him in the dark, Virgil ran for the cane patch. 'Fonso cranked up the motor and pretended he was leaving. Then he quietly *rowed* back without being heard, caught Virgil, and took him home. Virgil told me later that while he was hiding in the cane, rattlesnakes were buzzing everyplace he stopped, and at every jump, he was afraid a panther was gonna grab him by the seat of his pants. But in the end, it was his dad who done the grabbing.

By 1933 I'd earned enough money to buy my own motorboat, with a little one-and-a-half horsepower motor made by the Kelly Company. We called them Kelly kickers. Instead of a wheel, there was a small rope on each side of the boat for steering. Times were so hard most people were still rowing, so you can imagine how proud and excited I was, a kid of thirteen, when I took hold of the steering lines of that little kicker and captained her away.

I really done some work to get that boat. When we went to the island for supplies, I worked every moment I could, cutting out nets for fishermen. The job involved taking an old, worn-out net and cutting away the ropes, corks, and leads to use on another one. It was a full day's job, but believe it or not, all I would earn was ten to maybe twenty-five cents. Some days I rowed a big skiff over to the mainland shore and cut a boatload of firewood for Aunt Bessie and Aunt Annie on the island (Dad's sisters, married to the Daniels brothers, Jack and Cap). They burned the wood to boil water for the family wash. Their husbands usually overpaid me—a dollar-fifty for a seventy-five-cent job.

Me at about age thirteen and baby sister Audrey, about four, in a banana patch at Chatham Bend.

Once I got my own little kicker, us boys usually went by ourselves in to Chokoloskee for supplies. Around then I was spending a lot of time with my cousin Albert, who my dad had nicknamed Kelly when he showed up at church one day wearing a green necktie. (There was a popular song then that went "Has anybody here seen Kelly, Kelly with a green necktie.")

Getting my own kicker also made a big change in our ways around Chatham Bend. We done a lot more fishing and hunting. By now Peg had learned to throw the cast net himself. Us kids towed a skiff out to the fishing ground, and while Peg threw the net, the rest of us rowed the boat. Other days we went down to the mouth of the river to go graining. We had a two-prong spearhead called a grain (something like a frog gig, only stronger) which we slipped over the end of a long, slender pole with a light cord tied to it. We threw it like a harpoon, and the grain came loose from the pole after striking the fish. One of us would row the skiff while the other stood in the bow and struck the fish. Dad could throw that thing like he could throw a rifle ball from his rifle, and Peg was no slouch himself. I, of course, watched and learned from their every move.

We still hunted coons, too. We'd tow our hunting skiffs down to the mouth of the river and rowed around fire-hunting for the coons coming out on low tide to catch fish.

Coming in from hunting, we tried to make sure our guns were unloaded before leaving them in the corner of the big screened porch. One morning after coffee, my cousin Kelly, Peg, and I were on the porch and Sport, our big old hound dog, was in the corner looking out on the river. Kelly picked up Peg's gun, pulled the hammer back, and aimed it at Sport's head just as the dog looked around. Kelly says, "Ol' boy, if this gun was loaded, it'd be your head." And sure enough, it was—the gun went off with a roar and so did Sport's head! That shook us all up, Kelly the most. He dropped the gun and out the door he went, running around and around the house. We thought he'd never stop—that's how upset he was.

*   *   *

The winter months were always the best. The nights were cool and there weren't many skeeters, making the coon-hunting and camping-out especially good. It was always the most fun to go hunting with Dad. There was something to go after—deer, birds, coons, or gators—most every day through the winter.

When Dad went gator-hunting, I went along occasionally and once he helped me catch fifteen little gators, from one to four foot long. I kept them in one of Watson's old abandoned cisterns near the dock and put wooden floats in it for the gators to sun themselves on.

Watching them just about every day, I learned their habits. Late summer and fall, they ate anything you threw in and would fight over it something terrible. The first part of winter, they ate coon carcasses like they were going out of style. But in the spring, they ate nothing and went into hibernation. The water was about four foot deep in the cistern, and during their hibernation, the only movement they made (which was very slow, like for hours) was from the bottom to the top for air, and then they only stuck their nose holes out and back down again.

Many times I took one of the gators out into the field, as much as a quarter of a mile from the river. No matter how I turned the gator around, it headed straight for the closest water every time. You can lay a gator down on his back, stroke his stomach very gentle for a minute or two, then turn it loose, and it'll lay there for a while like it's asleep. I tried putting one of my little gators to sleep like that out in the cane patch, and every time it rolled over, it headed for the river. A gator's instinct never fails.

We had a problem at Chatham Bend with one big boar gator. In the first part of the winter, before he went into hibernation, this gator hit our trap line again and again and took several coons, traps and all. This was a big loss, but there didn't seem to be much we could do about it.

Some gators can't be killed in the daytime, even with a high-powered rifle—they are smart enough to sink before you get a chance at a shot. And some are too smart for the headlight at night. A gator like this has usually been shot at before, doesn't care for any more of it, and is wise enough to feel the vibrations, or hear your sounds, or see you first—and pull his snout down when you come by.

In early 1934, a man came upriver and stopped by for a chat. He was about fifty years old, a hunter from Texas, and he'd come to Florida because of the Depression. His name was Arthur Leslie Darwin, and he claimed to be a fifth cousin of the famous Charles Darwin. This Mr. Darwin told us how to catch boar gators using a fishing line and a hook.

Dad didn't put much stock in this, but us kids did. The next day, Kelly done exactly what Mr. Darwin said. He got a fishing line with a no. 8 hook, then killed a heron for bait. He tied one end of the line to an overhanging limb with plenty of give to it, put the hook (inside the bird) on the other end, and laid the bird on a log where the gator could get to it easy, which he did. Mr. Darwin told Kelly that when he went back the next day the gator would be right there, lying on the bottom. Then, if Kelly pulled on the line very easy-like, the gator would slowly come to the top. When the gator's head cleared water, Mr. Darwin said, Kelly had better be ready to put lead in his eyes. Sure enough, it worked just like he said. Kelly killed a twelve-footer that would have cost us many more traps and coons.

Mr. Darwin lived out his life in this country. In the 1940s, he became a hermit at Possum Key (the same camp where we used to live). He died in 1975 or thereabout, in his nineties, still at Possum Key—the last white man ever to live in the Everglades National Park.

*   *   *

While all the hunting and fishing and farming was going on at Chatham Bend, Dad finally got far enough ahead with his 'shine to put 110 gallons away to age in charred-oak barrels. He knocked the end out of two 55-gallon barrels and set fire to the inside to char 'em. Then he put back the ends, buried the barrels in the cane patch (to keep out the Prohibition bugs), and filled 'em with 'shine that we carried out there in 5-gallon demijohns. He let the 'shine set in the barrels for six months or more before starting to sell it. That was the first and only whiskey ever to be aged in this country around here and was considered the best.

When someone came by to buy a gallon of 'shine, Dad sent me after it. He'd rigged up the barrels so we could get the 'shine out of them while they were still buried in the ground. He put an airtight tire valve on each barrel and ran a copper tube to the bottom. He then connected Ma's syringe hose from the tube to the jug, screwed a tire pump on the valve, hit it about twice, and out come the prettiest colored 'shine I ever did see. My cousin Kelly didn't know where the 'shine was hid and tried hard to get me to tell him, but to no avail. I was a big boy now and Dad had told me that no one was to know. But Kelly pulled a fast one on me: he sneaked up on top of the house, watched my every move, and saw just where I went to fill that empty gallon jug. But so far as I know, Kelly never told anyone about those mystery barrels in the cane patch.

*   *   *

Sometime in 1934, we moved again, this time back to Chokoloskee. After the park rangers took over in 1947 and run off everybody who was living there, someone burned the Watson place down. It was probably the rangers, who had burned everything else the old settlers had built since the 1880s.

Looking back on Chatham Bend, it certainly offered a good, clean, wonderful life to a youngster growing up. There were times the mosquitoes were so thick you couldn't hardly bear 'em, and I didn't have any toys like kids today, and sometimes nothing but flour gravy and grits or beans to eat. Still, it was so far beyond the life of today. It's a shame every youngster don't get a chance at a few years of that kind of living. As for me, if I had my life to live over, I'd put most of it in Chatham Bend.

8 / School days on Chokoloskee

Good as life seemed to me at Chatham Bend, in the spring of '34 Mother put her foot down and said she was moving back to Chokoloskee to put her kids in school, especially Audrey. Mother's father, Grandpa McKinney (known as the Sage of Chokoloskee), had encouraged her to take a few college courses, which she did, in Tampa, Florida. Back then very few women in these parts got a chance at high school, let alone college. Naturally, she wanted the same for Audrey. By now, Peg and I had both had a shot at working at something far more exciting than school. I guess Dad and I would have stayed at Chatham Bend forever, but we all knew Ma was right and one day we loaded up ol' *Nelly* and headed out to Chok for good. But Dad just couldn't give up Chatham Bend completely: he made sure to leave enough supplies around for him to camp there part-time—and also go hunting, brew some moonshine at nearby Liquor Still Bay, and do a little commercial fishing with his brother Mick. Once again we moved into Grandma McKinney's big house with a partition down the middle.

*　　*　　*

In October 1924, Grandpa McKinney had written in his newspaper column: "Our school teacher . . . is going to give up her school today; it is too much for her nerves. She seems to be a nice refined lady and we are sorry for her. She had a trying time here, but we can give her praise for her endurance." The following month, he reported worse news: "We have . . . no school. We heard of a he-teacher who started down here and got as far as Marco and found out he did not have his fighting spirit along; so he went back up the coast."

Seven months later, in May 1925, things hadn't gotten much better: "Our school is moving slowly, being somewhat crippled up, the swamp angels being so fearful just now. It is hard to run anything here successfully now except a spray gun."

By 1934 Chokoloskee had a fairly nice grade school. But getting me back into school now was about like trying to cage up a wildcat. Mother had taught us what she could while we were at Chatham Bend, but most of what I learned down there sure never came out of schoolbooks. By the time we got back to Chokoloskee I was going on fourteen, and I managed to make it into the seventh grade before I quit completely. Mother tried her best to keep me in school, but I was capable of doing a man's job now, and I finally talked her out of it.

There's a few things about Chokoloskee School that have stuck in the back of my mind. One was the ding-dong bell with a pull-rope hanging down to make it ring; the cistern to catch rainwater, with its cedar bucket and dipper; the little outhouse with the Sears, Roebuck catalog and the boys trying to peep at the girls; my teacher, Mrs. Rollins; and the prayer every morning. Mrs. Rollins told me once that every time you learn something, a new wrinkle comes in your brain. I often wondered how many wrinkles I'd have by the time I was grown.

Us kids didn't go much for games. We were more interested in the country ways of life, like hunting or going fishing in our little boats with nets or hooks. The only games I remember was hopscotch, marbles (Peg was tops at that), and baseball, with a buttonwood stick for a bat and corn sacks full of broke-up oysters shells for the bases.

Some evenings after school we sneaked into Joe Lopez's (Gregorio Junior's brother's) field and stole sugar apples, pears, and rough lemons to eat with salt and pepper. Rough lemons are very easy to peel, and even the thick peeling is good to eat. They're a little different kind of sour than a regular lemon, and I never saw them anywhere but on the shell islands. There wasn't much for us kids to munch on, so a rough lemon dunked in salt and pepper went pretty darn good, even to the thick peeling—especially if we stole 'em out of Joe's field! We also picked Spanish limes from Ted Smallwood's trees, and then run through his guava grove when we saw him coming. Sometimes we even stole a chicken or two from Mrs. Smallwood and had a chicken roast in the grove.

The main hangout was the old tamarind tree, and the best of that was to let the girls get there first and then run under the tree and look up their "flower sack" dresses. Everyone in the neighborhood spoke of that tamarind (the largest one I've ever seen, and still standing today near the Parkway Motel). We met at the tree and went out from there.

If that tamarind tree could talk, what tales it could tell about the boys and girls I grew up with! But don't get me wrong—I'm not talking about making love, like today. Yesterday was different: a boy seldom got to hold a girl's hand, let alone put it around her waist!

'Most every evening after school there was someone at the tree. If the tamarinds were ripe that was fine. If they were green that was better, because then we dunked 'em in salt and pepper like rough lemons. Anytime we were doing a little sneaky thing (like maybe smoking Bull Durham or Prince Albert tobacco rolled up in a piece of brown-paper bag), it was in the tamarind tree. The trouble was, all the parents knew about that tree and, if they were looking for their kids, that's where they'd come first, and they'd usually catch someone up there, smoking or whatever.

Another one of our hangouts was the old shell mound (gone now) on the east side of the island. Made of pure shell, oyster mostly, and a hundred foot across the top, it was a good twenty foot above sea level—and for this low mangrove country, that was something to see and wonder about. The east edge of the mound was only a few foot from Chokoloskee Bay and was about as steep as land gets. We had a piece of tin we slid down on, right out into the bay. But the biggest thrill was the wire-and-pipe trick.

Out in the bay in about four foot of water we drove a post down and tied a good strong wire to the post, and the other end to a tree on top of the mound. The wire was stretched taut and threaded through a piece of pipe about three-quarters of an inch in diameter by one foot long. We climbed up to the top of the mound, took hold of the pipe with both hands, and turned loose, sailing through the air hanging onto that pipe until we hit the water. We had a string tied to the pipe to haul it back up to the top of the mound.

We played a lot in the little creek near the mound, especially catching fish such as porgies. We even went there at night with a headlight and waded along, blinding the fish and catching them with our hands. The mound was also headquarters for skinny-dipping— just us boys, of course; we never even thought of girls that way. The girls didn't make it to the mound that much anyway. It was too hid-out and too far from home to go without a chaperone.

Chokoloskee Bay is only a few feet deep and the bottom was cov-ered with "trout grass," which is where the little minnows hide that the trout feed on. The bay was full of large speckled trout and redfish. When the tides were right of an evening after school, it was nothing for a couple of us kids to row over to one side of the bay and drift back across, fishing with a twenty-foot cane pole with cut mullet for bait, and catch fifty pounds of trout, redfish, and jewfish. They were so plentiful in the Islands you could catch a hundred pounds on one tide with a hand line, using clothes-hanger wire for a leader and a net lead for a sinker.

Sheepshead and snapper were in the Islands in schools. We could go out any time and catch all we wanted. The little baby fish around the dock—snapper, sheepshead, grouper, pinfish, and others—were so thick that we caught 'em by the dozens with a hand line, a bent pin for a hook, and fiddler crabs as bait. But today, I never see one around the docks.

There was never any conchs in this country that people ate as a regular thing, but there is a small "snarly" conch about the size of a golf ball that us kids ate for fun. We gathered up a few and threw 'em on the hot coals (shell and all) for a minute or two, then pulled the meat out. With a can of pork and beans and a piece of onion we had a picnic.

"Sea-graping" was always fun for us kids. It's only a few miles' rowing from Chok to the coastline, and the beautiful white-sand beaches filled up with sea grapes in the fall (if we didn't have a hur-ricane), especially the beach we called Picnic Key. We'd spread a blanket under a grape tree, shake the tree, and then dump the fruit from the blanket into a washtub. Back home, the women cooked 'em up into sea-grape jelly, and was it ever good.

*   *   *

Some of the most exciting trips—with boys and girls together—were when we went "turtle-turning." On these trips, we walked the beach

in couples, but the chaperons didn't let us stay away from the campfire for long.

First you need to know a little something about loggerhead turtles.
By instinct, they come ashore on the coastline by the dozens in May,
June, and July to lay their eggs—the same coastline they were
hatched on. They crawl out on the sand beaches at night, usually on
full or new moon, because the high spring tide makes it easier for
them to get out. Once a turtle has left the water and is on her way up
the beach to the high land, she's no longer scared of anyone. Most of
the laying turtles are rather large, two foot or more wide and three or
more foot long, and very heavy—over 100 pounds and sometimes
much, much more. An average laying is probably 125 eggs, laid every
twelve to thirteen days through the laying season. The shells of the
eggs are soft and very tough, like canvas.

The turtle first digs around in several different places, trying to
make it hard for other animals, like raccoons, to find where she actually buried her eggs. Once she decides on the spot, she digs a hole
with her back flippers, first one, then the other. She turns her flipper
edgeways like a shovel and as she shoves it down into the sand she
slowly cups it. Then all at once, very quick-like, she throws the sand
up and out. Then the same with the other flipper, until the hole is
about a foot deep and a little bigger around than a football. It's
amazing how such a clumsy thing can dig such a perfect round, deep
hole. Once the hole is ready, she starts laying her eggs in little
bunches, like a half-dozen or so at a squirt. After she's finished
laying, she covers her nest up and pats the sand down real tight with
her back flippers, one at a time. When that's all done she scratches
around, doing a little more camouflaging, and heads for the sea.

Now for the sad part. The minute she heads out, the raccoons that
have been just waiting for her to leave start digging the eggs up to eat.
Very few eggs make it, but don't blame us natives for that—*we* don't
eat them. In fact, when we "turn a turtle," we always let her lay her
eggs first. Then we follow the turtle down to near the water and turn
it over on its back.

Because a turtle cannot turn itself back over, she can be left there
near the water's edge until time to load her on board. Then she is

turned up on her side against the low-sided skiff and flipped into the boat. Back at Chokoloskee, we butchered the turtles on the beach and took them home for dinner.

Turtle-*timing* is when you see where a turtle has crawled out on a beach to lay her eggs, then count twelve to thirteen days ahead and she'll be back then for her next laying.

By the way, did you know that alligators also lay eggs? They do—about twice the size of a hen's egg—and after ten weeks in the hot Florida sun, out come the last of the dinosaurs.

* * *

In my time there was only one church on Chokoloskee, the Church of God. In my courting days the church house was an old-time wood building setting up on buttonwood posts with wooden shutters for windows, no ceiling, a kerosene lamp for a light, and an old brass bell that Grandpa McKinney gave them. (He also gave part of the land the first church was built on, around 1900, and the more modern one they have now is on the same spot.) What little courting there was back then usually went on either in church or in the front room of the girl's home under the brightest of lights.

Before the road was built in 1956, most people on the island were natives and very religious—not every member of every family, but usually some in most families, especially the older people. You never saw a woman in pants and they usually had long hair, very little makeup, and very little jewelry, if any. It was a very strict community in that respect. 'Most everyone went to church on Sunday morning and again on Sunday night. Most of the net-fishing was done at night, but on Sunday nights the church members didn't go out on the water until after the evening service. Until I got married and went to work so hard, there were very few Sundays I missed church and Sunday school.

Grandma McKinney and Grandma Brown were full-fledged members and never missed a meeting, not even when they had revivals, with prayer meetings every single night for a month at a time. The first revival, held in 1913, was followed by a baptismal service at the landing near Grandpa McKinney's home. In one of his columns, Grandpa said he wished they'd gone somewhere else for the baptisms because he didn't want all those sins washing up in his front yard.

The revival was conducted by a preacher named J. J. ("Babe") Whidden. "Brother Babe Whidden has been with us all week," Grandpa McKinney reported, "preaching with some good attendance, sometimes very few. . . . [He] baptized four of the disciples. Mr. C. A. Row was a backslider and thought it best to take another dip after being reclaimed."

There was more or less an agreement among the fishermen to take Saturday night off and "rack up" (put the nets on long poles to dry and to be mended) on Sunday, giving the fishing grounds a rest. Saturday night, except for churchgoers, was show-time at Collier's movie house. There was no road, no ferryboat to get us there, but Jim Demere always had a nice boat and everyone was welcome to ride with him. Or with my brother Bert, who had one of the fastest boats in the bay: a twenty-six-footer with a Chrysler car motor.

There was no ice-cream or beer joints on Chokoloskee, so when we hit Everglades City they some kinda knew it. (I can still see those cops shaking their heads when they saw us stepping out of our boats.) Some of the boys ate ice cream and goodies till they got sick, some drank beer at the old bakery till they didn't care whether they saw a movie or not, and some wound up in the town jail for disturbing the peace (they were really just letting off steam after working hard all week). But most of us outran the law, pushed out in the river in our boats where they couldn't get to us, and headed for home.

9 / A man at fourteen . . . the squall of the panther . . . fifty long miles in a rowboat

On March 12, 1934, I turned fourteen. It was that year I took on a man's job and I haven't forgotten yet how I enjoyed every minute of it, fishing for mullet with a 300-yard gill net and an eighteen-foot skiff, a big rowboat with eight-foot oars.

The year before, the wholesale fish companies got down to paying only a cent a pound for mullet, ten dollars a thousand. But in '34 the fishermen, especially in the bay area, organized a union. The Chokoloskee boys (including me) started it on our own. We all paid $1.50 a month dues, but it was worth it: the selling price of mullet went up to *three* cents a pound! (Today mullet sells for twenty-five cents a pound.) In spawning season, which is only three weeks long, red-roe mullet goes for a dollar a pound. The Japanese make caviar out of it; we like it fried.

Through the winter I'd saved up enough money from coon-hunting and working part-time for the fishermen to buy what I needed to make a full-length commercial net: webbing, ropes, and twine. For months I bought second-hand net leads and floats at a cent apiece from other kids.

After making the net, I still needed a fish skiff, so I took out my first loan: thirty dollars from the Bank of Everglades City for thirty days. An older fellow co-signed my note. (From then on I was able to borrow on my own signature.)

Thirty dollars bought me enough cypress lumber for an eighteen-foot skiff. My older brother Bert had just built one for himself and now he built another for me. The two of them were top-notch boats that could each haul about eighteen hundred pounds of fish. I could never tell it in words, just how proud and happy I was the day I boated my own net on board my own fish skiff and rowed away like a full-grown man!

During our stay at Chatham River I had just kinda grew up overnight. I proved myself enough to establish credit 'most every place—the bank, stores, and above all the wholesale-fish companies.

Credit with those companies meant a lot to a fisherman: there were times when nets, boats, and other gear was hard to come by, but if you had good credit with the companies, most of your worries about fishing gear were over.

I must add that Bert had more'n a little to do with the man I turned out to be. From the time I was fourteen, I was with him a lot more than with my parents. Bert always took out time to show me how to do it right. I done as he taught me. I tried hard to keep everything I owned in tip-top shape and just a little better than anyone else's. My plan was to become a captain and own my own launch and skiffs, but that was still some ways down the road.

It was Bert who gave me my first full-time job as a fisherman. He also gave me a place to live while fishing with him. Bert had gotten married in 1933 to Vivian Braman and they'd rented a house from Gregorio Lopez, Jr., on the northwest beach of the island. With Bert's patience and good teaching, I soon learned my way around, along with some tricks of the trade.

Because of the Depression, motorboats were still very scarce. Fortunately, Bert had just gotten a good buy on a twenty-six-foot open launch (no cabin), meaning he could tow both our skiffs out to the fishing grounds and back. If you didn't have a launch, it was hard work rowing an eighteen-foot skiff most of the night, especially if it was loaded with fish. (Most mullet fishing was done at night, at certain phases of the tides and the moon.) Many times, rowing back to the Island after fishing, I've heard the roosters crow at the break of day.

Out at the fishing grounds, we would anchor the launch and get in our skiffs. There was times we put our nets out together and other times we each went our own way. We call putting the nets out "making a strike." First, though, we had to determine if there was enough fish to strike for. One way was to listen for them to jump. Another way, a lot more interesting, was listening for them to "grunt."

When fish are scared into moving suddenly, most of them make a noise that sounds just like a grunt. At night, mullet gather around oyster beds to rest and get away from the sharks. A fisherman then can row up very quietly and punch the bottom with his oar. The fish make a grunting sound that comes up through the oar; a good bunch of fish will sound like thunder. The fisherman then gets into place to make his strike. When the net is put around the mullet, they'll jump out of the water like a shower of raindrops. If they're thick enough, they can be heard for a mile or more as they "shower" and "roar"— along with the fisherman hollering "Whoopee!"

At first Bert and I couldn't afford a camp cookstove, but we still had a way of getting a hot cup of coffee when we rowed back to the launch all wet and cold. We filled the one-gallon bail can two-thirds full of water, added a cup of gasoline, laid a couple of old wrenches across the top to let in air and to set the pot on, then set fire to the gasoline/water below. Because gasoline floats on water, the flames were up near the top of the can, heating the coffeepot just fine. But did the pot ever get sooty! And if there was any wind at all, it looked from a distance like the launch was on fire. Occasionally people stopped by to help put out the fire; instead they probably got a cup of boiled coffee.

Later, we did get us a little two-burner gasoline stove, and the fish we fried up out there beat any steak I've ever chewed on.

*   *   *

In the late fall of '34 Bert and I had an experience that's still a mystery to me. We got together with a couple of our friends, Dexter Hamilton and Raymond Demere, and went mullet-fishing up the Fakaunie, a river north of Chokoloskee (Faka Union River on the charts). We put my net on Bert's skiff and the two of us went in one boat.

We took off in our three skiffs in the afternoon. The river was covered in places with overhanging limbs entangled together, so it was like paddling up a tunnel. Now and then a big alligator or an otter slid off the bank into the water and swam around near the boat. After a couple of hours we came to the first bay in the river and Dexter suggested we stop and build a fire for coffee.

Sitting there on the bank, we could see schools of mullet coming upriver, some of them jumping as much as three foot out of the water. We could even hear 'em from around the point. Raymond says,

"We're really gonna mop up tonight, all these mullet jumping around here." Dexter says, "Yes—but listen for a minute. I hear something jumping that don't sound like mullet to me."

We all listened very close and, sure enough, we heard a large animal of some kind walking in the water alongside the riverbank. A little bit later, with everything quiet and still, it fell or jumped out of a tree across the river from us, about fifty yards away. We only got a glimpse of it—a reddish-brown animal like a panther—but we could plainly hear it splashing water as it ran off. Just in case, Dexter drug out his single-barrel shotgun and loaded 'er up for action, the only gun among the four of us.

All this time the mullet were pouring up the river, jumping like they were having a party. Just at dark we put the nets out. Bert and I tied one end of our net to the mangrove roots on the shoreline. Dexter and Raymond had theirs out in the open. We all bumped and beat on the boats to scare the fish into the nets. By this time it was black dark and very quiet, and suddenly Raymond says, "I hear something."

Sure enough, we could hear the panther on its way back to the same shoreline Bert and I had tied our net to! Then it let out a blood-curdling squall. Usually a man in the Glades isn't much scared by the wildlife, not even a Florida panther. Three of us were full-grown men, but this ol' cat sounded so different and dangerous he had us all scared to death, and the oddest part was that for a change we weren't ashamed to admit it.

This time the cat sounded far away, but every time it let out a yell it seemed a little closer. We soon decided to pull in the nets and see just how quick we could get out of that cat's stomping ground. The hard part was that to get our net, Bert and I would have to go into the mangroves on the shoreline, with the panther getting closer every squall. I wished I had Dexter's old shotgun, but he hung onto it like a baby to its bottle.

By the time Bert and I had gathered up all of our nets except the one end tied to the mangrove roots, the panther was getting too close for comfort. When it got up to within twenty or so yards of the water, it stopped making any noise whatever, and then we couldn't tell *where* it was. By sticking both oars down in the mud for an anchor, we managed to drag the rest of the net into the boat without going ashore. All the while we were there so close, the panther didn't make a sound, but once we rowed away it started again, and a constant growl followed us down the shoreline.

As we went back downriver, Dexter made sure he was in front with the gun, and Raymond made sure he was in the middle. Then came Bert and me, with the cat bringing up the rear. We had a large window-weight in our skiff for an anchor. While Bert paddled from the bow, I had the weight in my hand ready for action, but the action probably wouldn't have amounted to much because that cat had me shaking like a dog passing peach seeds. The cat stayed right with us. When we stopped, he stopped—every time. Finally we came to a fork in the river and took the west branch. The panther continued on down the east branch, growling, screaming, and carrying on like he was ready to tear us apart, till at last he went out of hearing.

I still can't understand why that cat acted so strangely. But one thing's for certain: if everybody through the years had been as scared of panthers as we were of that one, there'd be a dang sight more than twenty-eight (or whatever) left in Florida today.

* * *

On December 10, soon after the panther ran us out of Fakaunie, the season closed on mullet; it would reopen January 20, after the spawning season. Meanwhile, Bert, Vivian, and I went coon-hunting. But this time, instead of camping on the shell or sand islands, we camped on our boats. Bert stretched a tarp over most of his launch for a place for us to eat and for sleeping quarters for Vivian and him. I stretched a tarp over my fish skiff for sleeping.

Late in January '35, we started mullet-fishing again. Because Bert and I both knew the Chatham Bend and Huston areas so good, we decided to put in the season there. In a little bay between the Chatham and Huston Rivers, we built a dock alongside the channel, and Bert tied his new houseboat to it. With the help of our fishermen's union, he'd made enough money fishing (plus the coon-hunting) to get himself a nice boat, large enough for us all to live on—Bert, Vivian, their brand-new baby Bobo, and me.

My oldest brother, Bert,
with his baby Bobo,
around 1937.

We had a perfect layout for the summer and fall, living in the middle of the fishing ground, with a wholesale-fish house four miles south at Turkey Key, practically in our backyard. When time came to go fishing, we usually left the launch tied to the dock, stepped in our skiffs, and rowed away.

I soon learned how to run the launch by myself, and took our fish to sell at Turkey Key while Bert got some sleep on the houseboat. Afraid to leave the houseboat unattended, we took turns going in to the island for supplies. Bert, Vivian, and the baby went in one weekend and I the next.

One weekend, while they were at Chokoloskee, I had some excitement on my own, a little to my sorrow. It was a very still, quiet day with no ripple on the water. I was on the dock, mending the nets, when I noticed a couple of manatees (sea cows) "blowing" (coming up for air) out in the bay. I decided to take a crack at one of 'em with my shotgun. I knew it wouldn't be easy: we'd kill one occasionally for food, if times were really hard, and it usually took a whole lot of shooting, using a high-powered rifle. Not having a rifle,

A wholesale-fish house on a scow, pulling out for Turkey Key with a houseboat, launch, and fishing skiffs in tow. (Courtesy of Ted Smallwood's Store.)

Brother Bert's thirty-two-foot mackerel boat, his eighteen-foot mullet boat, and his hunting skiff.

I cut a 12-gauge shotgun shell in two (if you do it right, the fine shot in the shell stays together and becomes like an ounce ball—very effective). I got all set and pushed out to the cows in my skiff. When one came up, I let 'er have it. I only fired the one shot and when I didn't see the cows anymore, I thought maybe I'd missed.

About a week later, I went upriver to where Dad was camping on the Watson place all by himself. Did he ever raise hell! He said that a dead sea cow had drifted up to his dock, "killed by some s-o-b just to be killing something," and he wished to God the people around here would learn some sense! You can rest assured I didn't tell him *I'd* killed that sea cow, and did I ever make a quick getaway. Dad had taught me not to do that kind of thing and I was so ashamed I just couldn't admit it. But I can tell you this: from that day on, whenever I pulled a trigger it wasn't for play.

Once during a commercial-fishing strike, one of my best friends, Albert Daniels, and I killed a few sea cows for the community to eat. We examined one we'd killed and found their brain is more in their neck than their head. The next (and last) one we went after, instead of plugging away at its head all day with a high-powered rifle, we killed it with one shot in the neck from a little 32/20 Winchester.

*   *   *

By the mid-1930s raccoon and otter pelts were selling at their best and played a big part in our livelihood, especially during the closed season on mullet. Two weeks before Christmas in 1935, I went on a two-week coon-hunting trip with Ike Smith, a native of the island who was about twenty-five. I was going on sixteen.

By this time my little Kelly kicker from Chatham Bend had had it, and Ike only had a twelve-foot hunting skiff. I had the eighteen-footer Bert had built for me, plus my little hunting skiff, the *Hockey Pot*, from Liquor Still Bay. Ike and I rigged a big sail on my eighteen-footer for the trip. We took all three boats, loading up with what supplies we could afford, like shotgun shells, nails to tack the hides on the coon frames, carbide for our hunting lights, and a few staple groceries. As always we planned to catch fish and kill saltwater birds to eat.

We first rowed our boats out Rabbit Key Pass to the coastline and then stretched our sail. Just as we started south down the coast, a northwester (cold front) began blowing, but not so hard we couldn't continue on. With a quartering wind at our backs, we were hauling tail, "like a wild Indian heading for the saw grass," as they say. It was too rough for the little *Hockey Pot,* so we put her on board my fish skiff and towed Ike's.

Sometime after dark we made it to Big Shark River. We pulled in for the night at an old hunting camp called Graveyard Point. We were then about forty-five miles from Chokoloskee and had just another ten to go to our destination, Little Sable Creek; but it got so rough on the way we began to wonder if we were ever gonna make it.

It was certainly a good feeling when we finally sailed our rig into harbor next night at Little Sable. At the very mouth of the creek was a perfect little high-sand campground. It's been fifty-some years since Ike and I stepped out on that little piece of dry sand, and if I live another fifty years I'll still remember just how wet, scared, and worried we were when we turned that little skiff crossways of the sea to head into that harbor.

Northwesters back then seemed to be stronger cold fronts than today, but even then they usually started letting down after about the third day. But not this time. After several days there was no change—the same fifteen- to twenty mile-an-hour wind kept coming out of the northwest, quartering down the coastline. During those first few days, with nothing else to do, we made ourselves a real camp. Ike had brought along three dozen traps to set on the shore, but the high wind made it impossible to put 'em out there. It seemed like that cold wind would never quit blowing. To keep from using up our matches, we kept a fire going twenty-four hours a day.

'Most every day I went out along the creek, hunting for meat or fish. I had a long-barrel .22-caliber revolver-pistol I played with, trying to kill birds to eat, but usually I ended up killing 'em with my shotgun. There wasn't many curlew so we settled for the Louisiana herons Ike called "crankies" because they never set still. There was no problem catching fiddler crabs for bait and hooking mangrove snapper, sheepshead, redfish, and occasionally a snook. But after about two weeks we began getting low on groceries.

We walked the two miles down the coastline through the woods and roots to North Cape Sable, and cut some swamp cabbage (hearts of palm) to eat. One evening the wind let down just enough for me to chance rowing out of our little creek and down the shoreline to another creek. While I was hunting there, the wind sprung up and I had to stay there alone that night and like to have frozen. I got so hungry I tried roasting a piece of coon I'd killed. It made me sick all the rest of the night.

After nearly three weeks we were down to almost nothing to eat and getting low on fresh water, too. Ike said there was a surface well about 100 yards back from the point of North Cape Sable, two miles away, and we'd better go looking for it, so next morning we did. Ike could remember that the well was near two cabbage trees growing close together, parallel to the beach. After finding the two trees, Ike said to look for a low place and a barrel-top even with the ground, that would be the well. We looked and looked but couldn't find it.

Next morning, we came back with knives, a hatchet, and a machete to dig our own well. It took most of the day, but finally we hit fresh water about five foot down. Within thirty minutes after digging the well, I spotted something white in the grass about twenty foot away. It was a marker for the old well, a short stick drove in the ground with a white rag tied to it. It turned out to be a twenty-gallon barrel with the bottom knocked out and holes bored in the sides, and just as full of good, fresh water as it could stick.

That day, while walking through the woods to the cape, we heard a boat running. It soon came in sight but not close enough, I guess, for the crew to see us. Motorboats were so few that, along with the bad weather, there probably wasn't three boats that passed by during our stay—all of 'em too far away.

Next morning, the wind had calmed. But before we could load up to get out of there, it started blowing again. This day made three weeks we'd been stuck on Sable Creek and we'd only brought supplies for two weeks. We'd planned to be back home for Christmas, and I was sure Mother and others were worried about us, but there was nothing we could do.

Ike, being more experienced, said the wind most likely would calm down next morning about the same time as today, before daybreak, but the calm would last a little longer. That afternoon we got all packed and loaded up and at four o'clock next morning we were sitting around the campfire, waiting for the wind to let up. Right on time as Ike had figured, it *did* let up, and we jumped in our skiffs and started pulling on those oars.

Ike said that if the wind came up again, we'd have to either make it to a creek he knew about up the shore or turn back to our camp. The wind had calmed down enough so we could just barely row our skiffs against it, and we only made it to the creek by the skin of our teeth. Ike said he expected the wind to calm down even earlier next morning and stay calm longer and, if it did, we'd make it to Little Shark River, a few miles to the north.

Again, Ike hit it right on the button, and we did make it to Little Shark and a piece of high land. Next morning, Ike woke me up before day and the wind had died down to nothing—"a slick calm," with the water smooth as glass. The sand flies soon ran us out and we were on our way. From then on there wasn't one breath of wind to sail with! We had to row every inch of those fifty-five hard miles back home. Sometime after dark we made it to the mouth of Broad River. We each stuck an oar down, tied the skiff to it, and fell asleep.

Next morning we tore up a small wooden box, built a fire on top of the carbide can, and cooked up the little bit of nothing we had left to eat. Then we headed for Lostmans Beach, about two miles ahead—the first high land we'd seen since leaving Shark River, and one of the first homesites to be settled in the Lostmans River country. Wallace Rewis and his wife, an older couple, had lived there for many years. The cluster of tall Australian pine trees at their home could be seen from offshore farther than any other landmark on the coastline and was called "Rewis Pines." (In the 1960s the National Park Service destroyed all the Australian pines along the coastline, because they weren't *native* trees!)

Reaching the pines, we had it made. The Rewises were both at home, and Mr. Rewis said, "Go put on a big pot o' coffee, Ma, we've got company." Mrs. Rewis already had some deer meat stewed up, along with several different kinds of home-grown vegetables, and she soon had several pans of soda biscuits baked and ready for us. After our big feast, we sat in the shade of the pines with Mr. Rewis for a while and then headed out again, with some cooked food and other supplies from Mrs. Rewis to make it back with. Mother was sure glad to see her little teenage "man" safe at home again.

*   *   *

I hunted hard the full hunting season of 1936, from January right into March. I camped on the highland spots throughout the Islands, particularly the sand beaches on the coastline.

Peg and I camped on one trip near Gun Rock, at the mouth of Huston River. Peg was still pulling tricks on me the way he'd done at Camp Huston when I was ten. One night, before I got back to camp, he took the shiny bottom of a Prince Albert tobacco can and, with black mud, rigged up a perfect set of coon eyes. He nailed the "eyes" to a limb in a big black mangrove tree on Gun Rock near our camp, where I couldn't miss shining my light on my way in.

That's just what I did: I saw the "eyes" and blasted away at 'em with my 12-gauge shotgun. But what I thought was a big boar coon kept sitting in the fork of that tree in perfect view and I just couldn't bring him down. I decided maybe I'd killed the coon and it was laying there dead, looking my way. When I finally climbed up that old tree and found only a piece of tin nailed there, my feathers fell. You can imagine how embarrassed I was when Peg met me at the landing and asked, "Did you get 'im?" But at least I had a good answer this time: "Nope. Shot 'im the first time and missed 'im. Shot 'im the next time and hit 'im in the same dang place."

*   *   *

After fishing with Bert a couple of years, along with coon-hunting, I went out on my own in '36. Someone on Chokoloskee had been building a twenty-four-foot launch but couldn't finish it up. I bought the boat and finished it myself, a step at a time, as I earned the money for lumber and parts. Marine motors were very expensive and there were few around, so the first motor I put in was a used-car motor, a four-cylinder Maxwell from a junkyard in Miami.

While working on the launch, I was going out fishing with different people, and sometimes rowing out by myself. There was one fishing trip I'll never forget. At the time I needed seventy-five dollars to finish my new launch, and I just couldn't wait to put it in the water and become Captain Totch for the rest of my life. Three of us boys— Ernest and Marks Hamilton and myself—went on a week's fishing trip down the coast.

Ernest had brought along a jar of Ovaltine, something we'd never seen before. After we got down around Chatham Bend, about fifteen miles south, we decided to have a cup of it before starting to fish. After the Ovaltine, Marks said he felt sleepy. Falling asleep during a good fishing tide was something we just normally didn't do, even if we had to put tobacco juice on our eyes to stay awake—but that Ovaltine put all three of us to sleep and we lost the tide.

After the little Ovaltine party, we put in a full week of hard fishing in mosquitoes about as thick as they come. Our first stop on getting back was at the wholesale-fish company to draw our pay. We'd cleared seventy-five bucks apiece, just what I needed for my new boat. But our second stop was the dock at Grandpa McKinney's old store building, and a poker game was going on there. That suited me just fine. I'd been lucky at poker lately, winning a little whenever I played, so I stepped right in.

Before morning I'd lost the seventy-five bucks I'd worked so hard for, and owed Scully Brown twenty or thirty besides. From then till now, that was my last poker game! I don't remember how many fishing trips it took to pay off Scully and finish my boat, but I do remember the proud feeling I had when I took hold of the wheel and became captain of my own crew.

10 / Showdown at Jewfish Creek . . . a dolphin and her baby

In 1937, several crews of us from Chokoloskee went mullet-fishing down around Jewfish Creek, near Key Largo in the Florida Keys. We'd never ventured that far southeast before and we soon found out the "east coasters" didn't like the idea of "west coasters" fishing in their territory, especially with us putting it over 'em as we did. Once we got into a good run of fish (after scratching so hard back home), we really laid it on 'em. The season only lasted a few weeks, but before it was over we ended up in a big feud.

The first thing was a fight one night at the Pelican Roost, a juke bar near Long Sound Bridge, on the old overseas highway. A few nights later there was a bigger fight at the old Last Chance, the last bar on U.S. 1 from South Miami to Key Largo. Scully Brown (who only had one good leg) got beat up pretty bad by a big, overgrown brute who also hit him in the eye with a Coke bottle.

This of course went across the grain with all of us, and from then on we were on the lookout for that guy. One dark night while we were in port because of a northwester, one of the boys stumbled up on him in a houseboat. The boat belonged to an old man named Henry. Another old-timer, K. Irwin, lived on it too, some of the time. Henry had a reputation as a bad actor because of killing a man once, and K. Irwin was pretty famous, too, for the way he could handle his .30-.30 Savage rifle.

The big brute was having a drinking party on the boat with his buddies, including Old Man Henry and K. Irwin. Back then we all carried guns on our boats, and we went and got 'em and headed down to the houseboat. Luckily the whole gang was inside. Jimmy Brown stuck the barrel of his double-barrel shotgun in the front door while another of us locked their back door with their own padlock. With Jimmy and two others watching the front door, Bunk Hamilton and I went inside and took the east coasters' guns out of the rack: a shotgun and Irwin's .30-.30 Savage.

Old Man Henry got awful angry and I thought all hell was gonna break loose, but Jimmy settled everybody down fast by cocking both barrels of his shotgun at the same time. When he pulled the hammers back on that ol' two-barrel you could've heard a pin drop. Meanwhile one of the east coasters managed to get on top of the boat. Jimmy heard 'im and yelled, "Hit the water or I'll shoot!" That fellow hit the creek and came swimming back like a wet puppy!

We'd come aboard for two reasons: to get even with the big brute for beating up on Scully and to let those east coasters know that we aimed to finish up the fishing season, peace or no peace. Bunk and I together got the brute down on the floor and I held a big rock over his head, turning it loose and catching it just before it hit 'im in the face. After I done that a few times, he began to beg for mercy. Before leaving we hid their guns in a skiff tied to the houseboat.

That night we threw a party at one of the bars—with Scully right in the middle of it—to celebrate settling the score with the east coasters, as we thought we'd done. But next morning, when we woke up at our camp near Jewfish Creek, we saw a small open boat coming straight for us. In it was K. Irwin and Old Man Henry.

They pulled right up to our landing like it belonged to them. K. had his .30-.30 laying across his knees in plain sight and Henry had a double-barrel shotgun across his. They'd come to tell us something and they didn't beat around the bush. Old Man Henry spoke up loud and clear: "You fellows had better be thirty miles from Key Largo before the sun goes down." Then he turned the boat and off they went, just like that.

What a load of nerve those two men had, and what a pile of guts to go along with it—sailing up to our camp in an open boat, guns across their knees, and telling us straight out to leave the country! Even so, if K. or Old Man Henry would have made a play for it, they'd been both dropped by the two boys in the bushes with their shotguns ready.

But they'd left us sitting in a death trap. Our camp was completely surrounded by thick bushes, except along the water's edge. It'd be so easy for them to slip through the mangroves and shoot us down like rats. There were a few older men in camp that wasn't involved in the feud, and they right away suggested we load up and get out of there.

That seemed like a good idea. For one thing, the fishing had slowed down at this place and we'd been planning to move farther down the keys to Lower Matecumbe. For another, there's no doubt in my mind but what Mr. Henry's gun laying across his lap helped convince us the fishing might be better anyplace else.

But we couldn't just turn our backs and run. We were all from Chokoloskee, and men from the island had a pretty good reputation for standing their own ground. We couldn't let 'em think they'd scared us off. After we got everything loaded on board and we'd anchored out in the bay, we started making some special ammunition. All we had to defend ourselves were shotguns with bird shot, and we needed more firepower than that. We cut off a few net leads from our nets and made some ammo that would sure as hell turn a man around.

A net lead is about an inch-and-a-quarter long and as big around as a dime, with a quarter-inch hole through it. It's just a little bit too big to go through the barrel of a 12-gauge shotgun but, with a little hammering or cutting, it's perfect. By taking the bird shot out of a 12-gauge shell and replacing it with a net lead, you get a two-ounce slug. When it starts skipping across the water whistling "Dixie," if you're in the way you're gonna run for it!

While I was hammering the leads down to size, Bunk Hamilton was loading 'em in the shells, and pretty soon we were ready for action. We sat there all day with our little cannons. Just before sundown, here come K. Irwin's boat, stopping now and then and starting up again, but getting just a bit closer each time. The one who could be seen in the boat turned out to be K.'s son, Art. He said his father wanted to compromise. We hollered back, "Okay!" Art turned the boat and was soon out of sight.

After that we felt like we could leave. Next morning right after coffee, we headed out for Lower Matecumbe. First, though, we had to go through Jewfish Creek, and at that time there was a perfect spot for an ambush in the creek—the old train trestle, the same place the Homestead Bank robbers had their shoot-out. It was scary going through, but nothing happened. The feud with the east coasters just kinda faded away. Some years later, while fishing at Flamingo, I met up with K. again. The feud was never mentioned and K. and I became the best of friends. I even borrowed his .30-.30 rifle to go deer-hunting.

*　*　*

Back home after our little feud with the east-coasters, I was out mullet fishing in a little bay one afternoon and had put my net out in such a way that it cut off most of the pass from the bay to the Gulf. After a while, along came a couple of dolphins, a mother and her baby. They could've gone around the net, but instead the mother chose to take the shortcut and jump over it. Now, to a dolphin, jumping a net in muddy water is no more'n jumping for play. In muddy water they use their radar and it never fails, no matter how muddy the water is. But they can be caught in clear water with a net.

The jump was perfect, only it put the two of 'em inside the compass of my net, completely surrounding them. For some reason the mother seemed uneasy about the baby having to make a second jump, over the far side of the net, to get out. She swam all the way around the inside of the compass, the baby close by, looking for a way to escape. Then she went over the net like a horse jumping a low fence, but the baby got caught underwater in the meshes of the net.

I had been getting ready to quit for the day, and by this time I had part of the net on board my skiff. To go and help the little one, I'd have had to put the net back out or cut it in two. Before I could make a move, the mother dolphin stuck her nose under the baby and raised it up to the surface to breathe. She did this over and over again, just like clockwork. I decided she'd take good enough care of the baby until I could get there, so I carried on.

Close to the dolphins, I could hear them talking to each other and squealing desperately. The baby was the smallest I'd ever seen (three foot or less), and the thought came into my mind to take it home and keep it for a pet in an abandoned cistern on the island.

When I took the little one out of the net and laid it in the bottom of my skiff, the mother was right there, begging me for dear life to let it go. Then she swam around the skiff, blowing and squealing constantly. She began sticking half her body out on every squeal, and the baby answered every time. With the mother dolphin standing by, begging, I finished pulling in my net and rowed to my launch. She stayed right with us. After tying on the skiff and boarding my launch, I pulled anchor and headed out. I was running about ten miles an hour with the mother dolphin still alongside.

By now I was starting to feel like I couldn't steal a precious little infant from its loving mother. I got back into my skiff, picked up the little fellow in my arms, hugged it like a baby, and eased it over the side.

Mother and baby headed west for the Gulf as hard as they could go. When dolphins are traveling in a big hurry, they jump completely out of the water to blow and don't lose a minute. I set right there and watched 'em go, jumping on every breath, until they went completely out of sight. Since then, I've often wondered who felt the best about that—the baby dolphin, the mother, or me sitting there that afternoon, watching them go for the sunset.

11 / Dying on the full moon . . . the Queen of the Everglades . . . a terrible fire

I kinda believe Dad knew for a long time before he let the family in on it, that he was dying with cancer. For some reason he just simply wouldn't give up that old river. Looking back at it today, I'm sure his sickness had something to do with him hanging on there so long.

Dad was just simply a different sort of man than most of the natives. He was always a loner and never one time went for the same type of work they did. He always managed to find something different. He was an extraordinary talented man and was highly respected. Like so many others, Dad's talents never made big time, what a shame. I guess Dad enjoyed living in the wild better than anything he ever did. Especially hunting what he needed to eat. It was nothing for him to camp out for weeks at a time with no one knowing where he was. He was down-right crazy about nature in every respect. He told me time after time, "Son, never kill anything you can't use." I remember Dad getting so mad when he'd find an animal someone had killed just for the fun of it.

Dad still had his ol' Gibson guitar with 'im down there and before leaving he wrote a lot of songs about South Florida and the Glades. I still have the words and music to all of Dad's songs—us natives think they're great—plus a few of my own, like "Chatham Bend" and "Down in the Everglades."

He usually came into the island about twice a month for supplies and to see us. We also went down there occasionally. But remember there was no telephone or radio to call and find out what supplies he needed.

Mother was a lot happier on Chokoloskee with little sister Audrey in school. She started a little grocery business on the northwest beach the very same place Grandpa McKinney started his in 1890.

Mother's little business turned out well for a number of years, but credit finally got her. I ended up taking over the store but only to get her out of it. I ran it on a cash basis long enough to bring it out of the hole.

Dad in 1936, after he was already sick. He took this picture of himself using a string to trip the shutter.

In the late fall of '36, Dad was still living part-time at Chatham Bend. One day he came poling in with a bandanna tied around his head, a knot pressing on each temple. He said the headaches he'd been having were more than he could stand. He had first taken BC powders (they were more popular then than aspirin) and, for a while, they gave him some relief; but then his stomach began to hurt too. (We had our own remedies back then, and doctors were few and far between.)

We finally talked Dad into seeing the general practitioner at Everglades City. He diagnosed the trouble as an ulcer, but the medicine he prescribed didn't help in the least. Dad went on and on in terrible pain, even though he didn't seem to lose any weight.

In December, Dad's brother Mick checked around and found that commercial fishermen were entitled to help from the Public Health Service, and Dad had fished enough to get it. Uncle Mick called the Coast Guard in Miami, and I'll be darned if they didn't land a seaplane near the northwest beach at Chokoloskee, picked Dad up, and took him to the nearest P.H.S. hospital in Key West. Seeing an airplane land around here then was about like seeing a flying saucer today! The gathering at the beach that evening when we put Dad on that plane was a big event.

Instead of flying him direct to Key West, they flew him to Miami, where they'd come from, then by car to Matecumbe in the Florida Keys. There they put him on a ferryboat that was taking cars from Matecumbe to No-Name key. The 1935 hurricane had blown out the seven-mile train track across Bahia Honda. I remember Dad telling me that on the ferry he had to lie on an old tool box that felt rougher than a gator's back.

At the hospital in Key West, the doctors operated and found cancer. They advised Dad to take radiation treatments in New Orleans. At first he went out there by himself, then with Mother, and later with me. But he wasn't physically able to take the treatments for long; he was just too far gone to start with. There wasn't anything they could do but give him shots of morphine to ease the pain. When they discharged him from the hospital they showed Mother and me how to give the shots and we brought him back to the island.

Dad had unbelievable courage and willpower. He never once mentioned pain or dying—only what he was going to do when he got well. He died on Chokoloskee in August 1938. He was only forty-six, but he'd had a couple of years to talk with God and from the way he talked, I'm sure he was saved.

The night before Dad died, Uncle Doc, Peg, and some of us were standing around the yard talking. A big moon was coming up above the trees and Uncle Doc said, "Tonight is full moon. John will probably die on this moon." The next day, Dad passed away.

Many years later, in August 1986, my wife and I were driving to Miami to see Peg. He was in the hospital with cancer. We were driving east and a big, full moon was just coming up. I told my wife what Uncle Doc had said in August 1938, and said that Peg would probably die on this moon. Sure enough, he passed away at noon the next day, at sixty-nine years old.

*   *   *

Life went on, as it always does. That same year, the year I turned eighteen, I started a little courting. About the only place on the island for us teenagers to get together was around the church house. Most kids regardless of age had to go to Sunday school and church services with their parents. So it just came natural for the old churchyard to play a big role at courting time—and one Sunday evening in the summer of 1938, that's where I found Estelle Demere.

Two Sunday nights before that, Peg had walked Estelle home. Seeing her walk by with him, looking like about a hundred and seven pounds of nothing but natural-born beauty, was a-gettin' to me. Probably about the first thing that caught my eye was her tiny little waistline, so small I could have reached my big hands completely around her. She had beautiful wavy brown hair that lay softly on her shoulders, and big brown eyes. The blue dress she was wearing showed off her most perfect shape, and her quiet little smile made me want to climb the wall. As Grandpa McKinney used to say, right then I began "stirring up my thinking tank." On this particular Sunday night, I knew that Peg had planned to walk Estelle home again, but I also knew that something had come up and he wasn't going to make it. Standing outside the church with the boys, I saw Estelle sitting inside by the back window. I slipped up and tapped on the old wooden shutter. She looked out to see, and I stuck my head up and whispered a little fib. "Peg said to tell you he can't make it tonight," I says, "and he wants me to walk you home in his place."

Estelle was a native like me; she'd been born on a houseboat at Sand Fly Island near the edge of Chokoloskee Bay. I'd gone with a few other girls before, but somehow it never amounted to anything. The first time I walked across the key holding Estelle's hand in mine, I knew without a doubt. We both fell so hard that a few months later—on October 14, 1938, in the evening, at the old courthouse in

Everglades City—our good ol' country judge S. S. Jolly married us and she became my Queen of the Everglades.

The knot we tied that night sure must've been a square one, for it's held for fifty-five wonderful years and is still hangin' in there, tighter'n ever. After all the years and the kids, the hardships and the good times, we still stroll across the key hand in hand.

Estelle turned fifteen a month after we were married, and I was only eighteen, but the way we'd been brought up in the Depression, we were both much older than our years. Still, when I took the Queen for my mate she'd never given me more than a few little birdie kisses. On our wedding night, on the way home from Everglades City in a small boat loaded with people, we ran out of gas and had to drift around in the bay half the night, with no privacy whatsoever and the mosquitoes thick enough to carry us off.

At first we lived in an old storm-beaten house that belonged to Mother, near Grandpa McKinney's homesite just off the beach. At that time I was commercial-fishing for mullet and pompano. Estelle got to go coon-hunting with me that winter, the last year they were hunted professionally. (At that time, alligators weren't even worth skinning.)

Eleven months after we were married, our first child, Lorna, was born. Estelle went to stay with a friend in Fort Myers shortly before the baby came, so she could be near the doctor. We had never been apart more than twenty-four hour at any one time, and when she left we both broke down and cried. Estelle was so young and little, we both really thought she might die. But everything went fine, and I made it there in time to hold her little hands and cry right along with her. The baby was nothing but beautiful, and she took her first steps at eight months. Even though Estelle was only fifteen, she took care of her baby like a grandma.

Everything went along smooth for some time, but then in 1940, for some reason (probably too much rain), mullet got so scarce in Chokoloskee Bay we couldn't make a living at it. We heard about fish being very plentiful at Flamingo, near Cape Sable seventy miles southeast, and several of us went down there. We had a rough time sleeping in our little open boats in the mosquitoes and rain, but there were lots of fish.

Estelle's father, St. Clair Demere (who I called "Saint") was fishing with me at the time. He helped me build a two-room tar-paper shack on Flamingo, where several other families were living. One room was for my crew, the other for Estelle, Lorna, and me. Estelle was pregnant with our second child, but she was happy as a lark to live in that shack.

Others from home soon joined us on the fishing grounds, going through the same routine we did: first sleeping in their boats in the mosquitoes and later building a tar-paper shack. It's hard to believe how bad the mosquitoes were in those days. It was before you could buy a good rub-on repellent, but we did have an aerosol spray that done some good when we squirted it out of an old-time spray gun. Any time we walked over to see a neighbor, they met us at the door with the spray gun to try to keep the skeeters from swarming in. In May, June, and July, they were so thick on the screens you couldn't hardly see the sun until about ten in the morning.

After a few months we got ahead enough to rent an apartment for Estelle and Lorna up in Florida City, near Homestead (forty-five or so miles away) but there was no way I could keep her in it. The wholesale fish truck ran up to Homestead from Flamingo several times a week—every day, if fishing was good. Estelle loved me so much she came back on the next truck every time, and her long-gone pregnant with our second daughter, Judy, who was born at Homestead in 1941.

The following year, fishing got better at home and we moved back to the island. World War II was on now and fish were selling good, as they usually do in wartime.

*   *   *

One evening in 1943, Estelle and I took the children—Lorna, four, and Judy, two—out fishing with the fleet. We were in Rabbit Key Pass, about three miles south of Chokoloskee. While we were running along, I began to smell gasoline. The gas tank was under the foredeck of the boat, up high for gravity feed, right near the bed in the little cabin. The back end of the cabin was open, no door. I looked in and saw Lorna asleep on the bed, and I also saw that the hose had

Estelle and baby Judy at Flamingo. Our tar-paper shack is in the background.

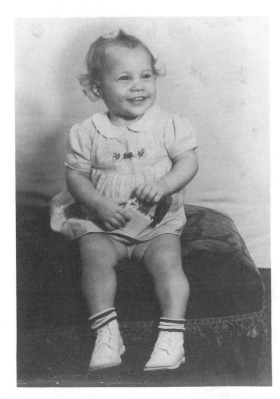

Judy at age two.

slipped off the tank and gasoline was pouring out on the floor. I grabbed Lorna and shoved her on deck outside the cabin and then I dove for the hose—but at that very moment, the gas exploded!

Next thing I knew, the cabin was a solid ball of fire and so was I. I dove overboard. When I came up, Estelle was in the water, too, with Lorna in her arms (the explosion had blasted 'em off)—but Judy was still in the boat, on the engine box, with flames licking at her. I swam toward her, hollering at the top of my voice, "Judy, jump overboard! Jump!" But she just held out her little hands, looking at me and crying. By the time I made it to the boat and got her out of the fire, she'd been burned real bad.

Ernest Hamilton and his wife, Mary, were coming along behind and picked us out of the water right away. Back on Chokoloskee, Ted Smallwood's son, Little Ted, heard the explosion and saw the smoke. He came out in a very fast boat, picked us up, and took us to

Everglades City. From there my cousins, Mutt and Jimmy House, drove us in a car to the Jackson Memorial Hospital in Miami. Next morning, just before day, Judy died from burns over 95 percent of her little body. She was buried at the mouth of Barron River where my father had been laid to rest five years before, in the little burial ground Grandpa Brown had set aside on his old homesite.

Estelle, Lorna, and I couldn't come to the funeral. We'd been burned, too, and had to stay in the hospital a long time. Most of the exposed skin came off our bodies. Sulfa drugs had just become available, and I think we were among the first burn victims they treated with 'em. The drugs sure worked, because our burns left very few scars. While we were healing up, Mutt and Jimmy stood by us like brothers and so did the rest of the island community. Some of the boys were able to save my net, but the boat was a total loss.

After the fire, I sold all my commercial-fishing gear and our furniture, too. I bought an old broken-down Model A Ford and repaired it myself. We rented a furnished apartment in Homestead and I went to work on the water pipeline to Key West. There's never been a freshwater well on the Florida Keys. The sixteen inch pipeline I worked on runs 100 or more miles from Homestead to Key West; later on a much larger line was added. Today they also distill salt water into fresh.

I only worked on the pipeline about a week and then went to Key West, carpentering. Because of the war, the government was building barracks, boatyards, and lots of other wooden structures. My friend and first cousin, Godfrey Daniels, was working with me, and we slept in my old Model-A Ford in the parking lot of the Busy Bee Restaurant until we could afford apartments in Key West. Then we brought our wives and kids down. But taking me away from the water and boats was like taking a fish out of the sea, and within a few months I was back commercial-fishing.

After getting back to Chokoloskee, I fished with first one and then the other until I made enough to get myself a small motorboat—an eighteen-foot skiff with a five-horsepower air-cooled motor. It wasn't much but done the job well enough to get me started again.

Flamingo was running over with fish, especially pompano and mullet, and good money could be made there. To get caught up from

Estelle, Lorna, and me.

my loss, I loaded up my motorboat, hung my fish skiff in tow, and headed down the coast all by my lonesome.

At Flamingo I camped around at first any way I could, then ended up in the same tar-paper shack I'd built back in '41. Later, Estelle joined me there with Lorna, but this time I really fixed it up for the Queen. I managed to buy another shack, set it up within a few feet of the first one, and screened in the whole space between 'em to make a breezeway for her to wash clothes in, out of the mosquitoes. For wash water, I cut the tops out of a few oil drums, coated the insides with hot asphalt, and set 'em in the breezeway to catch the rainwater that ran down from the two roofs.

There wasn't much at Flamingo but a fishing camp—no electricity, no stores, nothing in the modern way of life. On Saturday mornings we usually cranked up our ol' Ford and went into Homestead to pick up supplies and unwind a little. The Flamingo area was all clay, very slippery. When it was wet, you never knew which way you were going to go in your car, sideways or ahead. One time I had pulled out my eighteen-foot skiff but forgot to untie it from the Model-A, and Estelle took off in the car to visit one of the neighbors. When she got there, she had my skiff with her—the wet clay was so slick she couldn't tell she had it in tow! One of the men says, "I've seen boats drag anchor but this is the first time I ever saw the anchor drag a boat."

Eventually I got ahead enough to buy a twenty-four-foot open launch. It didn't have a motor, but I got an old car motor and installed that in it myself.

As I said, it was about a forty-five-mile drive from Flamingo to Homestead, and five miles of it was a narrow, clay dirt stretch through a mangrove swamp full of mosquitoes. Because of that stretch, it sometimes took me half a day to make the trip in the rainy season (when the mosquitoes were at their worst), and many times I wasn't able to make it at all.

One Sunday afternoon, we were coming back to Flamingo from a nice weekend in Homestead, and the ol' Ford was loaded to the moldings with people and supplies. We hit the bad stretch, made a few hundred yards, then down we went in the mud, and I mean to the bottom. It took hours, but about sundown we finally got out of the bog—only we'd burned up all our gasoline doing it.

There we were in the middle of a mangrove swamp, out of gas, with a load of women and children, in mosquitoes so thick you could rake 'em off by the handful. We poured a quart of whiskey in the tank but that didn't work. Then someone pulled out the spray gun for the mosquitoes, and a thought hit the back of my mind. I poured a gallon of mosquito spray in the tank, and away she went. That Model-A drank skeeter dope like it was high-octane gasoline!

12 / World War II . . . remembering the River Rhine

About eight o'clock in the morning on June 6, 1944, my friend and uncle, Lloyd House (known as Barrelhead for the way he paid cash on the barrelhead for fish), knocked on the door of our tar-paper shack. He'd come down from Homestead with the mail, and when I opened the door he said something along the line of "Today is D-Day and here's your call to the Army."

Many of the farmers and commercial fishermen on the Gulf coast were getting deferments from military service. My brother Bert, thirty-one, was deferred because of his kids, but Peg, twenty-seven, also married and with kids, accepted the draft and was already overseas with the Seventh Army as an automatic rifleman. (Eventually Peg was awarded two Bronze Stars for valor in combat, but none of us knew it until I found them in his army records when he died in 1986.)

Though I was only twenty-four, I probably could have been deferred, especially since my mother was on the local draft board. (That was because she was one of the better-educated people on the island and in Everglades City.) Even though I wasn't all that brave, or any too happy about leaving my wife and daughter, I didn't go for a deferment. Instead I sold my fishing gear, all but my little launch (which I stored in a warehouse in Everglades City), and got Estelle an apartment in Florida City, where her mother and her three sisters were living.

I was inducted at Fort McPherson near Atlanta, and took my infantry training at Camp Wheeler near Macon, Georgia. I'd tried for something on the water, but because I was color-blind they marked my card "infantry only." When training was over, I was the only soldier out of 250 who qualified for Officer Candidate School, though I only had a seventh-grade education. Maybe I was wrong, but I told 'em I knew enough, without any more training or schooling, to do the job: "Just give me a gun and show me the enemy."

Estelle and her sister, Faye Gooding, made it to Macon with Lorna by the first weekend. (Faye's husband, Earl Gooding, was already overseas in combat, so she and Estelle had decided to pool what little money they had and live together until either he or I came home again.) The buses were so crowded Estelle had to stand up most of the way, holding five-year-old Lorna on her hip.

The first week after us rookies got to Camp Wheeler, the officers let us know that to get a weekend pass we'd have to have ourselves and our gear in absolutely tip-top condition. Knowing that little wife and daughter of mine were coming to Macon that weekend, I had myself and my rifle so clean that the lieutenant marched me around my platoon to show 'em a perfect soldier. I was very proud of myself, being one of the few in my platoon to walk out with a weekend pass. Just like I knew they'd be, Estelle and Lorna were waiting for me with their arms wide open when I arrived. The place they'd found to live in for the time I'd be in training was a rat hole—an old barn converted into a six-room "motel" with one bathroom and one share-all combination kitchen and dining room. Each bedroom only had one bed in it and the room wasn't any bigger than the bed. To get into the room, you had to get *on* the bed!

Why Estelle and Faye picked this place was very simple: other places were worse. In 1944 there wasn't any such thing as a respectable apartment available anywhere near a training camp. If one did turn up, the serviceman's pay and the wife's allotment was so little they couldn't afford it.

The other women in this barn-motel were servicemen's wives, too, and very cooperative. They shared the kitchen with no problem. Estelle and Faye got a kick out of showing the northern girls how to prepare rice and tomato gravy. Whenever I got a chance to spend the night with Estelle, one of 'em was nice enough to let Faye move in with her.

On my last weekend at Camp Wheeler, we rented a little rowboat at a lake near the motel and rowed out with Lorna for a family picnic. We found a nice place for it: one side of the shoreline was full of beautiful big trees covered with Spanish moss (*without* any red bugs). The terrible thing was, Estelle and I both knew this was our last time together before I went overseas, and only God knows how much it hurt us to say goodbye.

Brother Peg was awarded two Bronze Stars.

The first of December, 1944, about 9,000 of us infantrymen boarded the USS *Wakefield* on our way across the Atlantic to help whip the Germans. Seven days later we landed in Liverpool, and two days after that we were crossing the English Channel to Le Havre.

About the time we landed, the Battle of the Bulge broke loose and they rushed my outfit to the border of Luxembourg and Belgium near Bastogne and Metz. We went in as replacements for the Golden Acorn Division (87th Infantry) of Patton's Third Army, which had been hit very hard in the first part of the battle.

The morning of the day we went into combat, I was squatted down on the latrine when a tall, lanky, middle-aged man with no brass on squatted down beside me and started asking about my line of work and where I came from. I gave him a few good answers but some I cut short. I didn't know it, but he was my company commander, Captain Kidd from Starke, Florida. The captain assigned me as gunner on a new five-man machine-gun squad—"new" because the old squad had been wiped out, except for the leader. When we went into action, the leader was hit after only a few hours, and Captain Kidd moved me up to sergeant and squad leader.

After the Battle of the Bulge was won—and the 87th Infantry done its share to win it—our next job was to break through the Siegfried Line. This was a fortified line 500 miles long the Germans had built along their western border—a chain of concrete pillboxes in the hillsides, with concrete dragon's teeth, four foot high, between the strong points and in front of 'em, too.

One morning we were just starting to make some headway against the line when the Germans opened up with their 88-mm. guns and pinned us to the frozen ground. I tried to dig myself a little protection with my trenching tool while holding onto my carbine, but a shell hit within a few foot of me and tore my gun to bits with my hand still on it. God must have been watching out for me that morning, because outside of a concussion and a temporary hearing loss, all I got was a nick near the eye from a piece of shrapnel. But the concussion, and the job it done on my ears, kept me in the hospital for three weeks.

When I rejoined my outfit, we were still in the thick of the action. We helped take a real prize, the big city of Coblenz on the west bank of the Rhine, but then came the hard part. To go forward, we had to cross that river in the face of the German guns. For the Germans, it was do or die—they *had* to stop us, or else.

Our officers were smart enough to know that our best chance of beating the odds was to practice the crossing over and over. We took the little rowboats we were going to use out into a forest, drew imaginary lines to represent the river, and for ten days went through dry run after dry run, with me teaching my landlubber buddies how to handle a boat and row it quietly.

Finally we were ready, and one night, a few minutes past midnight, we put the boats in the river. I was in the first wave. Where we crossed, the Rhine is maybe a mile wide. We only got halfway over before the Germans spotted us—and then the flares and tracer bullets, along with real bullets, came at us until hell wouldn't have it. But we made it across all the same and hit the shore on our bellies, crawling forward like loggerhead turtles into a steady hail of machine-gun fire. We'd known in advance the Germans were dug in all over the riverbank, with trenches from one machine-gun nest to the other. Our plan was to take 'em out with hand grenades. We were loaded up with them, and we threw 'em ahead of us for all we were worth.

Once we'd knocked out a machine gun or two, we had it made, and blasted our way through their trenches. But it still was the roughest battle I was in over there, and one of the hardest parts of it was that we had orders not to take even one prisoner. Whoever gave that order knew his stuff, for we would have been in sad shape trying to hold a prisoner with one hand while throwing grenades with the other.

* * *

The skills I'd learned shooting and surviving in the Glades helped me a lot over in Germany, and I was also able to help some of the men in my outfit, especially the boys from the big cities. For me, the way we had to live wasn't much rougher than what I was used to every day back home, but there were some who suffered about as much from living outdoors as they did from the fighting.

One kid in my outfit was a little fellow who wasn't quite as bright as he might've been. I called him "Doughboy." He kept telling me that back home in Miami he lived across from a drive-in movie theater. Doughboy stuck with me like a child, kinda putting his life in my hands, and I watched him like a mother hen. I used to holler at him in combat, telling him what moves to make.

One morning after we crossed the Rhine, the outfit was moving forward, on foot, only Doughboy had "the GI's" (diarrhea). He stuck with me as much as he could, but time and again he just had to "go." I stopped with him each time, keeping an eye out for snipers, but the last time, I didn't stop—I felt I was needed up the

Me (kneeling) with my squad near the end of the war.

line, with the rest of my squad. Doughboy never more'n got his britches down, and I no more'n turned my back, before I heard sniper fire. I ran back, but too late. Doughboy's mouth was closed but his eyes were open. Then I knew why he'd been so careful about telling me where he lived in Miami. I could still see it in his eyes: "Across from the drive-in." He'd been as good as saying, "If I don't make it back, Sarge, you go there for me, huh?" Well, I tried, many times, but I never could bring myself to go tell his parents how we'd served together and how hard he'd tried to be a good soldier. I knew if I did I would break down.

I lost Doughboy, but sometimes I saved a youngster's life with only words—kids who just didn't know how to keep from exposing them-selves to the enemy. One morning, as day was breaking, I saw a squad of GI's crossing a little open field with no cover between them and the coming-up sun. I called 'em over to my foxhole and they had no more'n got there before a couple of German artillery shells landed right where they'd been.

My squad always followed me faithfully, and I believe that my use-fulness to them and whatever good I did came from the knowledge I

All dressed up after
World War II.

brought with me from the Everglades. My rewards were a Purple
Heart, a Bronze Star, three battle stars, European and African The-
ater campaign ribbons, a sharpshooter's badge, and a Good Conduct
Medal.

When the war in Europe ended on May 8, 1945, my outfit was sent
back to the States for a thirty-day furlough before going to the Pacific
to take on the Japanese. The idea of going to Japan after fighting the
Germans went a little across the grain with me but, like always, I
accepted what I couldn't change.

A few months before I got home, Estelle gave birth to our third
child, Marie Faye, but the baby had an enlarged heart and lived only
ten days. About the same time Estelle's father, Saint, a man of only
fifty, died from aftereffects of the mustard gas he had been exposed to
in World War I. The first half of 1945 was a sad time for Estelle, and

Happy to be back with
the Queen of the Ever-
glades, after the war
was over.

she couldn't help worrying all over again when my furlough came to
an end.

Then, on my very last evening at home, I went out for a walk with
Bert in Everglades City. As we passed Sheriff Thorp's house, his
daughter Mary Divine rushed out, threw her arms around me, and
hollered, "Isn't it *wonderful*?" I asked, "Isn't *what* wonderful?" And
she says, "The war is over!" A few days before, we'd dropped the

atom bomb, and now the Japanese had surrendered. Those were probably the sweetest words I ever heard anyone speak: "The war is over."

Two months later, I was given an honorable discharge at Fort Benning, Georgia, and went home for good. Estelle and I rented an apartment in Everglades City, and I took my twenty-four-foot launch out of storage and started back fishing for our living.

13 / Stone-crabbing with Dollar Bill

The first winter after the war, I was fishing with Estelle along the coast near Chokoloskee when I noticed that every time our net touched bottom we caught stone crabs. The thought come to my mind that they hadn't been commercialized any place in the United States, and there ought to be some way to do it.

A short time later, up in Naples, I ran into Dad's brother, my Uncle Dollar Bill, and told him what I'd been thinking. Right then he said, "Let's trap 'em!" Dollar was a real promoter, never satisfied with commercial fishing. "There's more to the Everglades than catching mullet," he told me time after time. He was always looking for something new, different, *big*, even though all he was doing then was painting houses. And he was well known for his promoting. A man named Ben Dunn was walking one day with Dollar past old Ted Smallwood's trading post, with Dollar trying hard to talk Dunn into something. Someone sees the two of 'em and says to Ted, "There goes Ben Dunn." The old man takes a look and says, "Ummmm—if he ain't been done, he damn soon will be!"

Dollar Bill loved the stone crab idea, and from then on he spent every weekend with me at Chokoloskee, talking about the Stone Crab Project. After several weekends we had it all figured out: we could tend a thousand traps a day; with two crabs to the pound and two to the trap, we were talking a thousand pounds a day. It didn't turn out anything like that, but the project *did* develop into the biggest thing of its kind, ever, in the Florida waters.

First we built eight sample traps to experiment with: cube-shaped boxes, roughly $12 \times 14 \times 12$ inches, made of wooden slats and looking much like the plastic traps of today. We took the traps out to Rabbit Key to finish 'em with a cement base to sink 'em to the bottom and hold 'em upright. We mixed sand from the key's beautiful white beach with seawater and store-bought cement, and "bottomed" the traps. Then we set them along the coastline, and the next weekend we pulled 'em. To our surprise and sorrow, there was a total of two crabs in the eight traps.

Chokoloskee natives Charlie Boggess, myself, and Thelma Smallwood in
Smallwood's store, about 1956.

A big letdown, but we didn't let it throw us. Instead, we moved the
traps to a new location. It didn't help—nothing did. Weekend after
weekend we moved the traps, but didn't catch a single stone crab. All
we ever caught was trash—queen and king crabs, and the spider
crabs we call "navel pinchers."

By now summer was coming on and mullet-fishing was not good.
Unbeknowing to us, it was also a bad time to catch stone crabs. Cliff
Goff was fishing with me and we took him on as a third man in the
crabbing project.

One weekend we went out in the Gulf looking for rough, rocky
bottom, because we'd noticed stone-crab claws were always worn
from chewing on clams, "pearl" oysters, and other shellfish found out
in such waters. Southwest of Chokoloskee, offshore of Pavilion Key,
where we could just barely see land and in about fifteen foot of water,
our drag began to hit gravel. We put our eight sample traps out, using
cork net-floats for buoys.

The following weekend, the traps were full of stone crabs, with

Stone crab traps get completely covered with barnacles; they're cleaned once a year.

more hanging on trying to get in! After emptying the traps, we left 'em there again, and Dollar went home that evening with a smile on his face, certain at last we'd found the way to a fortune. To cash in, though, we'd have to build a pile of traps. It'd take time and money, and we had neither; but I did have good credit with Jimmy Howell, then the president of the Bank of Everglades City, and I borrowed enough to build 200 traps. This turned out to be a much bigger and tougher job than we'd figured. With no electric current on Chokoloskee for lights or power tools, we had to saw all that hard-pine lumber by hand, under a carbide light. We worked into the morning hours of the night, but even with Estelle and Cliff's wife, Muggy, helping, we still couldn't turn out the traps fast.

While the building was going on, Cliff and I fished just enough to keep us all in food. Finally we got 225 traps completed, but they still had to be bottomed, and we also needed ropes and buoys.

The following weekend, Cliff and I caught enough mullet above living expenses to buy cement. Old net rope was scarce, but we finally gathered up enough. Now we were all set to go, except for the buoys.

There was no plastic or Styrofoam buoys then, only small-size net corks—too expensive for us. Dollar came up with the idea of using dried coconuts, tied to the trap by a rope, with a staple drove in the nut. Ted Smallwood's yard near the old trading post was covered with 'em, and he said we could have all that was on the ground, "but keep your hands off the trees!" The old man never knew, but to make all 225 buoys we did have to slip more'n a few dry nuts from the trees.

We used my twenty-four-foot open launch I'd stored away while I was overseas; Dollar named her the *Molly Hawk.* One summer morning Dollar, Cliff, and I pulled out loaded with traps, coconut buoys, and bait. About noon we made it out to our eight marker traps. Then we baited the 225 new traps and dropped 'em over the side.

The next weekend, those traps were filled to the brim. I imagine our eyes were about as big as the traps. We had three fish barrels in the *Molly Hawk* and filled all three with big crabs, probably about 600 pounds. We felt for sure that now we were on our way to what Dollar Bill had always said was there for the finding: a life far, far beyond mullet-fishing.

It took the three of us all day to pull the traps—much longer than expected. It was black dark when we got in that evening, and we knew that 225 traps was all that we could ever tend in one day. Pulling a thousand was out of the question.

Next morning at dawn, Dollar was on his way to Miami with the crabs. He sold the live crabs, claws and all, to the owner of Joe's Restaurant for forty cents a pound. (Today the fishermen get five to seven dollars a pound for the claws alone.)

Before this Joe had bought all his crabs from a man who was catching a few in the Florida Keys. With Joe specializing in stone crabs and helping Dollar and I work up a market for them, we soon gave him the name Stone Crab Joe. And his place eventually became famous as Joe's Stone Crab Restaurant.

After our first big day, some bad weather came through and we lost all our traps except the eight samples we'd put net-cork buoys on. The corks had stood up fine to the rough seas and strong spring tides, but the dried coconuts had become waterlogged and were down on the bottom now with the ropes and traps they were fastened to. On the plus side, we learned that rough water is good for catching crabs. The eight traps that survived the bad weather were just running over.

Even though we seemed to be right back where we'd started, I wasn't about to quit. Estelle and I had recently put a down payment on a house at Chokoloskee, and I needed to make a success. I went back to the bank and gave away most of the crabs we'd caught in the eight traps, trying to convince Jimmy Howell and the others that stone-crabbing was the coming thing. Jimmy finally let me have enough to build another 200 traps.

By this time we'd learned how to do it right, but there was still a lot of hard work ahead of us. Dollar quit the house-painting in Naples and stayed with us while we were building the traps. Cliff Goff said he'd had it with stone-crabbing, and we hired Horace Gooding, Estelle's brother-in-law, in his place. The three of us worked every night until one and sometimes two in the morning. For buoys this time we used one-gallon clear-glass jugs with a little black paint in 'em, so we could spot 'em floating in the water even in bright sunlight. Dollar got the jugs from drugstores in Miami for ten cents apiece.

After Horace and I put out the traps, we pulled 'em every day. Dollar sold the crabs in Miami and brought back supplies. The first few days we done good, but then the bottom dropped out. We eventually figured out that the problem was calm weather and clear water. Crabs crawl much better in winter months and in rough, muddy water, and only at night. We also found out that a tough bait, like jackfish or stingray, worked better than soft bait, like mullet. I caught the stingrays myself with a grain (harpoon) while they were feeding on low, rising water.

Then came another problem. Florida had never seen any amount of stone crabs before and there was no real market for 'em yet. But with Dollar's gift for promoting, he managed to sell all the crabs we caught that season.

The next year Dollar bought himself a launch and a truck to sell crabs from. Several others also went into the business, too, and Dollar sold everyone's crabs (mine included).

With what stone-crabbing brought me that first season, I paid off

Me and a stone crab, 1991.

the mortgage on our home—and more'n forty years later, we're still living in it. By that time the market was glutted, and I sold out my stone-crabbing business and went into pompanoing.

Meanwhile, stone-crabbing grew to be the largest seafood business on the southwest coast of Florida. (I just wish my Uncle Dollar Bill could have known that; he died of cancer before they really got it going). By 1965 or thereabout, the trappers had come up with a hydraulic device called the "puller" to bring the traps up. It boosted up their catch and doubled the amount of traps they pulled—400 a day instead of 200. In the early seventies, I crabbed a little and came up with the idea of two pullers instead of one, boosting the traps pulled to 800 a day.

Today, if a crabber doesn't have four *thousand* traps and up, costing fifteen to twenty dollars apiece, and a forty-foot boat or larger, costing $100,000 and up, with three men on board using two

A modern forty-eight-foot stone crab boat. (Photo by Oscar Thompson.)

hydraulic pullers pulling 700 or 800 traps a day (300 pounds of large claws is a "good" day), he isn't considered in business. Only it costs $200,000 or more to get started!

Because there's so many in the business now, a man really has to be on the ball to make a success. There isn't many crabs to the trap, and so many traps have to be pulled that the pullers don't usually take time to handle the crabs with care.

Both male and female claws can be taken, either claw or both, provided they meet legal measurements. The law requires that the claws be broken off on the fishing grounds and the crabs thrown back into the sea so they can grow new claws.

When the puller reaches his hand down inside the trap to grab the crab, he has to move very fast; a large crab can crush a man's finger with his claw. When he grabs the crab by the arm of one claw, he has to throw the crab into the box quick enough so the crab's other claw doesn't get him. Throwing the crab into the box makes the other crabs in there mad and they start fighting. By the end of the day, when time comes to break the claws off, some of the crabs have killed each other, some have just simply died, and others are so weak after their claws are broken off they can't survive. My guess is, maybe 10 percent (certainly not more'n 25 percent) live to grow another claw.

When the trappers bring in the day's catch, the wholesale dealers have their boilers ready and the claws are cooked right away. Cooking time is eight to twelve minutes in hard-boiling water. No claws are iced or frozen before being cooked (that makes the meat stick to the shell). Once they're cooked, they can be put in the freezer with no problem.

Stone crabs can be found now up and down the southwest Gulf coast, from the shoreline out to depths unknown. They probably got their name from the fact that their body-shell, while thin, is hard as stone (except for the very bottom). So are their claws, which are much thicker and harder to break. One claw is always much larger than the other. The claws of a medium-large crab weigh about three-quarters of a pound, the body a bit less; with its claws open out, a crab measures about eighteen inches across. When a stone crab isn't feeding, its claws are folded neatly back against its body, so from a distance it looks like a stone the size of a man's open hand.

14 / A new kind of fishing . . . pompanoing with the Queen . . . adventures in the *Fraulein*

When I first started commercial fishing back in 1934, it was mostly mullet we went after, fishing at night around the mangroves in mosquitoes and sand flies so thick you had to be careful when you breathed. Then came mackerel and pompano, an altogether different way of fishing. It was done in the open Gulf, in powerboats instead of rowboats, in the cooler months of the year —and out of the mosquitoes and flies. Instead of handling thousands of pounds of mullet at a few cents a pound, you caught a few hundred pounds of pompano "golden nuggets" at a dollar or so a pound. To most mullet fishermen, pompanoing was like a vacation.

However, fishing for mackerel, especially before modern times, was never simple or easy. Averaging about two pounds each, they were and still are caught by the thousands of pounds. For years the fish had to be split open and gutted to be sold. Some fishermen could gut 1,000 to 1,500 pounds an hour by hand, with a stacker beside them laying the fish in place. Mackerel have always been about double the value of mullet. Today they're fifty cents a pound.

The mackerel boats used to be 35 feet and the nets 20 feet deep by 500 yards long, and the catch would range from 2,000 to 5,000 pounds. Now, the boats are 50 to 70 feet with the nets 50 feet deep by 800 yards long. The catch can easily be 25,000 pounds or more, but not every day. Like everything else, it depends on your luck and your know-how.

At first all fishing was done at night. Commercial fishermen use many different ways to find schools of fish. It may sound like a joke, but a good fisherman can smell a heavy bunch of fish, especially mackerel. Some fish, when in a hard bunch, give off an oily substance that comes to the top; it looks like an oil slick on the water and has a strong odor. (If I was running at night and caught a scent of fish, I turned hard right, ninety degrees of the wind, for a few minutes; if I lost the scent, I'd zigzag, going upwind until I found the slick.)

Modern-day fishing with powered rollers. The weight of the fish laying across the roller pulls the fish on board.

At times there's phosphorus in the water: very small particles that glow when fish swim by and bump 'em. A good captain can tell what kind of fish is moving the particles and about how many there are. If he sees enough fish to "strike," a small, lighted buoy is tied to the top end of the net and thrown overboard. The boat makes a complete circle with the net around the fish. Once the fish are completely surrounded by the net, the boat's lights are turned on and the boat runs around inside the circle, scaring the fish into the net.

The best way to find pompano is to look for them to "skip." Sometimes they will jump out of the water when scared by a boat and a dim light. When the fish comes out, it falls on its side and slides across the water, hitting it about three times, then slips back in. This is a perfect sign.

Today most mackerel fishing is done in the daytime, and tricks of the trade include spotting the places where fish have muddied up the water while feeding. If you know about this and can tell "fish mud" from water that's muddied by wind, tide, or whatever, it's a big help.

This live pompano just jumped right into the boat!

In the end, you find fish mostly by instinct, along with knowing the tricks.

Fish-spotting by plane is done more for mackerel than pompano. Most fish are dark on top. Even though the fish may be on the bottom, if the water's clear the pilot can see what's called the "tar black" of a heavy bunch of fish. He then calls the captain of the fishing boat by radio and directs him to the area.

My first cousin, Buddy Daniels, had a fifty-seven-foot boat named after his wife, the *Janet D.* He made up a special net, put eight men on board, and headed out. (The average crew on a mackerel boat is six besides the captain). Buddy started that season in November and ended up in March with a *million* pounds of Spanish mackerel. It had never been done before, and I doubt it's been done since.

But mackerel fishing was never for me. I just couldn't see handling thousands of pounds of fish for no more than I could make handling a few hundred pounds of pompano. I guess maybe a lot of it had to do with what you were cut out for.

Sometime after I went into pompanoing on my own, Estelle became my fishing mate. By this time we had two more babies; Elaine was born in April 1948, Loren in October 1951. The Queen worked hard and stuck by me, rough seas and all. I can still see her as though it was yesterday, holding a baby under one arm and pulling net with the other.

The babies slept in a wooden bread box; with a Grandma McKinney quilt folded in, they had a perfect bed. But along with all the joys of having the kids on board, there was always the fear of one of 'em falling over the side and not being noticed until too late. Many times, up at night looking for fish, I noticed Estelle sleeping with her hands on the children's ankles, Elaine's on one side and Loren's on the other. I've never seen a more perfect and caring mother, not even my own.

One afternoon, on our way down the coast, she was putting away the groceries. All of a sudden she rushed out of the cabin, hollering, "Where's Loren?" Just then I looked past the stern and saw a couple of porpoises playing with something in the water. As I frantically turned the boat around, Estelle hollered again: "I found 'im!" Loren had crawled under the bunk after his little dog "Troubles."

We never had but one dog in the family at a time, but went through about six all told. We named the first one "Troubles" and from there on, nearly every one had the same name. Most of 'em were just common ol' runabout, short-haired dogs. None was as smart as the first Troubles. He was a crackerjack!

Quite often we took Troub along on the boat for company, especially for the kids. He liked to swim and play on the beach right along with them. When Troub wanted to go he'd put his feet up on the deck and began to bark, looking at the beach and then us. I'd ease him over and he'd swim to shore. There were no dogs or anyone living on the shore and Troub always spent a lot of time unsuccessfully trying to find signs of another dog. When it was time to go, I'd just give him a call and he'd swim right up to the boat for me to pick him up.

Troub was a little curious and uneasy about any unfamiliar fish we

Estelle and Lorna with our first Troubles.

pulled into the boat. He just had to get a good smell of each different kind, but once he got his smell everything was okay and he paid 'em no more mind, except for the sharks. If the sharks were any size at all, Troub somehow knew he had to be careful. To get his smell, he snuck up, leaning forward with his nose as far ahead as he could get it. If the shark moved, Troub would almost jump out of his skin. And you couldn't get him to have anything to do with an alligator.

The last Troubles we had was pretty smart, too. My dock is about a block from my home, on the edge of the main channel where many boats pass by. I could be out gator-hunting for a week and when I came back—night or day—before I could tie up my boat ol' Troub would be there waiting.

*   *   *

At first we couldn't catch enough pompano to eat, let alone sell. But I kept right on a-strikin', and finally one night we lucked up and

Me and our current Troubles ... a day in Paradise.

caught a swinging load. My problem had been that I was striking at every single pompano that jumped instead of holding back 'til they were packed in the water like sardines in a can. From that day on, catching a school of pompano was no more to me than catching a baseball.

Today pompano are the most expensive fish caught commercially in Florida—about $3.50 a pound to the fisherman in the round, which means just as they come out of the water, not cleaned or gutted. When first caught, they're silver-gold, then turn to pure gold; that's why they're called "golden nuggets." The average pompano weighs about a pound and a half. It's rather flat, short, and wide, with very small scales that scrape right off.

Pompano are very rich and tasty, with real soft bones that can be chewed with no problem. A large one makes a delicious chowder, and the small ones are especially good fried. (Season 'em with plenty of black pepper, roll 'em in yellow cornmeal, add salt, and fry 'em in smoking-hot oil to golden brown—and if you like fish, you just might swallow your tongue.)

Most of the pompano caught in the United States are netted in the Gulf along Florida's southwest coast, and farther south in Florida Bay near the Keys. The heart of the season is December and January, and fishing is done mostly at night.

For the first ten or fifteen years after pompanoing started in '36, the first run of fish each season was caught near home and south to Lostmans River. (You can't fish there now because it's part of the national park.) As the weather turned colder, the fish moved farther south to Shark River and Cape Sable (fifty miles from home). The boats were too slow to make it into port and back in one day. So we stayed out on our boats, going into port about once a week. We called it "going after a clean shirt."

The boats were equipped for sleeping and cooking, with iceboxes to keep the fish overnight. Then you took your fish to one of the run boats (operated by the wholesale fish companies) that followed the fishing fleet. The fish were weighed and iced, and you got a receipt for your catch. About twice a week the run boat carried the fish into Marathon or Everglades and brought back supplies for the fleet. Later on, as the pompano boats became larger and faster, with Styrofoam iceboxes that would keep fish for a week, the run boats were no longer needed.

The average catch would probably range from 50 to 200 pounds a night, but sometimes, night after night, you caught nothing. Several nights I got real lucky and caught 1,200 to 1,500 pounds at a time.

The little boats were mostly cabin cruisers, small and very cramped-up. (But I'd step aboard one right now, even if it wasn't but ten foot long, just for a little taste of some of my yesterdays with Estelle and the kids.) With the net on board along with the icebox, jugs of water, and extra gas cans, most of the time there was hardly room enough to move around. If there was any rough water at all, as there usually was out in the Gulf, most everything got wet. We had to dry out our bedding and clothing just about every day.

The cabin was very small, too, maybe six foot long and five or less wide, and portable. It was called a "hunting cabin." Underneath the bow was a space for storage, about four foot square. There was no

Me and Estelle with Elaine in our backyard, 1949.

bunks in the cabin, only a bare floor with nothing but bedrolls of blankets and sometimes a quilt or two.

We got our first cabin cruiser in 1950. I named her the *Fraulein,* and stuck with that name for every boat we had afterward. The name *Fraulein* had nothing to do with the German girls; the only fraulein for me was the Queen of the Everglades. I got it from a song I heard overseas.

The fleet pulled out a little before sundown, looking for a likely spot. When we found one, we each put out our net—designed to float several foot above the bottom—in about twelve foot of water, in a

Me with Lorna and Elaine on our front porch.

straight line like a fence. Since the average drift net is 1,200 or more yards long but only eight foot deep, you have to be very careful not to let it drift into rock piles or sand bars.

At dark, the pompano come to the top to feed, and while milling around, they simply bump into the net and then swim forward and get caught. Drift fishing is more or less a lazy way to fish. But sometimes it doesn't turn out so easy: bad weather comes down; or your net drifts into someone else's and the two nets get "pinned" together by the fish caught in one net swimming into the other; or you misjudge and your net drifts into a bank and fills itself full of coral and trash fish. There were times the big sharks, like blacktips, hammerheads, and tiger sharks, cut your net in two and you'd never see it again. Other times one of the fishermen would find it.

After sunup the big sharks would come around and tear the nets, biting at the fish, so we usually got our net cleared and back on board by 7:00 of a morning. But there were times we caught so many trash fish, we put the net on board, left the fish in it, and cleared them out after getting into harbor. There were times it took all day to clear out the puppy sharks, catfish, and other trash. After getting the net cleared and ready to go again we had a good meal of fish chowder, fried turtle, or whatever the sea had brought us.

*   *   *

In 1950 Estelle and I were fishing on the north side of the Seven Mile Bridge on the overseas highway to Key West. We caught so many pompano in a little basin near the bridge I called it "my sugar bowl." Not many people would chance fishing so close to the bridge, because their net might drift into the coral on the pillars, tangle up, and they'd never get it back without tearing it to pieces. But I've always loved to take chances, and fishing in this dangerous place was right up my alley.

We'd been putting our net out about dark, drifting up to within a few hundred yards of the bridge, knowing the tide would most likely change direction and take the net back away from the bridge with no problems. But this time we were both so tired from working all day on our first *Fraulein* that we lay down for a few hours' nap.

The nap lasted a little too long. A light north wind was blowing, causing the tide to run south longer than I'd expected. What finally woke us up was the eighteen-wheeler trucks rolling over our heads on the Seven Mile Bridge! When we awoke, our 1,500-yard net was laying broadside along the bridge. The boat had drifted completely through the arch to the south side of the bridge without even touching the pillars, leaving my net behind but still tied to my stern.

I sat down with Estelle and did some tall thinking. I figured out that if I tried to get the net back with the wind and tide both running south and the net on the north side, my boat would get torn up against the bridge. But if I waited until the tide turned back to the north, it would push my boat *and* the net away from the bridge and I might get it back with no problem.

Estelle with one day's catch, in the 1960s. And people ask why isn't there any fish left!

Sure enough, that's just what happened. When the tide changed, I took my boat back through the arch and then Estelle and I started getting the net on board. We'd caught twenty-nine arches (nearly a mile of that bridge) with our net. We had to tear it a little, getting it loose from the coral, but not too bad.

*   *   *

One afternoon in August 1953, Estelle and I were in that same *Fraulein* with our baby boy, Loren (nearly two), heading down the coast to Cape Sable for pompano. The sun was shining bright but we were heading into a heavy rain cloud—not unusual for that time of year. When we entered the squall it was pouring down rain so thick I couldn't hardly see anything but my compass. Still, I could tell we were approaching some very odd weather: what wind there was seemed to be going around and around. Then, all at once, the wind hit us so strong the boat wouldn't turn into it! We'd run into a water-spout (or, as we call 'em, a twister)—like a tornado, only drawing up water instead of debris.

Even with the motor at full throttle, the *Fraulein* would only hold quartering to the wind. It all happened so sudden I couldn't turn the wheel loose even for a second to help Estelle and Loren. (If I had, the boat probably would have started going around and around and could easily have turned over.) Estelle hung onto the doorway of the cabin with one arm and Loren with the other. He thought the boat was going to sink and kept begging for his "floats." (I'd just made him a ring of floats from net corks to help him learn to swim.)

The twister was pulling at us so hard I could just barely keep my place at the wheel. All at once, everything in the cockpit went straight up. A hatch lid, about eighteen inches square, came flying at me right through the windshield, but I ducked just in time. In the next moment, the twister lifted the entire canopy off the boat, straight up and out of sight.

Shortly after that, the twister moved farther out to sea, and it was all over but the rain. We were still scared half to death and headed for land as hard as we could go. But in thirty minutes' time it was just as pretty and sunshiny as could be. After a while, we built up enough nerve to go back and look for any of our belongings that might still be afloat. We picked up quite a few things, including the canopy. It was too heavy to haul aboard, so we tied it astern and towed it in.

That night we made it to the mouth of Big Sable Creek (an anchorage for the fishing fleet), tied the canopy to a tree on the shore-line, then went out to join the other boats that were busy fishing. My cousin Buddy Daniels saw my boat coming toward him, but didn't recognize it without the canopy. When I hollered, he couldn't believe his ears. He says, "Totch, what the hell are you doing on that boat? Where's the *Fraulein*?"

*   *   *

Later that same year, Estelle and I went fishing close in around the sandbars near Harbor Key, west of Marathon, taking along Elaine, going on six, and Loren, two. (Our oldest, Lorna, fourteen, was home on the island with her Aunt Betty.)

One evening about sundown, with everything going our way, we put our net out for a drift. We knew the tide was coming in and we'd have to take in the net within a couple of hours or it could wind up on top of a sandbar—but we were so tired we just had to get some sleep. After carefully setting our old alarm clock, we slept right through the alarm for another hour.

The *Fraulein* bumping the bottom woke us up to a world of trouble: the tide had made high, then turned back out falling, leaving us aground. I rushed out of the cabin like a wild man and cranked up the motor, trying to get the boat off the bar, but we were stuck hard and fast. Realizing there was nothing we could do about it, we crawled back in our bunks and let Mother Nature have her way. Through the morning part of the night, the boat listed over on her side so far it took all we could do to stay in our bunks.

At daybreak we could plainly see that we'd drifted onto the Lantern Bank sandbar. About 200 yards of our 1,500-yard net was bone-dry and all the rest of it was missing, nowhere to be seen. When the tide got turned out strong, with one end of the net stuck fast aground, the pull of the current had torn it in two at the edge of the bar—and 1,300 yards of it had gone out to sea with the falling tide.

With the boat laying on her side, it was no picnic making coffee and a bite to eat, but we managed. Then we all got out on the sandbar. While Estelle and I got the fish out of what was left of the net, Elaine and little Loren took 'em back to the boat in buckets. Next we cut the net into pieces small enough to tote to the boat, to be sewed back together later.

I didn't worry much about the rest of the net. Through the years I'd found that if there's no high wind or nothing unusual taking place, a net will drift back and forth in the same path. So I was kinda sure mine would drift in on the next incoming tide. And it did. About the time the tide had risen enough to float the *Fraulein,* we could see the net coming directly back to us, just as perfect as a martin to her nest. We only had to run out a few hundred yards to it and soon got it back on the boat (with a fair catch of fish in it), and by dark we were ready to go again.

Loren at age twelve drawing his first share.

Another time—in the mid-fifties, before ship-to-ship radios—Estelle and I were off Marathon in the *Fraulein,* well out of sight of land, when we saw a lone boat flagging us with a blanket. When we got there, the boat was about to go down with its two-man crew. I jumped aboard and found the problem: one end of a board beneath the bottom had come loose. I told one of the boys to dive under the boat and bump the board back into place, but they'd seen a lot of sharks circling about and was afraid to. So I dived under myself and fixed the board. Then I patched up the leak just enough to keep 'em afloat, took 'em in tow, and told 'em to bail for dear life with the buckets.

Me in my carbide light cap, about 1955.

Once I started towing, they quit bailing and asked if they could come on board my boat and let theirs go. They were just too lazy or scared even to *try* and save their boat! This really aggravated me. I got a big butcher knife and put it on the tow rope and told 'em to bail or else I'd cut it and leave 'em to sink. They went to bailing then with a bucket in each hand, 'til we made it into port at Marathon.

*   *   *

There's something about commercial fishing, especially pompanoing, that seems to get into a man's blood, and when it does, you're darn well hooked. Probably one reason is you're on your own, as free as a bird. And anytime you don't like what's going on, you can just drop your hook in your own backyard and let it all drift on by.

There's no better feeling than coming in from rough seas in the middle of the night, anchoring in back of a little key, with a fine ripple of water slapping the side of the boat while you lay there listening to the cold north wind howl through the mangroves.

When you come in from a northwester and anchor on the lee side of a key, the next morning you're always on the sunny side, with the sun coming up in the southeast. The sun feels so good when you wake up, and it's ready to dry out all that got wet overnight. Out there you can actually smell the fresh air, and even the rain before it gets to you.

And there's no better ride than cruising along the Gulf coast of southwest Florida with just a light chop (not rough enough to whitecap the water), so when you anchor it rocks your boat like a rocking chair. I never cared for the Atlantic; rough, rolling, deep water was never for me. I'll take the shallow, sheltered, smooth waters of the Gulf of Mexico anytime.

15 / Lost in the Everglades

In the dry season of '50, while the alligators were hibernating out in the Everglades in their lakeside caves and holes, I took my usual spring break from fishing and went lake-hunting for alligators. Lake-hunting is a hard job; it's not unusual to work a day or two, dragging a pit pan (a very small, lightweight plywood boat) across the mangroves and prairies to a lake, and find nothing when you get there. By this time, it was illegal to hunt alligators where I was going; in fact, it was right in the middle of the Everglades National Park.

Looking at my charts, I spotted a few lakes I'd never been to between Homestead and Flamingo, in the southern Everglades. I had a little extra cash on hand, so I chartered a crop-duster for half a day to look 'em over. Early next morning the pilot picked me up in his biplane on the airstrip at Everglades. I found that on a clear day like this one, gators could be spotted easy from the air. The pilot soon got so interested in the Glades and my way of life that he said he'd fly me all day for the half-day fee.

It wasn't long before we decided a little beer might make the Glades even more beautiful. We put down in Homestead, near a restaurant-bar called the Triangle, had a few beers, and bought a case to go. After getting underway, I told the pilot about my old friend K. Irwin, who had become known as the Sage of Flamingo. K. had gator-hunted himself in his younger days, and I suggested we stop there and talk with him about the lakes. By this time, the duster and I had both had enough beer to be ready for anything. So that even though there was no airstrip at Flamingo, just some open ground—down we went. That pilot just loved to take chances, same as me, and that probably had to do with us landing so perfect.

After a few beers, K. told us about every gator lake in the Flamingo country. We took off for where he said they'd be: a small canal with ditches running off to the side. I soon counted more than enough gators to come back for, and took some bearings on how to find my way there on foot. It was getting late now, so we made a beeline for Everglades City.

On the way back, I had to "go," but we'd filled up all the empty beer cans and thrown 'em out. Just then we were passing over Watson Prairie (back of the Watson place on Chatham River), and the duster says, "Why don't I put 'er down here and we'll both take a leak?" I says, "Okay, but let me tell you something. I've walked over every inch of that prairie, bird-hunting, and the ground isn't all that hard." The pilot says, "It looks dry and hard enough to me," and down we went again. But when he stepped out onto the soft ground, it probably scared the pee out of him before he even got his whang-dang out.

The sun was just going down, leaving us sitting in a mud hole we might not be able to get out of. First we tried taking off down the length of the prairie, but the ground was simply too soft. Then we started walking, looking for the hardest ground, while it got darker every minute. Just before it got too dark, we found some, but it was crossways, the short width of the prairie, and we had to take off headed toward tall black-mangrove trees.

After several tries that didn't work, when it was so dark we could barely see the mangroves, the pilot came up with the idea of lightening up the plane. We put everything out on the ground we didn't have to have, including me. Then I pushed on the bottom wing, walking at first, then running and hanging onto the braces and crawling aboard as we took off. I thought for sure we were going straight into the mangroves, but the pilot had the motor souped up so much that he pulled 'er almost straight up—and over we went.

Throughout the day, while we were drinking all that beer together, the duster had been talking about going into the gator-hunting business with me. He'd fly me to the lakes, put me out there, and pick me up again on a regular schedule. But that night, after we finally got off Watson Prairie and put those two little wheels down on the hard ground at Everglades City, he said, straight out, "Forget it!"

* * *

Two months later, my brother Peg and I took off for the canal K. Irwin had steered me to. We went by car to Homestead, to the home of my sister-in-law, Faye, and her husband, Earl Gooding. He took us down the Flamingo road (State Road 27) about twenty miles, as near the canal as he could get. The road runs from Homestead to Flamingo, the southern gateway to the Everglades National Park. Our target was a mile off the road on the south side: an abandoned ditch, dug many years before, right in the middle of what had become the park.

Earl dropped us off with our guns and gear at 4:00 P.M. on Easter Sunday. A light cold front was just breaking down, and it was beginning to rain and turn cold. We hadn't expected weather so bad this time of year, and neither Peg nor I had a raincoat, a tarp, or anything else to keep dry with. But it was too late to turn back. Earl left, promising to come back for us in three days' time, but shaking his head as he glanced at the rain coming down.

To get to the canal, we had to make our way in the rain across a mile of glades and willow heads (shrubby willow trees growing in low places). By the time we got there, the rain had turned into a constant drizzle and was just as cold as I've ever known it for April. But the worst of it was, the gators were gone! In the few weeks since I'd flown over this spot, the canal and the side ditches had dried up.

Peg and I decided that the gators hadn't gone far—probably holed up in the willow heads nearby. (Because willows grow in the lowest places, nearest underground water, the gators usually dig their holes there, too.) About an hour before dark, with the cold rain still coming down, we decided to split up and start walking, looking for gator caves. Where I went, I found half-a-dozen or so gators but didn't kill any of them. Just as it got dark, I made it back to where we'd started, but there was no Peg or any sign of him.

Neither of us ever carried a compass in the woods. We found our direction either by the sun, moon, and stars, or by the glow of lights from Miami to the east. But this particular night, the heavy overcast and constant drizzling rain blacked out everything in the sky.

After a couple of hours, I decided Peg had to be lost, hard as that was to believe. I waited around a few more hours and finally put my headlight on, took my gun, and went out looking. I shined my light and hollered for Peg 'til I was so hoarse I couldn't holler any more.

Just before day I gave up and walked back to the Flamingo road and headed for Homestead, planning on chartering a plane there to search for Peg in daylight. I didn't expect any traffic that late at night, but to my surprise I was able to hitch a ride with a writer who was working for the park. When he asked me, I told him my name was Goodery, I lived in Homestead (at Earl Gooding's address), and my pickup truck had died on me, leaving me out here in the middle of nowhere.

Pretty soon we came to the park headquarters, a few miles from Homestead and just off the Flamingo road. The writer said he was living in a trailer there and for me to wait in the car while he went in for cigarettes. I thought for sure he was turning me over to the rangers, because after tramping around in the mud and rain all night, I had to look like some kind of desperado. But when he came back, all he said was, "If I take you home, you won't knock me in the head, will ya?" I shook my head and sweet-talked him some more, and he drove me straight to Earl's place in Homestead. I tried to pay him, but he only took a couple of bucks for gas.

By that time it was breaking day and still drizzling cold rain. Earl was home, and when I told him about Peg, he said he would skip work that day and the two of us started looking around for a plane to hire. Some of our friends said they'd track one down for us, leaving Earl and me free to drive back and see if Peg had showed up yet. We made two trips down there by car, for nothing.

Then, that evening, we got word from a boy on the Homestead police force that the Rangers had Peg in the park headquarters. The boy and another friend of ours were monitoring the situation at the ranger station. The rangers had been questioning Peg, but for the moment they'd sent him into an adjoining room with a door to the outside. The boys standing by motioned for Peg to keep on going, out through the door. They had a car waiting and off they went!

Later, when we all got together, Peg told us he *had* gotten lost that night, and with all the rain and cold he came close to freezing to death. Just before day, he'd found a high cabbage hammock with a lot of dead cabbage palms, and his cigarette lighter lasted just long enough for him to start a fire with the palm fans. He said the fire saved his life.

Next morning he'd found his way to the road by afternoon, when there was plenty of traffic on it, and he soon caught a ride. He told the man who picked him up that his name was Jack Smith (a name too common) and made up some kind of story, the way I'd done, to account for being in the park. Only this fellow didn't believe his story and pulled in at the ranger headquarters. He told Peg he'd be right back, but instead it was the rangers who came back.

Luckily, Peg saw no one at the station who knew his face. At that time and for years before and after, Peg and I were the only ones bold enough or crazy enough to go gator-hunting in the park—and the rangers knew it. But they only knew our names. What they didn't know was who "Jack Smith" really was. Peg thought they'd just about figured him out, though, and only wanted to check a little further when they asked him to step into the next room for a few minutes. Our friends outside were a little too quick and slick, and so was Jack Smith.

One night that same year, Peg was gator-hunting near Flamingo when he run out of coffee. He stopped by the park's ranger station and visitor center and borrowed some from one of the home boys, a man named Hillburn, that was charter-boating out there. The next day Hillburn mentioned Peg's visit and one of the rangers says, "Why in the world didn't you call me? I just been dyin' to meet that man." Hillburn says, "I would have, only he had his boat loaded with alligators."

16 / The Seminoles in their Everglades

Before the Everglades became a national park in 1947, there were several different tribes of Indians living in the Everglades. There were Creek Miccosukee and probably others, but of so little a difference to me I call them all Seminoles. I believe all tribes in Florida call themselves Seminoles, but I haven't made a study of it.

When my grandfather first came to the southwest Everglades in 1880, the Seminoles were living back inland from the coast, on the ancient shell mounds throughout the Islands and also back in the Everglades. But as we began to move onto the mounds ourselves, they moved farther back into the Everglades. They had no desire to mix with the white man.

I find the Seminoles to be a special kind of people. Unlike most of us, they're still trying to hold on to their family traditions. Even though our government has time after time thrown them out of their homes and off their land, they are still living their own way of life. But their chiefs tell me the government is now telling them how to run their reservation—their hole in the doughnut, I call it.

The Seminoles were hunters. I never saw one do any kind of commercial fishing, or even fish with a hook and line. They used a long slender cypress pole with a spear on the end of it. They could throw that thing like a rifle ball, not only for fish or turtles but anything else they went after in the Everglades.

Unlike the Calusa Indians, the Seminoles never liked the coast. The only time I saw them on the coastline was when they were traveling south about fifty miles to Shark River. They had to come out on the coast for a short distance. They all used canoes. The only one I ever saw in a boat was Charley Tigertail. They didn't paddle their canoes, or sit down in them. They stood in the back end and used a long cypress pole. To build the canoes, they poled out across the Glades to the big cypress country while the water was up. Here they cut down a big tree but didn't start work on it until dry season. After the canoe was finished in the rough, come rainy season they floated it out across the Glades to their camp and finished it up there.

Charley Tigertail was the best-educated Indian in the Everglades, and he had a motorboat. George Storter, an early settler, built his boat, but Dad put the motor in it for him.

Charley ran a trading post way out in the Glades and often came into Chokoloskee to trade with Grandpa McKinney and to get Dad to work on his boat. He usually brought rough lemons and lots of other fruits he gathered from the Indian mounds throughout the Islands. I remember him counting the lemons. Because he could only count to twelve, he'd get to one dozen and say "One dozen one, one dozen two," and so on.

Tigertail's trading post, off the head of Lostmans River, was a problem to get to, even for him. He had to go about twenty-five miles south of Everglades City in his motorboat—which was seldom running, so he frequently poled it—then loaded his goods in a canoe and poled up a narrow little creek into the Glades. In rainy season with the water up, he could pole across the Glades to his camp, but if the water was down, he had to carry his goods on foot. After all that trouble, all he got for cigarettes was ten cents a pack and for Prince Albert tobacco, fifteen cents a can.

In Dad's young life, before he married Mother, he pretty much lived in the woods, hunting near the Indians. He became very close to 'em—closer, I'm sure, than any other white man in those parts; and he was still just as close when he got older. He spoke their language well and helped 'em out in many ways. He often went to their camps and bought their furs and gator hides.

When Dad was out in a motorboat, he never passed one Indian canoe he didn't stop and offer a tow. There were very few white men that the Indians would let give 'em a tow, but they would always let Dad.

One day, one of the Seminole leaders, Chief Charley, came and camped at our dock at Chatham Bend with his wife and kids. He did something very unusual for a Seminole: he asked us to help his wife, who was having hard labor (maybe it was because he knew Dad like his own brother). Mother, having helped Grandpa McKinney with his midwifing, knew how to deliver the baby. So we took her into our home and everything went fine.

Charley Tigertail.
(Courtesy of Ted
Smallwood's Store.)

Mother knew the Indians and their ways right well. Her knowledge come mostly from her father's trading post, the first on Chokoloskee, where the Indians stopped by all the time to trade. (Grandmother McKinney sold 'em most of their dry goods and beads for the famous Seminole necklaces.) From the way Mother talked, she was around the Indians a lot, playing on the beaches with their children while she was growing up—not only on Chokoloskee but at other places throughout the Islands.

*   *   *

As the rains came and went, so did the Seminoles and much of the game. In the dry season the Seminoles camped more-so in the rivers. To do their hunting they walked out into the Glades and marshes near the rivers. With the water up they could pole or sail their canoe across the Everglades from the Gulf of Mexico on the west coast to Miami on the east coast (ninety miles). Because of the water control that would be impossible today. The dams that hold the rainwater back from the southwest Everglades keep the land so dry you hardly get your feet wet walking on it.

In the Glades they camped on the cabbage palm hammocks. The ground was a bit soggy, but they were used to that. For all their woodwork they used cypress trees, a good tree for lumber. They built their open chickees with sides just high enough to walk under and cabbage palm fans for the roof. Inside the chickee was a cypress platform, several feet high, to sleep on; being high, it was out of the sunlight and much cooler. All cooking was done over an open fire on the bare ground. A tripod (three poles tied together at the top) stood over the fire. A wire or buckskin hung down from the top to hold a big iron pot for cooking.

The Seminoles did most of their farming in dry season, growing corn, sweet potatoes, and pumpkins. They kept the Everglades well cultivated. They burned the wet prairie lands yearly, keeping the growth green and tender and the ponds open. They hunted raccoon and otter for fur and alligator for hides, and never took more than they needed. They brought their skins in to trade with us and often

Indian dugout and typical Seminole village in the Everglades. I just wish to God I could call time back and be standing in the other end of that canoe. (Courtesy of Ted Smallwood's Store.)

brought in venison (deer meat), and sometimes wild turkey. When they came in to trade, they usually camped on the beaches of Chokoloskee for a few days at a time.

In the summer, it was hard for them to get their meat in to trade before it spoiled. They laid it between cabbage palm fans, which tend to be cool and help keep the meat. Black pepper helps keep the flies off.

When buying the meat, you had to pay for it by the piece, one at a time. They also paid for each article as they got it. Some of 'em wouldn't take bills, preferring silver.

The Seminoles were good hunters but no better than some of our old-timers. They may have had the edge on us a little bit with old Mother Nature. Hunting in the Everglades in wet season, we were usually wading in water six or more inches deep. At the first opportunity, we went for dryer land, but not the Seminole. He kept right on wading, to avoid rattlesnakes laying on dry ground.

Even though they walked all over the Glades hunting, you never saw one with shoes on. But to us there was nothing strange about that because most of us went the same—over oyster shells and all.

There was one meal they used to put together that was something else—turtles, garfish, and sofkee. The way it was prepared and eaten would really take the eye. They brought garfish with them and sometimes their little turtles from the Glades. We don't eat garfish but there's nothing wrong with eating one. Their turtles were streaked-heads, soft-shell, diamond-backs, mud, and alligator turtles. Alligator turtles have a tail with horns on it like a gator. They are bad about biting and are sometimes called snapping turtles. If they didn't bring their own turtles, they went out scouting around on the island, gathering box shells, a small highland turtle, about the size of an open hand, that we have on the shell islands.

After camp was set up, they built a small fire that didn't usually go out. The Seminoles don't build a big fire. They say, "White man crazy, big fire, stay far away, burn one side, cold other, build little fire, get close, stay warm." And the Seminoles are right.

Once they got a good bed of coals, they put on their sofkee, a coarse grits made from corn. While the sofkee was finishing up, they put on their garfish and turtles. This part would shock your modesty. I don't remember if they killed the turtles before throwing them in the fire or not, but I well remember they threw them in whole, just as they picked them up—guts and all. A few minutes after they've been put on the red, hot coals, they begin to swell and soon burst, and the goody juice started to ooze out.

And now came the feast. A big spoon made of cypress wood stayed in the sofkee pot and a big fork made of wood was nearby to work on the turtles and garfish with. In season, they added corn, and sometimes bread; they had a way of making bread you just couldn't turn down.

Everybody sat down on the ground with their legs crossed at their ankles, in a circle around the fire and sofkee pot. The chief first took the spoon for a sip of the sofkee, then put the spoon back in the pot. Going around counterclockwise, the next in the circle took his turn. While the sofkee spoon was going around, the chief used the big wooden fork to pull out a turtle leg or tail or maybe a head and neck, followed in turn by the other members of the circle, and so on many times around.

I probably knew Little Tiger better than I knew any other Seminole, but still not good enough, I guess. In 1937, when I was seventeen, I went on a deer hunt with a friend of mine nicknamed "Shine." We went up a narrow little river called Sweetwater (probably named so by the Indians because its water was fresher than most rivers). The Sweetwater runs all the way to the Glades before heading up into the mangroves. By the time we got to the upriver stretch, dark caught us. I was in the front of the skiff wearing the headlight. Shine was in the back. Halfway up the river, shining my light and looking for the way through the overhanging limbs, I thought I spotted the eye of an animal gleaming in the dark. Shine passed me a .30-.30 lever-action Savage rifle and I cocked it. Immediately somebody let out an Indian war whoop that could be heard for miles!

It was Little Tiger. He was living on a mound on the bank of the river. With the beam of my light I had picked up something in his camp that shone bright like an animal's eye, but when he heard that little sound he let me know in a hurry that he wasn't an animal.

Shine and I didn't figure it out until we came back down the river late the next afternoon. Little Tiger was nowhere to be seen. We investigated the abandoned campground and the first thing we saw was Tiger's name. There was a large green limb laying high just overhead of the pathway into camp. He had carved "Little Tiger" on the limb in the prettiest and most perfect way I'd ever seen. When it came to whittling, the Seminoles were hard to beat, and to my notion, Little Tiger was the best. I later found out that he never left a camp that he didn't leave his name carved on it that way. He usually carved a beautiful leaf on both sides of the name with even the little cores of the leaf carved in.

We could tell by the looks of the camp that he had lived there for a long time. But just because we happened to find him, he had checked out, camp and all. I was young then and didn't think much about it, but if the same thing should happen today, I'm sure I'd feel right bad about causing Little Tiger to have to tear his camp down, go find another hiding place and build another.

We seldom went up the Sweetwater, it was so narrow, grown over, and hard to travel. But that just suited Tiger. In the back country, up near the head of the rivers or out in the Glades where there wasn't much activity, the Indians were a little more leery about us coming around and would move camp if we did. But there were a few who lived more out in the open near Chokoloskee, especially in the earlier years, and didn't seem to mind us coming by or even camping near them for a while. But as a whole, the average preferred to live their lives to themselves. They believed in their tribes and ways of life. By no means did they intend to change and they didn't change in any respect until they were forced to do so by the U.S. government.

After the Everglades became a national park, they were forced out of their free lands in the Everglades and put into an Indian reservation in the higher land. I believe they were forced to send their children to school. Before then there was no mixing. If they did slip (which was very, very seldom), they were cast out of the tribe for sure and were no longer considered a Seminole.

I recently spoke with an old Seminole friend, Bobby Clay. He told me he was a counselor for the Independent Seminole Indians, who did not sign up for the reservation and mostly live alongside U.S. 41 (Tamiami Trail). Bobby says that today there are no rules against their tribes mixing among one another or with non-Seminoles.

I have a great admiration for the Seminoles. The way I saw it back then and to this very day, they were a part of the Everglades. I believe that no other people, without tools and with only the help of old Mother Nature, could have possibly cultivated their land as well as they did. If God would only grant me the power, I'd take the Everglades from the government and give it back to the Seminoles.

17 / Hunting for gators . . . the white ghost . . . Hurricane Donna

In September 1960, when Hurricane Donna was out in the Atlantic and not expected to hit Florida, I went gator-hunting down around Cape Sable and past Flamingo to Madeira Hammock, ten or fifteen miles north of the Florida Keys.

Anytime I went on a long trip, say about a week, my little sixteen-foot gator boat was really overloaded. If I was going below Shark River, as I was this time, I would stop at a little creek at the mouth of the river and stash away some of my supplies. This particular creek has good water in it even on low tide, and plenty of big trees and brush for good hiding. It's about forty-five miles south of Chokoloskee and by the time I made it to the creek, I'd used about one tank of gas. As usual I put out the empty tank and a full one to go back with—plus a jug of water, just in case.

Up to here, I'd been traveling the coastline. I still had to go around Cape Sable and on past Flamingo ten miles to Garfield Bight, a large, shallow cove. Making it to the bight was no problem, but getting to Gator Creek in the bottom end of it was something else. I had to get out and push the boat across a mud flat. Finally I made it, but only after lightening up my boat by leaving a lot of my supplies on Umbrella Key near the mouth of the bight, including the coarse salt I normally use on my gator hides.

When I got in the creek, I made my first mistake. I killed an eleven-foot gator so scarred-up from fighting that his hide wasn't worth a dime, but I had to drag him around in my boat all night because I couldn't afford to leave him for the rangers or the public to see.

My next problem was a low bridge, about a foot high, that the government built across the creek for the workers who cut and burn the wild cotton in the Glades, trying to kill out the boll weevils before they get to farmland. The bridge was too low to run the boat under, so I took my motor off, laid it up on the bridge, and let some water into the boat to get it low enough to pass under. Then I was on my way again.

I soon made it to the first lake, the Lungs, which is shaped like a pair of lungs. Seeing gator eyes all over the place, I knew I'd hit the jackpot. I went for the first pair of eyeballs I saw shining back at my headlight. The closer I got, the slower I traveled, and the higher I raised my light up over his eyes; as the light grows dimmer to him, he thinks I'm going away.

When I got within ten yards of the gator, I took the motor out of gear. The boat coasted very slowly as I crept quietly to the bow with my rifle. About fifteen foot away, I turned his heels up. (When a gator takes a fatal shot, he usually rolls bottom up, sticking his front foot just out of the water, but only for a few seconds.) I put down my gun at once, grabbed my oar, and paddled for all I'm worth, trying to catch hold of the gator before he sinks. If you fail to do this, you take your gator hook (a pole with a hook fastened on one end), feel around the bottom, and bring him up that way.

Killing an alligator isn't always that simple. They often hang out under overhanging limbs that are so thick I can barely make out their eyes, and my rifle-ball has to be put in a spot the size of a nickel. While I'm paddling around trying to get in position, the gator usually gets scared and sinks and will not come back up if I stay nearby. I have to paddle back out some distance and wait there in the mosquitoes, thirty minutes or more, for him to finally rise again.

The wise gator starts sinking the minute I see him and takes his time about coming up. Sometimes I can grunt like a gator and he'll pop right up, but not often. Other times, if the water is clear and I can see him lying on the bottom, I can very, very gently put my gator hook under his chin and slowly raise him to the top.

A much better way, if the water isn't too deep, is to stick the gun underwater, arm and all, put the muzzle within a half-inch of the gator's eye, and pull the trigger. This works because no water gets into the barrel. It's like sticking a bottle down into the water, neck first; not one drop will go in.

After a gator's been shot he'll flop around for hours, scaring away any others I'm trying to slip up on. I take the gator by the snout, pull his neck up over the side of the boat, push down on the snout, and then chop the spine in two in the back of the neck. If the gator is very lively, I chop him a second time on the back between the hind legs.

The problem with this trick is the blood. Alligators and sea turtles have more blood than any animal I've ever put a knife in and are the hardest to kill of anything I've ever shot. Cutting the head completely off makes no difference either, they don't even slow down. In fact, there's only one way to quiet down a gator you've just shot. After you chop the backbone in two at the four legs, run a small wire or reed down its spine. All hell is gonna break loose but by damn that's the way to stop him.

With my first gator laid out cold and gator eyes shining back at me like a Christmas tree, I went after another, and another, until I'm killing 'em by the dozen. After cleaning out the Lungs, I moved on through another creek to Long Lake. From there a third creek, short and narrow, leads to Cuthbert Lake. The rookery that a man named Cuthbert discovered at this lake maybe ninety years ago is still there: saltwater birds, especially egrets and other herons, including curlews, never quit their roosts. To keep anyone from disturbing the birds in nesting season and in the evening when they roost, the park rangers have put a swing gate with a padlock across the creek into Cuthbert Lake.

The gate is low to the water, but so was my boat, all loaded up with gators, so I didn't have to sink 'er to get under it. Past the gate, the creek is very short and easy to navigate, as the rangers keep it clear for their tour boat. After getting into the creek, in sight of Cuthbert Lake, I spotted a pair of eyes about a foot apart coming across the water at me like a hydroplane!

When the eyes got close enough, I could tell it was a twelve-foot crocodile. Was I ever glad I had my .22 magnum pump with me that night (lots of times I hunt with a single-shot .22). If a gator or crocodile is coming head-on, you really need a high-powered rifle to stop him; a small rifle won't penetrate the bone from the front. I held back till he got about two feet from me before I shot, to make sure I rolled him over.

There's thousands of alligators throughout Florida but only a few crocodiles, which are found in the upper Florida Keys. Florida crocs and gators are about the same length but not the same color. They both have a clear thin skin that slides over their eyes when they go under. The back of a gator is very dark (practically black) but the croc's back is green. A gator's snout is as wide as its head and rounds off into a chubby, blunt point, with the bottom teeth fitting into holes in the top jaw, while a croc's head and snout are narrower than a gator's, with two tusk-like teeth in the bottom jaw that stick up through the top jaw. Crocs go around with their jaws open, gators don't.

After I loaded my croc on board, I decided to name that creek Crocodile Creek. My boat had about all the gators I wanted in it for one night, and a dang sight more blood. In fact, I was darn nigh to sink, and that's the last thing I wanted to do, especially with twelve-footers swimming all around me.

It was the early morning hours of a moonlit night and as I went on into Cuthbert Lake, I could see the snow-white birds on the rookery. I knew the tour boat would be coming in during the day, and I'd better get into my hiding place. There was a good place on the shore-line that I'd used before, with trees thick enough the park plane couldn't pick me out.

I first threw all my gators over the side into shallow water. If the un-skinned gators were left out on the mud or mangrove roots, exposed to the air, the vultures would soon catch the scent and be sitting in the trees nearby where a ranger might see 'em and figure out why they were there. I cut a few limbs and stuck 'em up for a blind (turning the leaves the right way, to look like a live tree growing there). I cleaned out my boat real good, getting the blood out before it could dry hard (dried blood is a dead giveaway to the rangers).

With my boat cleaned out, mopped dry, and hid away so no one could see me if they rode by, I rolled out my skimpy little bedroll (with my boat cushion for a pillow), rigged up an army-green mosquito net in my skiff, and was soon tucked in for a few hours' nap.

I was about a hundred miles from home now, alone in a sixteen-foot boat, and I still didn't know whether Hurricane Donna was gonna blow me away or not. I'd been watching the weather, but it still didn't look bad. The big moon was well over in the west now, and day was breaking. I looked up through the mangrove to the heavens and watched the stars twinkle and the clouds go by while I listened to the calls of the wild.

The frogs were hallooing—the little ones nearby and the big bullfrogs with the deep drumming sound far away. Early in the night, usually about dark, the whippoorwill is the first to call. About the same time, the night heron will start squawking around and the great blue heron will make its funny sounds. Then the raccoon will give its whistling call, and soon, usually, you hear the mate answer.

About dark that dang screech owl's bound to tear loose and another is sure gonna answer; they just simply give me the creeps. Then, late on a dark night, about thirty minutes after the moon comes up, the hoot owls get started. As I've said before, they have two sounds I love and a third I don't. Their normal hoot is a loving sound, and when two of them get together, they have a "laugh" that's nice to hear. But now and then, right out of the middle of the night, one will let out a scream that would curdle the blood of a grizzly bear.

For the birds, the best time is just as day is breaking. The hoot owl gives its wake-up call and the little birds begin chirping and chattering. The wrens seem to get started first, then the catbirds, the mockingbirds, the redheaded woodpeckers, a kingfisher or two, and then the larger saltwater birds, especially the Louisiana heron. Sometimes a heron will light on an overhanging limb right by me, not knowing I'm there, and sing for a minute before it starts looking for minnows to catch. Sometimes the crows gather up over me like crazy, flocks of 'em in the trees and in the air; they do also do this over four-legged animals, why I don't know.

At sunup on Cuthbert Lake a fish hawk made a few peeping sounds, hit the water like a ton of brick, and came up with a catfish. After the hawk cleared the water and got well up high, a big bald eagle dove on him with his mighty talons, and the hawk turned the fish loose. The eagle caught the fish before it hit the water.

I laid there a few minutes more, listening to hear if everyone had found a mate, and soon dropped off to sleep. When the sun was up good, I woke up and noticed a couple of buzzards sitting around and I knew there would soon be a flock of 'em for the rangers to see. I shot down one of the buzzards from a tree. This drove 'em off—but back they came again. This time I knocked one out of the air and that did the trick.

All my gators were over the side in the water, with everything moved out of the boat for skinning. Because I didn't have the gator up on a stand and had to bend over, this was a back-breaking job. The only parts of the hide that are worth anything (except for special orders) are the soft belly and sides, and you have to be real careful with your skinning knife. If there's even one pinhole in the pattern between the front and back legs of the hide, the value is reduced one-third. On a gator from seven foot up, almost all of the hide has to be cut off bit by bit. On the small ones, most of it can be pulled off.

Through the day, while I was skinning away in my hiding place, the tour boat kept coming by. While the tourists and rangers were in the lake watching the birds, I didn't get many gators skinned. I dragged the twelve-foot crocodile into the mangrove roots as far back as I could and skinned him there, still half in the water. I threw the carcasses out on land so the buzzards could get right to 'em and dispose of them in a hurry. By the time I got through skinning, the birds were coming in to roost. The two keys they roost on were turning snow-white with herons, white ibis, American egrets, white egrets, and gannets.

The weather was looking a little odd, so I hurried along. By sundown, I was done skinning, and everything was going my way. After getting my boat cleaned out and my hides stashed in a couple of corn sacks, I dragged out my little propane-torch stove, made some real coffee, and ate the chicken Estelle had packed for me. Before leaving camp, I made sure all the fresh-cut limbs were underwater so they wouldn't attract anyone's attention when they started wilting.

By dark I was on my way after more gators. With the water so fresh from all the rain this year, there wasn't much wildlife in Cuthbert Lake. There isn't anything in pure fresh water for them to eat; it all follows the brackish waterline. Most of the gators had dropped down to the Lungs, where I had been the night before. However, I found a little bit of excitement right quick. Just as I got on the shoreline, straight across from the bird rookery, I flashed my light out and saw two more of those monstrous eyes coming head-on for me again!

At first I thought it was another big crocodile that had been out to the roost to catch a bird. But when this thing got close enough for me to see the bulk of its body, it seemed to change in size, from one foot high in the water to maybe two or three, and it was snow-white! I've never been one to believe in ghosts, but that's the first thing that came to my mind. There I was alone in the middle of the lake, with a snow-white ghost coming straight for me, with eyes like red balls of fire. The closer it got, the whiter it got, the scareder I got and the more it changed in size.

As the ghost sheered off to the side, I fired away with my .22 magnum pump and laid him in the shade. The ghost was just another old alligator, with a live white wood ibis in its jaws! What made it change size was the ibis opening out its wings as it struggled. Gators don't go out into open water much, but this one had gone out to the roost, caught the bird, and was on its way back, paying me no mind.

Killing gators was a job I had to do at that time to survive. However, taking the life of this one went a little across the grain with me. The poor devil had gone so far for its prey and was just making it back home. But then I got an idea: I went out to the rookery and shot another gator trying to catch a bird. (They do it by knocking the bird off an overhanging limb with their tail.) This gator gave me a second idea: I picked myself up a couple of young, brown curlew fryers to eat later.

That did it for Cuthbert Lake. But I still had to make it back out through Crocodile Creek. I was always afraid someone in a plane might see my light or hear my gun, and half a dozen rangers might be in that little creek, waiting for me at the gate.

But everything was okay at the gate, and I made it out of Cuthbert, back down to the Lungs, and into an out-of-the-way place to skin the "ghost" and a few others I'd picked up on the way. Now for Gator Creek, the one way in and out, and that low bridge, only a foot above the water in the creek. It'd be so easy for the rangers to trap me there.

I took all precautions. I hid my hides underwater, cleaned all the blood out, and got everything shipshape. When I got up close, I shut the motor and the light off and started a-paddling, so quiet even a gator couldn't hear me.

I eased up within a few yards of the bridge and I thought for sure I saw a light flash there. I stopped and listened, but nothing happened. Finally, I eased right up to the bridge and popped *my* light on.

Nothing. I even got out and walked down the road a ways. Still nothing. I knew I wasn't seeing things, but there was nothing left to do. I went back, got my hides, and just as I got near the bridge, the light flashed again. This time I turn my light on at once, and again there's nothing there, except the biggest lightning bug I've ever seen!

Then came the mud flat that I had to get out and shove my boat across. When I made it back to Umbrella Key, where I had left my salt and supplies, I was so tired I just crawled right out on that bare ground with a blanket and caught myself a little nap.

Getting up next morning, I grabbed a quick cup of coffee. Picking a nice place under a sea-grape tree, I laid out the big twelve-foot crocodile hide, put the smaller ones on top of it, and started salting. I rubbed a layer of salt over the flesh side of the hides and rolled 'em up tight. What salt I lost on the small hides I caught on the big one. Then I put the hides in burlap bags and stashed 'em away in a good safe place.

I was still intending to complete my trip by hunting Madeira Hammock. My plan was to leave my hides at Umbrella Key, along with enough gas to get me back to Shark Point, and pick everything up on my way back home.

By now I was starting to get a bit hungry. I had the brown curlew I had shot at the rookery, and everything I needed to cook it: a fry pan, some oil, flour, a little coarse gator salt, pepper. After eating, I set out for Madeira Hammock. As I got near, the weather started looking stormy. Several different signs can tell you if a hurricane is heading your way, and they were all stacking up on me now like Grandpa McKinney's cordwood. There had been squalls for twenty-four hours but not any rain to speak of.

I was in hopes the hurricane was passing by (as the Weather Bureau had predicted before I left home). But then a squall brought plenty of rain, and right after it clear skies—a dead giveaway for a hurricane. The sun was just going down. While I was trying to make up my mind whether to stay and hunt some more or head for home, nature decided for me. Right out of the clear blue sky comes a bolt of lightning, and one rumble of thunder. You don't normally have lightning in a hurricane, but I knew that all signs *except* the lightning were perfect for a hurricane. It didn't take long for me to decide nature was looking after me once again, that lightning bolt was my warning to start for home.

After I got back to Umbrella Key and loaded up, the weather turned terrible. The wind rose strong and steady with frequent squalls—too much for a boat the size of mine. East Cape Sable, where I was heading, stuck out in the Gulf like a sore thumb, and under these conditions, the open water on the way there would be no picnic. Frankly, I doubted I could make it if a squall hit me near the point of the cape.

I stopped in behind Joe Kemp Key, about a mile from the canal that goes into the Flamingo ranger station (and from there into the Wilderness Waterway, the inside route to Shark River). I thought it over while I dug around in my boat for something dry to put on. If I tried going around Cape Sable, I'd probably wind up stranded on it. Finally, I decided to go through the ranger station and the canal. The wind was from the southeast, and by going through the canal and on through the inland route, I'd be in the lee of the storm winds pretty well all the way.

First I made sure all the blood was out of my boat, and my salt, too (that's another giveaway). Next, I piled up a few things in the stern, on the port side where I'd be sitting, and put my hides on the starboard side looking to the bow. Going through the canal past the station, everything would be on my left—the rangers, their boats, the works—with nothing to worry about on my right. I had my hides sitting handy on my right behind the junk I'd piled up, so if there was a problem, I could ease 'em over the side without anyone seeing me do it. And I had my gun in my right hand over the side of the boat, just under the molding, with my shells handy. If anything went wrong, I could drop the gun and hides overboard, and other than my name and looks I'd only be a "tin-canner," or tourist.

When I went through I passed within a few feet of the rangers, but they were so busy with their own problems they paid me no mind. The look I gave them from the corner of my eye was so strong it's a wonder they didn't feel it. The sigh I let out after slipping by was enough to back the wind down that canal.

By the time I made it to Shark Point at the mouth of Shark River, the wind was blowing real hell. The rest of the way, I took a pounding. It was some kinda rough water for a sixteen-foot boat. It took a long time to beat my way home, and it was broad daylight when I pulled into the dock.

When I first walked into the yard, I thought they'd done had the hurricane. The whole place was full of big tree limbs. But the fact was, Estelle had already gotten Loren and one of his cousins to cut off the limbs, as we usually do before a hurricane hits. At the same time some of the boys had put my nets and gear in my thirty-foot *Fraulein,* and my twenty-six-foot launch, and had tied 'em up with theirs in the Islands.

I'd made myself some perfect shutters after the '48 hurricane and I'd also put extra blocks under the house, so it didn't take me long to get set for the big blow.

I'd made it back home okay, got everything tied down, and had a thousand dollars' worth of hides hid under my house. So I just crawled inside with Estelle and the kids, locked the door, and Hurricane Donna huffed and puffed, but she couldn't puff hard enough to blow my house down.

18 / Hell and high water

Weathering out bad hurricanes in the early days of the Chokoloskee Bay country was like walking into hell. We never stayed in our homes. Many of them were too low and weren't strong enough to stand hurricane winds and water. We went up the river in our little fifteen- to twenty-six-foot boats into the narrow creeks. We tied four lines to the riverbank, one on each side of the bow and two aft, with enough slack in the rope for the rising water. The tall overhead trees and the tight narrow creek slowed down the wind considerably. But the pouring-down rains kept us bailing water out of the boats constantly. A few had cabin boats but a lot of us had to sit it out in the blowing wind and rain, usually about a day and a night.

Today the homes are built strong and up on stilts or landfill above hurricane water. But we still have to take our boats up the river and tie them down.

The Hurricane of '26

When I was six, we were living at Grandpa Brown's at the mouth of the Barron River, and along came one of the worst hurricanes that ever hit southwest Florida, the 1926. It struck just when Dad was only half finished with a boat he was building, but he managed to tie it to a tree before the floods came and that saved it. At this time we had a little twenty-foot open motorboat, the *Duck*. Dad put a few supplies in the *Duck* and topped it with a canvas, and when the water came we all climbed aboard and rode her out. After the water rose some, Dad tied the boat up in a little creek near the riverbank.

The very worst part of the hurricane hit during the night. Next morning, we could see from the creek what the hurricane had done to Everglades City. The chickens were setting all over the rooftops or whatever they could climb up on. The water must have been four feet deep in the front yards and probably two in the front rooms. Barron G. Collier just didn't pump his city high enough.

Hurricane Labor Day

The 1935 hurricane known as Labor Day was probably the strongest and most dangerous hurricane ever to hit south Florida before Hurricane Andrew in 1992. It struck the Florida Keys and the lower southwest mainland at Cape Sable and Flamingo. The eye of the hurricane hit Matecumbe in the mid-Keys and the winds reached at least 200 miles an hour. The barometer reading was 26.35 inches, the lowest ever recorded in the Western Hemisphere.

As bad as Labor Day was, there was only 408 deaths and only $6 million in property damage, but we have to take under consideration that the Florida Keys (except for Key West) was nothing but narrow bits of land ranging from only a few yards to a mile or so wide, plus bridges. There weren't many people living there at the time, and most of them were evacuated. The amount and value of homes and property was nothing like today.

In '37 I was commercial-fishing out of Matecumbe and, a few years later, around Cape Sable and Flamingo, and I saw some of the ruins from Labor Day 1935. At Matecumbe, railroad tracks were twisted up like corkscrews and heavy equipment had been shoved across shallow mud flats, leaving a channel deep and wide enough you could row an eighteen-foot skiff up it.

Around Cape Sable and Flamingo, miles of mangrove swamp were completely killed out—not only the red mangrove, but forests of huge black mangrove you wouldn't think wind of any kind could kill. The wind had actually twisted the trees until the bark was blown off.

At Flamingo, the Riggs Fish Company had a barge-type houseboat that was tied to pilings about a mile from land. The boat was at least seventy-five foot long and very heavy with its living quarters and walk-in iceboxes, but the hurricane winds blew it clear across a mud flat onto dry land a mile away!

My dad's old friend Bill Gandees was living at Flamingo when the hurricane hit. Bill said the wind first come from the land blowing in an easterly direction (as it usually does), blowing all the water out to sea. Soon after, he heard something roaring. It was the water coming back, in a wave several feet high. Flamingo itself was very low, maybe two foot above sea level at high tide. When the tidal wave hit, it took all of the people with it, into the mangrove swamp in back of the open land they were living on. Bill said they hung onto the mangrove trees in water over their heads. While trying to hold onto a tree himself, he lost one of his children from his arms, and the child drowned.

The hurricane also hit a work camp for veterans of World War I at Islamorada. They were working on the highway through the Keys, and many were killed. Their bodies, and dozens more, were found as far away as Cape Sable and Flamingo—a distance of twenty to twenty-five miles. I've been told that Ernest Hemingway wrote a piece for a New York magazine about what happened to the vets; he called it murder because they hadn't been evacuated in time like they should've been. The veterans' bodies were cremated, buried, and a monument was placed over their graves that still stands today at Islamorada in the Florida Keys.

Hurricane Northwest

In September 1948 the Chokoloskee Bay area was hit by a hurricane in which the highest wind came from the northwest, which was very unusual. After it passed over, there wasn't much left of the northwest beach; several homes were torn completely up.

Mother's home was on that side of the island. As soon as the wind let down enough, I more or less swam across Chokoloskee in the late hours of the night to check on her. I believe the most relieving sight I ever saw was the light from Mother's kerosene lamp as she walked by that window. The first thought that came to my mind was the old song about the mother who keeps a lamp shining in her cabin window, as she waits for her boy to come home from the war.

Mother's house was up on stilts, and during the hurricane it probably felt to her like it was going to fall off any minute. But bless her heart and thank the Lord, she'd weathered out another one. (My home sits on a hill back from the beach, and received very little damage.)

After this hurricane, the Red Cross came to Chokoloskee for the first time. Several families had lost their homes, and others had been left without much of anything. The Red Cross done a fine job at this time of need, giving aid to all and building new houses for the homeless.

Hurricane Donna

There was some question with the old-timers at Chokoloskee whether or not Hurricane Donna in 1960 had them all beat. They finally all agreed that the 1910 hurricane was the worst in our area until Donna. (We didn't get much from Andrew in '92.) The wind may have been stronger in 1948 than in 1926, but there was far more water in '26. We estimated the water in Donna to be nine feet above sea level, the highest since 1910.

I believe Donna done more damage on the south side of the island. Brother Peg's home was on the south side, and it was torn apart and scattered all over the island. There was nothing left at the homesite. During the hurricane, Peg and his family stayed in the Blue Heron Motel, high above hurricane water. The only thing they had left was the clothes on their backs and what few things they had carried with them. Peg got a government loan and built the house that stands there today in the same spot as the first one.

Chokoloskee was a disaster after Donna. Again, the Red Cross came with aid for Chokoloskee and, to my opinion, done a good job. Fortunately, my home was built strong and is on a high hill above hurricane water. Even though the water came within four feet of the house, there was no damage.

Somehow, since Donna, we've been lucky and haven't had a blow that's done much damage. I don't usually worry that much about winds less than 100 miles per hour. If we are on the ball and take all precautions, a 100-mile wind doesn't do that much harm. It takes a high wind, with water, to destroy much at Chokoloskee. However, if a 100-mile west wind hits on full moon with the spring tides coming in, the rising water can make a mess. I've heard some say their wind instrument broke at 185 miles per hour wind in Donna. If that's true, it probably reached 200 or more.

I notice hurricanes in the later years are going farther west before turning to the north, causing them to miss us in south Florida. They used to make their north turn before getting to Cuba and either hit us or go up the Atlantic coast. Nowadays, they go by Cuba and then turn north toward Texas, Louisiana, Mississippi, and Alabama. In fact, they've even been going into Central America.

19 / Stranded in the Okefenokee Swamp

Someone once told me "Okefenokee" means "trembling earth" in the Creek Indian language. But in April 1962, when I was hunting the Okefenokee Swamp on the Florida-Georgia border, it was *me* doing the trembling.

That year I was selling alligator hides to a dealer in central Florida. He came down to pick 'em up about once a month, and each trip he told me about a professional gator-hunter near Gainesville, how great he was, and also how thick the gators were in the Okefenokee. At the same time, he was telling the Gainesville hunter how great *I* was, bragging on one to the other 'til he got us to the point we just *had* to meet and go to the Okefenokee together.

I joined up with the dealer at a truck stop in Wildwood and we went on in his car to Gainesville to meet this great pro (let's call him Joe). After each of us got over the shock of meeting the most famous gator-hunter of all time, we headed out with the dealer for Fargo, Georgia, just over the Florida line. We stopped there overnight and next morning went down a long road into the Okefenokee National Wildlife Refuge. At the very end of the road was a marina and animal park set-up, with tame deer, raccoons, and a few other animals, and small outboards for rent.

We rented a boat and went through a short, narrow canal into Jimmy's Lake, actually part of the Suwannee River. It's several miles long, half a mile wide, and dammed in, so it's three to four foot deep even in the swamps around it. We counted enough gators in Jimmy's Lake to figure there had to be about 300 of 'em, six to twelve foot long, plus a few larger; maybe even a few fifteen-footers. But there was problems. The swamp was very famous for its alligators and one of the park rangers was an old-time gator-hunter who'd caught many poachers. Also, there were people living at the marina, only a quarter of a mile from the middle of the lake—close enough to hear gunshots and report 'em.

Because of my years of living and hunting in the Everglades park,

Joe left it to me to do the planning. I figured that to get our boats and gear into the swamp past the rangers, they'd have to be special boats, custom-built. As for the gunshot problem, Joe said he had "grained" gators lots of times with a harpoon tied to a long pole. Though I'd never hunted gators that way myself, I went along with it and said I'd make the grains and build the boats.

Back home, I went to work. In the daylight hours, I was building two small, lightweight boats out of quarter-inch plywood, each about ten foot long by three wide. At night, I worked in my shop on the harpoons and other gear.

I didn't put the plywood boats together. I left 'em knocked down and laid the sections inside my fourteen-foot, V-bottom boat (after taking the flooring completely out). This boat was high-sided and rather wide, just right for my plan. Along with the plywood boats, I put all of our salt (for the hides) in the bottom, plus other gear I didn't want the rangers to see. Then I laid new floor timbers high above all the gear, using hand-tightened bolts instead of nails. On top of the timbers I put a new plywood floor but didn't nail it down—only a screw here and there. Outside, on the hull, I painted a new, higher waterline.

When I was loaded up, I kissed the Queen of the Everglades goodbye, patted her pretty little butt a time or two, and was on my way. Again I met the dealer at the truck stop in Wildwood and we hooked my boat and trailer behind his car. Then we picked up Joe and headed for Fargo and the road into the Okefenokee.

Just before getting to the marina at the end of the road, Joe and I got out and walked through the woods, around the marina, to the canal leading into Jimmy's Lake. The dealer, alone, put the V-bottom boat in the water at the marina and picked us up on the way to the lake. That part went perfect.

We went down the Suwannee River in the V-bottom and found a hideaway to put the plywood boats together. After helping us unload, the dealer went back through the marina by himself with no problem. The plan was for him to pick us up in seven days, but not by boat; we were to walk back through the woods to the road.

Being afraid the noise of hammering might give us away, I'd designed our plywood boats to be put together with screws and brought along a speedy-type screwdriver. By dark, Joe and I were together in one boat in Jimmy's Lake, ready for action. When I turned my light on, gator eyes shined back at us like the lights on a Christmas tree.

The first gator Joe threw the harpoon into was about a nine-footer, and he took us for a ride like Moby Dick took Cap'n Ahab. Then, all at once, he "sounded"— went straight down to the bottom. The harpoon line was tied to the boat and once Joe pulled on it, the gator started rolling, which is their way of defending themselves and killing their prey. The more Joe pulled on the line, the more the gator rolled, turning over and over, winding up the line until he rolled right up to the side of the boat. It looked like he was coming on in!

It was my job to knock the gator in the head with an axe once he cleared water, but with him turning over and over it wasn't that simple. Either I had to stop that gator or give him the boat, and I wasn't about to do that in a lake full of the biggest alligators I'd ever seen. I finished him off just before he rolled into the boat, but we made more noise fighting that gator than if we'd emptied a 12-gauge automatic.

There we were, in the middle of the Okefenokee, afraid to use the harpoon again or shoot a gun because of the noise. But we still aimed to get those gators somehow, and we needed to explore our hunting ground. We started combing out the small ones that we could handle without making too much noise. In the daytime we laid around in our boats, hid away in the woods.

About the third day, I got a fever. I knew what was wrong because I'd had this problem before: we were drinking river water and sometimes it makes you sick. From then on, I boiled what little water I drank and took it easy, but for two days I ran a high fever.

When time came to meet the dealer, we found a good place to stash our boats and walked through the woods to the road with what hides we had—enough to pay all expenses. The dealer was right on time.

*　　*　　*

Two weeks later, we returned with the intention of hunting with a .22-caliber rifle—not in Jimmy's Lake but in Minnie's, farther north on the Suwannee, so far that no one at the marina could hear us shoot from there. The dealer put us out for another seven days.

Because we were in the two gator boats, we couldn't afford to be seen in the daytime. With no one allowed in the Okefenokee after sundown, paddling around at night with a headlight was also risky, if the rangers were out after dark. As far as we knew, though, they didn't have any reason to be.

That first night, just as we started paddling up the Suwannee into Jimmy's Lake, we found a skinned gator carcass! We knew right then that we were in the middle of a predicament, and we would have given anything for a way out. But the dealer was long gone.

We'd had in mind to paddle quietly across Jimmy's Lake into Minnie's, without turning on our light. Now we didn't know what to do. But we did know two things for certain: that carcass had been skinned by a pro, some time after our first visit to the swamp, and Jimmy's Lake had been "shot" (hunted). To get out of Okefenokee without the dealer would be hard and dangerous. To hide out in our little gator boats for a week wouldn't be so easy, either, with the rangers looking for the hunter who'd shot Jimmy's Lake and blaming us for it if they spotted us. Either way, it looked like hell to me. To top it off, it started drizzling rain.

"Well, start hunting," I says, "and if they catch us, they'll take us out." Joe grins and says, "Let's go."

In case the rangers had set a trap in the creek we were in, I took the lead in my boat and Joe brought up the rear in his, but far back and without a light, so at the worst they'd only get one of us. Everything was quiet going to Jimmy's Lake. When we took a chance and turned on our light, we saw the lake was clear of gators; that other hunter had cleaned 'em out completely. Then we really got scared; so much killing *had* to put the rangers on the warpath. But we still continued on in the rain—there wasn't much else we could do.

After getting to the far end of Jimmy's Lake in the pitch dark, we were afraid to tackle the very narrow creek that led to Minnie's. If the rangers had set a trap, it would almost certainly be rigged for that narrow stretch. We pulled into a little hole in the woods and sat there in the rain until daybreak. Soon we were on our way again.

Everything went well through the creek. Just before Minnie's Lake, we came to a little rest stop with a roof that could keep us dry for a while in the never-ending rain. We were so tired and cold, we stashed away our gun and salt and crawled under the dry roof for a little nap. (I was so down at the time I do believe that if the secretary of the interior had walked up on us, I would have just rolled over.)

Late that afternoon, we started stirring around again, to find a place for a camp. But there was no land above water anyplace; that's one problem with the Okefenokee, it's all dammed in. Then, off to one side of the creek (just before it opens up into Minnie's Lake), we found enough stumps and broken-down trees to put our junk out on, to make room in our boats for sleeping, skinning, and hunting. We even found a big cypress stump to build a small fire on, and fixed up a little supper and a cup of coffee. Just before sundown the rain quit, with most all our clothes wet and us about frozen.

By dark, we were ready for action. The plan was for me to do the hunting and Joe the hauling. We paddled out into the creek in the two boats, leaving everything at the makeshift camp, and fired up our light for the big kill.

Sure enough, when I turned on my headlight, there were enough gators looking at us to scare us out of there. Most of 'em were big—eight to twelve foot—plus quite a few grandpas. It didn't take me long to load my boat with the biggest alligators I'd ever seen. Joe switched boats with me and headed back to camp to unload while I hunted on toward Minnie's Lake in his. Even before I got there, I had another boatload, with over half of 'em grandpas.

I waited a while for Joe. When he didn't come back, I hid my gators in the woods and killed a third load. Then I turned out my light and hid at the lakeside, waiting. But no Joe. My first thought was, the rangers had him. But if so, why didn't they come on up after me? I sat tight until about two or three in the morning, with everything quiet as a mouse. Then I hid the gators I'd killed, cleaned the blood out my boat real good, and very quietly eased down the creek to our camp. But Joe hadn't been back and was nowhere to be found, certainly not in the dark.

Just before daylight, I got up nerve enough to look for him, but found no sign of any kind. I went back to Minnie's Lake and got all my gators hauled into camp just as day was breaking. That put another thought into my head. The boats were small and Joe's had been loaded with gators. The slightest wrong move on his part and he would've sunk for sure; with the weight of the gators, his boat could very easily have gone to the bottom, ten foot down, and stayed there. Of course, Joe still would have swam out and headed for the river-bank—unless a big gator got in the way. I'd seen some big enough to eat him in a minute!

I lay down for a nap, but Joe was on my mind so strong I couldn't sleep. I made some coffee and started skinning the gators. Because some boats passed by, it took a little extra time to get the gators skinned and the hides salted. Every time I heard a boat, I paddled away from the camp until it passed out of hearing distance. I was quite sure that whether or not the rangers had picked up Joe, they knew there was a hunter in the Okefenokee, and I wasn't going to chance getting caught skinning gators.

Not knowing when I might be back, I salted the hides extra heavy. I put them in an army duffel bag I'd brought my supplies in, stuffed in my gun and skinning knife, and hid the bag in some thick trees far away from the gator carcasses.

Late in the afternoon, I finished up and moved out to a new hiding place. I rolled out my bedroll in the bottom of the boat. By this time, I was so tired I dropped off just like that. When I woke up, the sun was going down, always my lonesome time of day. I can make out okay by myself until sundown, but then I want to go for home. As the sun went out of sight, I'd have given all I owned to be able to walk away from this problem and back home to my wife and children with an easy mind, knowing Joe was okay and I was out of the Oke-fenokee forever.

Then I got this thought: if the Rangers *had* caught Joe and were planning to catch me in the creek between Minnie's Lake and Jimmy's, they'd start waiting at first dark. So the later in the night I tried to get through, the more likely it would be they'd have given up and pulled out. It was 3:00 A.M. when I headed downstream, pad-dling just as quiet as I could.

I'd just come to an especially narrow stretch in the creek when all at once a light popped on. In its bright beam, I saw a shotgun and a revolver pointed directly at me. "Hold it right there!" Almost in the exact spot I'd expected, there were two rangers, with a rope tied across the stream to block it.

While one held a shotgun on me, the other put the cuffs on—he was so shaky I was afraid he might shoot me with his revolver without meaning to. Right away I told 'em I didn't have a gun and wasn't going to run. They believed me and settled down a bit. (I never met a ranger in the woods while I was hunting, night or day, who wasn't shaky. I even saw a park ranger drop his revolver once!)

After they got me handcuffed and put away in their boat, they looked mine over but found nothing. "You're all cleaned out, are ya?" one said. I didn't make so much as a grunt. They tied my boat on tow and off we went: a free ride out of the Okefenokee, the hard way.

They took me to Waycross, Georgia, and threw me in the jail. Before locking me up, they let me make a phone call. Luckily the dealer was waiting for it. The rangers *had* picked up Joe, he said, and he'd bonded him out and would be there in four hours to bond me out. He was true to his word.

On my way home, I didn't stop in Gainesville to see Joe. I went straight back to Chokoloskee and my Queen Estelle.

An attorney in Everglades City advised me to get a lawyer in Waycross, where I was going to be tried, and gave me a name and number. I called the lawyer and he agreed to take my case for a hundred bucks, which sounded good to me. I mailed a check and continued to fish and hunt (but not in the Okefenokee).

The Waycross lawyer called about six weeks later, gave me the court date, and told me to get two letters of recommendation from important people, which I had no trouble doing. I arrived in Waycross on a Tuesday, the date I thought he'd given me, but he said I should've been here the day before, Monday. Joe had been tried and then given six months' probation and a small fine. Today, the lawyer said, the rangers weren't here to testify, neither was Joe, so he didn't know what the outcome would be. "We" would just have to take "our" chances.

He walked me over to the county courthouse and, right in the middle of whatever was going on, he drug me up to the judge's desk and said a few words to the prosecutor. The prosecutor said a few words to the judge and at the same time handed him my two letters of recommendation.

Everything was very quiet while the judge read the letters, then he says, "Well, let's see. We have this gentleman here from the Everglades, charged with trespassing in the Okefenokee. I'll read out his letters of recommendation." After he did, he said, "It wouldn't be fair for a man with his record for military service and helping his community to be put in jail just for trespassing. Mr. Brown, I fine you twenty-five dollars."

*   *   *

A few days later, we took a little family vacation trip to the Okefenokee—Estelle, our three children, and myself. Just before getting to the marina, I got out in the woods. While Estelle was renting the boat and putting the gear and lunch on board, I walked around the marina, through the woods and the rattlesnakes. The family picked me up on their way out of the canal and we headed for Minnie's Lake. First, though, we had to go through Jimmy's, being careful not to pass close to any of the boats on the lake.

It'd been two months or more since I'd stashed the hides away, but they were right there in my duffel bag, still in good shape, along with my gun and knife.

Before we got back to the marina, I went into the woods with the duffel bag, and they picked me up again on the road going out of the Okefenokee. On the way home, we met the dealer near Gainesville and I sold him the hides. Then I drove up to Joe's trailer and laid the money on his table.

"Joe," I says, "how much was your fine?" Joe told me and I counted that amount out of the pile and handed it to him. Then I counted up what was left and gave him half.

Because he didn't have a phone, I hadn't spoken to him since the night he got caught. Now, while I was sharing out the money, Joe sat there with a puzzled look on his face. Then he stood up and took my hand in both of his. He looked down into my eyes and says, "Totch, I never expected to see you or those hides again. What kind of a man *are* you?"

20 / The habits of alligators . . . the Hamilton Lakes . . . hide-and-go-seek with Little Eddie

Alligators don't like salt water. In the dry season as the water in the islands and rivers becomes salty, the gators swim upriver to the Glades. Instead of crawling they get up on all fours and walk out into the Glades looking for fresh water, and also for a place to hibernate through the dry season. Some find a low place and dig their own hole down to fresh water, while others prefer something like a small lake ditch. After hibernation is over (around June or July) and the rains come again, back down the little rivers lickety split they go, eating everything they can grab. Their habitat changes from the islands in rainy season to a hole in the dried-up Everglades in the dry season. And I mean dry, since as we know some stupid politicians managed to get it all diked off.

Gators make three different sounds. One is the "grunt" used by young gators in distress to call their mothers. When you pick up a baby gator it'll start "grunting" every time. The mother will come to this sound right away. (With practice, you can imitate this "grunt" and often fool a grown gator into coming to you.)

Then there's a blowing sound gators make when they're more or less hemmed up, or cornered, and are good and mad.

The third sound is the gator bellow—a bloodcurdling sound that can be heard for miles across the Everglades. When one gator bellows, usually another will answer. When the big boar gators are bellowing in the deep stillness of the night and you're out in the bushes alone with all the other weird animal sounds (maybe a Florida panther scream or two), you start looking around to see what's coming out next.

When a twelve-foot gator bellows, he raises his head up as high as possible, his mouth wide open, and with a full breath, lets out his air. It's a sight to be seen! The bellowing is generally in mating season, the late spring, when the rains are about to start. The gators seem to be asking Mother Nature for a drink of water.

A wounded gator makes a goggling sound, and that gator is something to be scared of when you're in a pit pan. One night, Peg and I was hunting in Little Fox Lake, north of Flamingo, in a pit pan with very little freeboard. (Freeboard is the amount between the waterline and the top of the boat.) Peg was doing the shooting with a common .22-caliber rifle.

The water was a little rough that night, making it hard even for a pro like Peg to knock out a gator every time. When he shot one eight-footer, it wasn't a fatal shot. The gator started running around on top of the water with his mouth wide open. Soon he headed straight into the front end of our pan, into Peg's lap! When Peg tried to shove the gator away, he ended up with his whole arm in the gator's mouth. By a miracle the gator didn't clamp down and Peg was able to pull his arm back, torn up a bit.

While this was going on, I was trying to keep the boat from turning over. By the time Peg shoved the gator out of the boat, there was so much water in it we didn't dare move a finger. An empty milk can was floating around in the pan, but we were so near sinking neither of us could make a move to get it. Finally, by paddling carefully with my hand, I got ahold of the can and bailed her out.

$$*\quad*\quad*$$

Another hunt that sticks in my mind was in the dry season of '64, in the Hamilton Lakes about two miles out in the Glades off Lostmans River. Sometimes when you start hunting, the first dash out of the box something goes wrong, and from there on every move's the wrong one. But not this time: by daybreak of the second day I'd cleaned the lake out, except for a couple of grandpas I'm sure were over twelve foot. (I made darned sure I had a couple of bullets ready just in case one of 'em decided to take on me and my pan.) I'd been hunting all night and I went back to camp and crawled under my skeeter bar—but only for a couple of hours. I still had to gather up my gators, which I'd left in little piles around the lake. This took a little while—the pan couldn't haul many at a time, and the larger ones had to be towed. Finally I got 'em all piled up at camp. I skinned all day, stopped about sundown, and had a bite to eat. Then I put my light on my head and went back to skinning. It was late when I finished up but I got a couple hours' nap before day.

Coming home from a gator hunt. (Photo by Oscar Thompson.)

I hunted the Hamilton Lakes more'n twenty-five years ago. The larger of them is to me the most beautiful in the Glades. Now, remembering those piles of gators I killed and the bunches of birds I shot to eat, I wonder if I did right by Mother Nature. Then I think back to my grandfathers' time, when fishing and killing gators, coons, birds, and deer was the only way of life in this country. But if I face the facts, I know that what they done didn't give me the right to do the same. God, I'm sure, knew when He built the Glades that the cup would not run over forever. Regardless of the circumstances, I don't believe He thought it well of me to take the lives of the real owners of the Hamilton Lakes.

In the morning I sat around for a few minutes admiring my hides and the beautiful lake, and so did a big hoot owl that just wouldn't leave my camp. He seemed to be as proud of my pile of gators as I

In my pit pan near the Hamilton Lakes.

was. I'd killed and skinned eighty; at that time it was the biggest hunt I'd ever made.

I tied the hides up in bundles by running a small rope through the anus, exactly at the halfway point in the length of the hides. That way throwing them over your shoulder puts half over your back and the other half in front. I first carried my hides through the thick swamps around the edge of the lake to the Glades, then walked back and drug my pan out.

After going so long without rest, I was feeling kinda weak, but I'd left word at home when to expect me back, and time was running out. I should have made two trips across the marsh, to where I'd left my outboard—one with the pit pan and one with the hides. But to save time I put the hides in the pan and tried to drag both at one time.

The first two-thirds of the way I tried going without stopping. Then I came to a small, dried-up pond that was soft, muddy, and boggy. I was trying to drag the pan around the edge near the grass for better walking when, without any warning, I fell over. I found out later I'd had a heart attack. I had just turned forty-four. I didn't pass completely out but came very close. For a while I lay there on the mud and grass, not moving a muscle, trying to figure out what to do. The sun was very hot and I was laying there in the open, burning up. Then I noticed a bushy little mangrove tree right near me, on the edge of the pond. I rolled myself over to the shade of the tree, got comfortable, and dropped off to sleep. But the sun soon struck my face again and woke me up. After a while, still not knowing if I'd just fainted or what, I got up. Being afraid now to drag the pan and the hides at the same time, I first drug the pan to the head of the river, rested a while, then went back for the hides.

After getting everything back to the river, I put my pan in and started slowly drifting downstream. I stopped before I got to my outboard, and put my hides out in the bushes in case a ranger was waiting for me. (At this time I was in the dead center of the park.) Everything was okay at the outboard. After a nap and a bite to eat, I salted my hides, rolled 'em up, and dug out for home.

It was dark now and I had to go through two narrow creeks, Plate Creek and Gator Creek, but this time I hit 'em with my throttle wide open. I wasn't planning on stopping. If a ranger had been blocking the way, I probably would've jumped his boat or cut it in two.

Everything went well through the creeks but I still had a feeling I might have to outdo a ranger or two before I got home. I got that feeling every time I was out for a few days and knew the rangers would miss my boat at Chokoloskee and be on the lookout for me—especially Little Eddie. Some park rangers do their job, let well enough alone, then go home and let Mother Nature have her way. But the one I called Little Eddie was different. The more I outdone him, the harder he tried. He'd set up all night fighting mosquitoes just to get a peep of me coming in from gator-hunting.

I was still running at full throttle, with no lights. Just as I was leaving Sunday Bay and going into Lopez River, Little Eddie popped a light on me off from my port side—and the chase began. His boat was a little faster than mine and my only chance was to outmaneuver him. I knew every nook, crook, sandbar, and stump in this area, and lucky for me he didn't, and I wasn't long figuring out a surprise for Little Eddie. (Because guns are not allowed in the park, I threw mine out on the first sandbank I passed—but I still had my pit pan and the hides I'd worked so hard for.)

Ahead of me now was three sandbanks and two ways to go, with Little Eddie right on my tail. Coming up on the next sandbank (about two inches underwater) I pretended to go out the main-route channel; but instead, I pulled up alongside the sandbank, cut my motor for about two seconds, and turned my boat completely around, changing ends. Then I made a hard left about three foot from the end of the sandbank—and, sure enough, Little Eddie piled her up, high and dry!

I didn't stop or even slow down until I was about a mile away. When I did, I could hear him prying around with the oars, trying to get off that sandbank. To get home, I took Turner River, stopping only to stash my hides and pit pan in a little creek on the way.

Just in case some other ranger might be in Chokoloskee Bay when I came out of Turner River, I had my lights burning bright and legal. Lopez River, where I'd left Eddie, also comes out into the bay, and just before I got to my dock on the island he popped his light on me *again!* This time I stopped, looking surprised, and asked, "What's the problem, Eddie?" He just shook his head, knowing for certain it was me he'd been trying to catch, but he couldn't prove a thing.

My dock is about seventy-five yards outside the park and the rangers have no authority beyond park limits. But someone called next morning and told me Little Eddie was searching my boat. When I got there, Eddie was done gone. I called the park headquarters, and the top ranger said he had nothing to do with it, but he'd speak to Eddie. In the afternoon, Little Eddie came to my house and apologized. I went to Lopez River that same day and found my gun under the water where I'd thrown it. I checked on my hides but didn't bring them out until that night. The hides brought me $2,000.

Next day I went into Miami. The doctor told me I had hardening

The narrows of the Turner River in 1992, after Hurricane Andrew stripped all the leaves off the trees.

of the arteries. I had to quit smoking my three packs a day—just like that. ("Just like that" was down on my knees and throwing-up sick for two nights the first week, and darn-nigh dying for a little nicotine for five weeks more.)

With Eddie and me it was always kinda like playing hide-and-go-seek, but the one and only time he ever tagged me, he didn't know we were really playing the game.

It was on a summer day as hot as you'll ever see, and my old pal Buddy Daniels and I were slipping along the coast with about thirty gator hides stashed underneath the flooring of my sixteen-foot out-board. It was never my way to travel the coastline with gator hides in the broad open daylight, but this time I was so hot I just simply didn't give a damn. My fifty-horsepower motor had quit on us and we'd been traveling two days and nights, coming up from Cuthbert Lake south of Flamingo, with a little three-horsepower motor.

Just before sundown, approaching Buzzard Key south of Chatham River, I spotted Little Eddie. I'd just told Buddy that as slow as we were going, we were bound to hit a ranger head-on coming down the coast on his evening run.

With three horsepower there was no way I could outmaneuver him, get behind a key, and drop my hides over the side. But we didn't have to—because we were all set for Eddie. The hides and all the hunting gear was stashed under the flooring, with a couple of casting rods in plain view for a blind. Buddy stepped up on the high part of the boat and flagged Eddie down.

When Eddie got there, the surprised, happy expression on his face sure looked like a trip to park ranger headquarters for Buddy and me. But before Eddie had a chance to open his mouth, Buddy jumped over onto his boat and started tying ours on. He says to Eddie, "We've been out of food and water over twenty-four hours—how about giving us a quick tow home before we both starve to death?" Eddie hesitated a moment and then says, "Where you fellows been?" Says Buddy, smooth as silk, "Down to Shark River, guiding a casting party from their yacht." And before Eddie could figure out what he really should do, Buddy had him towing us home!

It all happened so quick, Eddie didn't really get a chance to check things out. Buddy just flat out-talked him. I stayed in my boat while he towed us and Buddy kept him occupied.

Eddie towed us into the mouth of the Barron River (which, like Chokoloskee, is just outside the park) and cut the switch. By now it was just getting dark and he couldn't see over into my boat very well, but he pulled his up alongside and did some eyeballin'.

First he says, "Are you fellows *sure* you were down there on a yacht-guiding?" Buddy says, "What else would I be doing at Shark River?" and stepped over into my boat. Meantime, Eddie was reaching for the lid on our storage box, but Buddy sat down on it fast and says, "There's nothing in there but ol' dirty clothes." Eddie knew my gator gun was laying in that box, but there wasn't a darn thing he could do about it but let us go.

On our way home we had passed a big fleet of pompanoers going out fishing. When they saw Little Eddie towing my gator boat with me in it, they naturally thought he'd finally won our game of hide-

and-go-seek. The fleet called into Chokoloskee by ship-to-shore radio, and word was out that a ranger had caught Totch Brown. When I opened my front door that night, the Queen had tears in her beautiful eyes and about half the women on the island was there trying to comfort her.

The Queen is always saying I got my best kicks from outwitting the rangers, especially Little Eddie. And the more I think on it, the more I get a feeling the Queen is right.

21 / Making a movie . . . charter-boating with celebrities . . . my second heart attack

By the '40s and '50s, Baron Collier's Rod and Gun Club in Everglades City was doing a business like you wouldn't believe. Whatever the drawing card was, it done nothing but draw! Not only did it keep its thirty-five or forty charter boats going steady, it brought in more than its share of celebrities. Maybe it was the perfect hideaway: a nice hotel on the banks of the Barron River deep in the Everglades, where no one was apt to bump into anybody they knew.

It wasn't unusual to see someone like President Eisenhower and his wife, Mamie, walking the dock of an afternoon looking over the day's catch. Ted Williams, the baseball great, put in his few weeks every year, fly-fishing and playing ball in the afternoon with the kids at the Everglades City school. Senators and other congressmen came by the dozens, and the big-timers, like Mr. Kraft (of Kraft foods) and Mr. Fleischmann (of the yeast company), usually spent a week every year.

The celebrities often gave us natives a big laugh. Probably the biggest laugh was on Richard Nixon, before he became president. He was standing in the bow of an outboard while the guide drove it through the narrows in the mangroves. The boat made a sudden turn and Nixon fell over the side. That evening at the guide dock, his friends more'n laid it on him.

About the time the club began to really bloom, Collier done away with his dairy farm, down on the point across from Grandpa Brown's place, and turned it into a golf course. He also had duck-hunting and skeet-shooting for the sport hunters.

During World War II, the government took over the club and converted it into a Coast Guard station for patrolling the coast and the Ten Thousand Islands. They also took over some of the charter boats and their captains, and you should've seen some of those captains' faces when the Coast Guard smeared gray paint over their boats' varnished decks!

In 1955 the club was took over again—this time by movie stars. Budd Schulberg and his brother Stuart set up in Everglades City to make Budd's movie *Wind Across the Everglades,* a thriller about illegal plume-bird hunting in 1910. I was lucky and wound up right in the middle of it.

The stars included Christopher Plummer, Gypsy Rose Lee, Peter Falk, the fighter Tony Galento, and Emmett Kelly, the world-famous circus clown. I probably hit it off best with the "heavy" in the movie, Burl Ives, who played a character named Cottonmouth. Through the movie he carried a fake cottonmouth moccasin wrapped around his arm, and in some scenes he actually wrapped a nonpoisonous water moccasin we'd caught in the mangroves around his arm. He fit right in with us natives as though he was one of us.

To me, the most exciting scene in the movie was on Cottonmouth Key one night between midnight and four in the morning. We were supposed to be acting drunk, but instead of pretending, we really laid one on! We'd planned ahead for it and made and drank our own moonshine. All but Chris Plummer—he didn't go for our 'shine, so we filled his jug with scotch. Burl kept forgetting his lines, but he was so funny that even the director, Nick Ray, had to laugh.

My role was a plume-bird hunter named One Note, one of Cottonmouth's gang. They needed someone who could play a guitar and make up a song or two about the Everglades. Having done so all my life, I was a natural for the part. Having the opportunity to work with all the stars and becoming friends with Stuart and especially Budd gave me the time of my life.

*   *   *

In 1965, I decided to try a little charter-boating. About that time, some new owners took over the Rod and Gun Club and its charter-boat dock in Everglades City. They spent a lot of money fixing up the club and, along with a lot of advertising, they had enough pull to bring in a lot of conventions.

My pal Buddy Daniels was one of the top guides at the club in the '60s, and he helped me get started in the business. My new thirty-

A scene from the movie *Wind Across the Everglades,* made in 1955.
Emmett Kelly is third from the left. I'm fifth from the left, then Christopher
Plummer, then another guy, then Peter Falk. Burl Ives is in the foreground
with his back to the camera.

three-foot *Fraulein* was the perfect cruiser for chartering, and it
looked great—a big help in getting the celebrities to hire me. I
charged five bucks a day more'n the others, and that helped, too.

As a guide I got to meet a lot of famous people—from Mr. Ferrari,
the race-car builder from Italy, to Jimmy Ellis, then the heavyweight
champion of the world, along with his managers, Chris and Angelo
Dundee.

One time I had Congressman Robert L.F. Sikes of Florida for several days. Each day we had fried fish and hush-puppies for lunch.
The guide always cleans and prepares the fish, but the lady of the
party had different ideas. First she says, "Clean those big sheepshead—they're the best fish you've got." (Back then, before fish got so
scarce, a lot of parties turned their noses up at a sheepshead; today
they're darn glad even to get a saltwater catfish!) Then she followed
me into the galley, rolling up her sleeves, and says, "You go back

My favorite out of all my boats, the thirty-three-foot *Fraulein,* in 1965.

there and talk with Mr. Sikes 'til I get these fish fried." After lunch, when I took the dishes into the galley, she came right in behind me, pointed her thumb out the door, and says, "You're always in my way."

Sometimes big shots will give a guide a fit, but not those two. They were as fine a pair as I ever had on my boat. Congressman Sikes wore an old beat-up straw hat and while they were on board, you couldn't tell either one of 'em from a native.

Arthur Godfrey, the old-time radio and TV star, was a different sort of man but I thought a lot of him too, same as it seemed he did me. On one trip, I had him out on my boat for several days, while he was making a TV show about the Everglades. Someone threw an empty beer can overboard and it made Godfrey so mad I thought he was going to call out the National Guard. Later on that day, we were walking down a little nature trail on Sand Fly Island (same one the Queen was born on) and came up on a little dead fire someone had built. They'd left some cigarette packs laying around, and Godfrey threw another fit.

It was right then and there I first noticed how we change as we grow older. The first thing that came to my mind, and I spoke it out loud, was: how many cigarette packs do you guess Mr. Godfrey ever threw out his car window onto the highway or city street when he was younger? There's something about the way we change with the years that isn't fair to the younger generation. Seems like no matter what we did when we were young, we don't want to allow them to make their own mistakes and learn their own lessons.

*   *   *

In my few years of guiding I done a lot of tarpon-fishing, and I never saw a day it wasn't exciting. The best time to catch the big hundred-pounders is in May, the peak of their spawning season and of the tarpon tournament. (To my mind, that's when the season on 'em should be closed. Instead, that's when we're out there knocking the hell out of 'em.)

Most fishing, especially for tarpon, is done a little different most anyplace you go. Around here, fishing for tarpon in the hundred-pound range is done with the boat anchored and the bait laying on the bottom (mullet with their heads cut off). The free-spooling reels are carefully laid down in a row in the stern of the boat, giving the fish time to swallow the bait before the drag and hook are set. There's usually at least four good jumps and about a thirty-minute fight. When it's over and the tarpon is caught, the guide cuts the leader off as far down its throat as possible, and releases the fish. (We believe some of 'em live; their stomach acid eventually eats up the hook.)

You don't always catch a big tarpon every time you go for one—a wild guess would be you have a fifty-fifty chance. You might go for a week and not even get a jump. Then, many times, the tarpon throws the hook its very first jump, or you might get lucky and catch several in one day.

Usually a tarpon party will go down the line changing rods, giving each one a chance to fish with each rod. But once I had four men come with a different idea. When I threw the bait out, each man picked out one rod for the whole day, and by 4:00 P.M. every one of 'em had caught himself a big tarpon.

While tarpon-fishing, it's nothing to catch several big sharks

A 100-pound tarpon caught by this lady on a charter trip.

weighing several hundred pounds apiece. And it's not uncommon to bring in the head half of a hundred-pound tarpon; twelve-foot hammerhead can cut a tarpon in two at one bite.

My brother Bert once took out a tarpon-fishing party that couldn't catch anything but sharks. They were pulling the anchor to leave when a big tarpon suddenly got on one of the lines. Most tarpon run away from the boat, but this one ran under it and out the other side—probably running from the sharks. The man holding the rod got excited and dropped it overboard. Bert was on the deck, and by the time the rod hit the water he jumped over after it! He came up with the rod on the other side of the boat and passed it to the man. Bert then crawled aboard and they landed the tarpon, but only half of it—the sharks got the rest!

Charter-boating was never really my piece of cake. It was expen-

A soupfin shark caught on a charter trip.

sive for the people in the party and at times the fish were so scarce I simply couldn't feel free to take their money. Then in 1970 or thereabout, when "Florida lobster" (crawfish) and stone crabs had become the thing for a commercial fisherman down here, I had a forty-three-footer built and went crawfishing.

Instead of fish for bait (as in crabbing), we used live shorts (undersized crawfish). Crawfish feed at night only; when day breaks they look for a hiding place. The trap being black like a dark hole, with three live crawfish already in it, they go for it.

The problem with crawfishing, there was never an end. The old Big Ben alarm clock went off at 3:00 A.M., we left the dock at 4:00 and were back at the dock at sundown. By the time we get the boat ready for next day and have a bath and something to eat, it's ten or eleven o'clock, and the old Big Ben is gonna ring again at three.

In 1973, Buddy Daniels and I got in a race on the opening day of the Florida lobster season. We both pulled every crawfish trap we could possibly pull and still make it back by sundown.

It was an extra-good season for crawfish and an extra-good catch.

Buddy, with two mates, caught 3,380 pounds. My son Loren and I, with one mate, caught 3,340 pounds of whole crawfish. But I also had 300 pounds of illegal-size crawfish tails hid away on board that we couldn't mention at the dock. So in the dark I won; in public, Buddy won.

Regardless of the hard work, there was something about crawfishing that I just loved. When we pulled up one of those big ol' traps half full of crawfish jumping around in it like grasshoppers, I got a thrill. But the hours were long and strenuous, and I was beginning to have chest pains.

In '77, I gave up crawfishing. Not long afterward, I had a second heart attack. The light attack I'd had while hunting the Hamilton Lakes in '64 hadn't given me any more trouble. But this time it was caused by blockage of the arteries. The doctors advised me to watch it from then on, and never again lift as much as fifty pounds.

The first few months I took their advice, with Estelle watching me like a hawk and afraid for me to lift even a matchstick. But, as active as I'd always been, there was no way I could just sit down and throw my hands up. Just before Christmas, I felt like maybe a little light work wouldn't hurt.

Estelle agreed to a little pompanoing with me that winter, thinking it wouldn't be too much of a strain. It was very cold, which usually makes a good pompano season. We loaded up my big forty-three-foot *Fraulein* with supplies, including 1,200 yards of sink net, a new kind that was designed to sink to the bottom, so it wouldn't drift with the current and get hung up on the crab and crawfish traps and buoys. At that time I also had a twenty-six-foot open launch which I called *Little Boat*. On it we put 1,200 yards of strike net for shallow water fishing on the sandbars.

We spent Christmas day at home with the whole family as usual. The day after Christmas, Estelle and I headed out with our puppy dog, Benji, a cocker spaniel we picked up after Troubles Number Six. The *Fraulein* had a lot of diesel power and moved right along, even with *Little Boat* in tow.

We were headed for Port Marathon in the Florida Keys. One night, not long after getting started, we pulled up to one of my favorite spots just at the right time. We first put out the sink net from the *Fraulein*, leaving a buoy light tied to the net to find it by later. Then we anchored the *Fraulein*, leaving it with an anchor light, and ran the *Little Boat* to the bank.

Putting the sink net out had been more or less guesswork, but when we hit the sandbar, I knew I'd guessed right. The pompano were "showering"—jumping out of the water, then dropping back like a shower of raindrops. We put out our 1,200 yards of strike net into the biggest school of pompano I'd ever seen in one spot.

After beating the fish up by running around in the boat with a bright light for a few minutes and framming on the gunnels to scare 'em into the net, we started taking the net up. It was so full we couldn't take the fish out while bringing in the net. We "roped it" on board, leaving the fish in the net, to clear out later. On this strike alone we caught 2,000 pounds of pompano!

After getting the strike net up, we were really worn out. Then Estelle says, "What if the sink net is full, too?" We went out to the *Fraulein*, anchored the *Little Boat*, and started on the sink net. There was a thousand pounds in it, making a total of 3,000 pounds in maybe less than three hours.

Once we had all the nets and fish on board, we tied the *Little Boat* on tow and headed up Spanish Channel. Next morning, at Port Marathon, we started clearing the net, and here come a crowd to see our big catch of golden nuggets. Fishermen of all kinds, and tourists with their cameras, were all over our boats.

The following night we done the same identical thing again: both nets were full; and another 3,000 pounds!

Sometimes, in the right kind of weather, you can catch a few pompano in the daytime. One morning after a big catch the night before, our net was tangled up a bit. I decided the best way to clear it for the night's fishing was to put it overboard. I picked a good spot and put the net out, then we had something to eat. Soon after, we started taking our net up. The way our luck was running, we'd caught 250 pounds of pompano and several hundred pounds of mackerel without even trying! My nephew Vince Brown happened along just as we got the net on board. Vince says, "It's the damndest thing I ever saw! I can't catch enough damn pompano to eat, and you can't keep the damn things out of your net!"

The trip had turned out to be so strenuous that I began getting a little chest pain. I was enjoying the fishing so much, as well as needing the money, that I didn't let on to Estelle until one night when we got stuck on a bank in the *Little Boat* with the tide falling. With my boat pole against my chest, I was pushing for all I was worth when a chest pain hit me that wouldn't let up. I had to lay down until after daylight.

Next morning, after the boat floated clear, we went into Port Marathon. The doctor there told me, "No more hard labor. No more skinning alligators and no more commercial fishing." We gave up the pompanoing and I did take it easy, but only for a little while.

22 / Pot-hauling and passwords

Heart attack or no heart attack, I still had to make it somehow for me and the Queen. How was I going to work for a living *and* keep on living? Well, I knew some of my fishing buddies were hauling a little marijuana, so I told Estelle I was thinking maybe I ought to try it, too. She hit the roof. "If you ever even *mention* pot-hauling again," she said, "I'll have you arrested!"

A bit later though, in 1978, a fisherman friend of mine (let's call him Sonny) heard I was in need and offered me a pot job that didn't call for any real labor, only running the boat. I told him I'd have to check with the Queen first.

This time I approached her a little different, explaining that marijuana wasn't a hard drug, only something to smoke; that it probably wasn't as harmful as cigarettes or alcohol; and that the Mafia had nothing to do with it. For a while we had both had the idea that only the roughest kind of people hauled pot and that once you got involved, they'd kill you if you even thought of quitting. But I'd found out from Sonny that the pot-haulers in the Glades were plain people just like myself; in fact, most of 'em were my own friends. Then I pointed out that we were starting to hurt real bad for money.

I also reminded her that we had no medical insurance and that sooner or later I'd be needing open-heart surgery (which in the end turned out to be a quadruple bypass that cost over $40,000). She suggested mortgaging our home, but I knew we could never make the payments.

With help from the county and from other people, I possibly could've made it *without* hauling pot. But I'd always been one of the best providers on the Island; I was proud of everything I'd ever done, and tried to do it right, better than anyone. In other words, my pride stuck out on stems and I felt I'd go right down the drain if I accepted help from anyone.

I finally convinced Estelle there was no risk to speak of, and with the money I'd make on this one run we'd be set for at least a while.

She cried a little and said she guessed it *was* our only way out. "But you've got to promise me," she says, "that you'll never go again." I gave her my word.

* * *

Sonny's part in the pot business was arranging for off-loading the "mother ships" that brought the marijuana up to Florida from South America or wherever. These ships usually were freighters that could haul a 100,000 or more pounds of marijuana at a time. It was off-loaded onto boats that could haul about 10,000 pounds each (my boat would be one of these), and then onto outboards that brought it ashore.

It was a couple of weeks before Sonny's job came through and I was kinda glad of the delay. It gave me a chance to look over a few creeks for a hideout to stash the pot away in case of a bust or problems of any kind. My buddies told me it wasn't necessary, I was just looking for trouble, but I figured it was best to know where I was gonna run to if I had to run. Sonny finally gave the let-go, and four boats of us went offshore from the Gulf coast about 150 miles to meet the freighter. Running back took all night—too late for unloading. Through the next day we all pretended to be commercial-fishing (for a blind, some of us had a few crab traps on board, others a little piece of net).

Just at dark we pulled into the coastline with everything looking good. The outboards and my twenty-six-foot launch met us right on time. I transferred to the launch and loaded her up to the moldings; several outboards trailed after me. But just when I sighted the dock, Sonny called me by CB radio and says, "The sharks are bad tonight—they're eating me up!" (That's what fishermen say when sharks tear up their nets; this time, "sharks" meant the law.) I was only a few hundred yards from the dock but managed to turn back without being spotted, taking the outboards with me to one of the hideaways I'd picked out beforehand. There we stashed the pot away.

From that point on, *nothing* went right. Most every crewman was new at pot-hauling, like myself, and the boats we used were too small and were overloaded. Several sank; others were leaky and the pot got wet. Above all, bad weather brought in the tidewater higher than normal and soaked some of what we'd stashed away.

One night during this job, about dark, I brought one of the big boats into the Islands near the creek where we'd stashed the pot, and the outboards piled a load on her, a good 10,000 pounds. The pot was stacked high in the cockpit, out in the open, but it was a dark night and I intended to get to my destination in the Florida Keys before day. After midnight, however, halfway down the coast, the motor quit. By daybreak, with the tide and wind in my favor, I'd drifted to the crabbing grounds. I threw over the anchor and by sunup here come a crabber, a man I'd known all my life, out to work his traps. I got on my CB and said, "Crabber, can you stop by a moment?" When he pulled up alongside, I says, "I'm broke down. How do you feel about pot?" He says, "Damn good. You got some?"

There was no way to hide the pot in his boat below deck, so we put it in the open cockpit and cabin and then picked up enough of his traps to cover it up. Through the day we stayed in the trap lines while working our way south to the Keys. The marine patrol plane circled over us twice but they must've thought we only had a boatload of traps.

It had taken four weeks to set up the job; now it took four weeks more to get rid of that load of wet, rotten marijuana. In the end, Sonny barely made expenses, but he gave me a little stake to hold me over.

Because this project took so long, Estelle was afraid I'd worked too hard and maybe done myself some harm. I told her Sonny had just put me in charge of the boats, and all I'd had to do was drive 'em and give advice, especially about the islands the others didn't know that well. What I didn't tell her was that I could plainly see the excitement of pot-hauling was about to win me over.

I told Sonny, but not the Queen, to count me in on the next trip. A few weeks later he stopped by and says, "I've got a pop-up [an unexpected job] that I can't do." He couldn't do it, he said, because he had promised to take his kids on vacation to West End in the Grand Bahamas for the weekend. The funny part was, the pot had to be picked up there that same weekend.

Sonny gave the entire job to me and a friend of ours, with the understanding I'd be in charge of the boats getting the pot from West End to Fort Pierce, north of Palm Beach on the Atlantic side, while our friend stayed on shore there and arranged for the unloading. It would only be a two-day job, and risky just for one night. The profits would be split fifty-fifty between the two of us (with nothing to Sonny), which meant a lot of money for me—and after the "big bull" (screw-up) when all the pot got wet, I could certainly use it.

I went to the Queen with this deal, making it sound better than it really was, and finally persuaded her to okay another run.

On a Friday morning, just a little before day, I pulled out with my crew from the Gulf coast on our way to the Grand Bahamas—two forty-eight-footers, powered with twelve-cylinder turbo-diesels (enough to put her on top like a hydroplane, even with heavy loads of marijuana). The weather was good and we hit West End on the nose and right on time, just before sundown.

A little red outboard with a big redheaded man in it was waiting there, as I was told he would be, to lead me to the freighter. But he didn't lead me anyplace until he was sure he was leading the right man. I'd never seen him before, or the two crewmen with him. I only knew I was to meet him and exchange a countersign with 'im. After making the usual boatman's talk for a minute or two, "Big Red" asked if I'd noticed any fish hawks while coming across. I says, "No, but would a bald eagle do?" He smiles and says, "That's pretty close, isn't it?" Then I pulled out the half of the dollar bill I'd been given when I took off from Florida and, with a bigger smile, he pulled out the matching half.

Big Red pointed out a little freighter kinda off to one side and says, "That's who you're looking for." He got to the freighter ahead of us and almost before we could tie up, the crew was throwing the bales at us.

The boat I was running was full of *Playboy* magazines and I knew crewmen were crazy about 'em. I pulled out a stack of magazines and told 'em if they could finish the loading in thirty minutes, the *Playboys* were theirs. They earned 'em for sure! We also gave 'em some cold beer.

By dark both my boats were loaded and "on top," headed back across to Fort Pierce as hard as we could go. The weather was just downright perfect. Everything was going our way, and it had to, for us to get there before day. We didn't take out time to stack anything below deck; instead we put it in the cockpit, covering the exposed part with canvas.

Going back, I only slowed down one time. The captain on my partner boat made the mistake of cutting across the bow of a big freighter, which is bad because freighters just don't stop for any small craft that gets in their path. In fact, they probably couldn't bring anything that big to a stop in time if they tried to. The freighter sounded its horn and flashed its light again and again. At first I thought it was a Coast Guard cutter and we were caught dead to rights. She missed the yacht, but came a lot too close for comfort. Sometime after that, I lost touch with my partner boat, but with him being raised at Fort Pierce, where we were headed, I didn't worry about it. Either he was ahead of me or not too far behind.

About four that morning, still right on time, I made it to the mouth of the inlet going into Fort Pierce. An outboard was waiting there to guide me up the channel and take my mate off. That way, in case of a problem with the law, they'd only catch me—provided they could swim that fast.

Everything went smooth going up the channel, but when I got to the dock the lights that should've been turned out were burning bright and there wasn't a soul to be seen. The unloading crew had let me down, and where was my partner boat?

At that moment I had three choices: hit the water and swim for it, head my boat back out the channel alone, with day about to break, or back her into the dock and go from there. My decision was to put her to the dock. While I was tying the rope on the stern, an elderly man and a teenager came rushing up and looked over into the loaded cockpit covered with canvas. The man didn't take a second glance—just grabbed the boy, ran for their little car, and made a quick getaway!

That was a real scare. I thought for sure they were going for the law. But, on second thought, I decided they simply didn't want any part of what they'd seen.

After all the smooth running and good luck going across to the Bahamas and back to Fort Pierce, there I was, on a boat loaded with marijuana, backed into a strange dock with lights burning all over it, and no one to tell me anything. And if someone did come by, I probably wouldn't even know 'em. I only knew two things for certain: the unloading crew had been scared off; and, as near day as it was then, there wouldn't be any unloading tonight.

While I was trying to make up my mind, a young man came running toward my boat as hard as he could go. He stopped before getting to me and yells, "This place is hotter than a firecracker. It's crawling with cops! Leave that boat and run for it!" Just as he turned and ran out of sight, my mate showed up. The outboard that had taken him aboard and guided me up the channel had put him ashore as planned; then he'd run through the woods to the dock to tell me what they'd told him: there'd been a bust there that day.

I started running, went about fifty feet, and then stopped dead still. I says to my mate, "Are you game to get on that boat with me and get it to hell out of here?" His reply was: "What are we waiting for?" Down the channel we headed with a swinging load and day about to break, with boats coming from every direction to go out fishing. To cap that, a big freighter was heading out the channel with a Coast Guard cutter alongside.

I pulled to the opposite side of the freighter, just as close as I could get without causing an alarm. By the time we reached the outside end of the channel, it was beginning to break day and my nerves were screaming. If it hadn't been for a six-pack I drank while hugging the side of that freighter, I don't believe I could've held myself together. And I still had to get by that cutter.

The problem was, I had in mind to go south, but the Coast Guard boat was on the south side of the freighter, and which way was *it* gonna go? By now, I figured they didn't know I was on the other side, so just as we approached the last channel marker, I turned completely around as though I was coming *in* and headed back up the channel—and the cutter steamed straight on out.

We waited a bit, then turned back around. After getting away from the inlet I put her on top, set the autopilot, and headed south. Then, forgetting chest pain and heart attacks, I handed the mate those bales of "hay" as fast as he could stow 'em away. Fortunately the boat had enough room below decks for the load. By 8:30 that morning we had everything put away and had reached the Gulf Stream, where the current runs like crazy (as much as twenty miles per hour, some say, and always to the north). When the mate came out of the hold, wet with sweat and smelling like rotten weed, he looks me in the eye and says, "Captain, can we shut this thing down for now and just kinda let her drift while we catch our breath?" "Yes," I says, "if ya got any left."

First we washed up and put on some clean clothes and threw the marijuana-stained ones over the side. While we were sitting there drinking a Coke, laughing about how close we'd come to losing our butts, including the boat and its load, it dawned on me we were drifting north like a bat out of hell.

I gave it some thought and decided to join up with the fleet of pleasure and charter boats, work my way south to the Keys through the day, and chance getting off-loaded that night into a house I knew about on the beach. But when I hit the starter button on my diesel, she didn't even grunt! I had two of the biggest batteries that could be found and both of 'em stone-dead with no battery-charger on board! The alternator had quit, leaving us floating along on our load of dynamite, drifting up the Gulf Stream without a paddle in waters too deep to anchor. The big freighters were coming by like speedboats, and we were expecting one to ram us any minute.

From what Sonny had told me about my partner on shore for this job—our friend we called "Mr. Brave"—I had all ideas he'd soon be out looking for us. Sure enough, about 10:00 A.M. he flew over in a small plane he'd chartered in Fort Pierce, made a circle, and gave us a big wave. We turned on our little CB radio, but his plane didn't have a CB. I opened the hatch and pointed at the batteries.

Circling back, he dropped a note in a little bottle, but he misjudged a bit and it fell far from the boat. Without a moment's thought, I hit the water—and until I picked up the note and started swimming back, it never dawned on me that a shark just might be eyeballing me!

In the note Mr. Brave asked if I needed batteries. On his next round, I nodded my head and again pointed at the hatch. He circled back and dropped his cap near the boat, but this time I surer'n hell didn't dive over. I gently eased into the water and done the dog paddle, keeping my arms below the surface to avoid making any noise that might draw the sharks. Written on the bill of Mr. Brave's cap was this message: "I'll have someone bring batteries to you."

Then came what was probably one of the longest days I've ever spent. Fortunately, it was very calm and not one of the boats passing by noticed that we were stranded. About 9:30 that night the boys with the batteries found us. We'd drifted much farther north than they'd expected.

After getting the new batteries on, I hit the starter button and that ol' diesel began to purr like a kitten, and did it ever sound good to my eardrums! Four hours of hard running, and we made it to the channel at Fort Pierce and went up it again.

When I backed her up to the dock this time, I didn't have to tie a single rope. Mr. Brave was standing there with the unloaders and he says to me, "Let's get away from here, Totch. They'll take care of this." As I'd requested when we first set up the job, he had a case of Budweiser iced down in the car.

Through the day, I'd been wondering what had happened to my partner boat. Mr. Brave told me my partner had hit the channel into Fort Pierce ahead of me the previous night. The outboard that met him filled him in about the bust that day. This scared him so bad he abandoned his boat, beaching it on the nearest land he could find, and ran for it.

When the outboard boy told Mr. Brave about that, he rushed to the boat and drove her up the inlet to the same dock I'd been to. But instead of tying up there, he docked her across the way with the engine box off, as though she'd broke down. Mr. Brave and his helpers put everything below deck and the boat, looking half-sunk, set right there until midnight the following night with no problem. They'd unloaded her just before I made my second run up the inlet. No wonder they called him Mr. Brave!

$$* \quad * \quad *$$

The very next day after I got back from Fort Pierce, Sonny stopped by and says, "You've gotta go again. I've got another pop-up that won't wait and nobody to pick it up."

I went on the *Fraulein*, my forty-three-footer, taking along a-

110-volt generator, a power saw, and some quarter-inch plywood to fix up a storage place below deck for the pot. It was good weather, so I set her on autopilot while my mate and I worked on the flooring. Our destination this time was Sylvia Light near Gun and Cat cays (the same lighthouse where the rumrunners used to pick up booze in Prohibition days and smuggle it into Chokoloskee Bay, then out by train through Everglades City). We anchored by Sylvia Light about sundown.

Our orders was to meet a fifty-seven-foot yacht there about dark. We sat up until 1:00 that morning, but nothing showed. I checked out my anchor, making sure it was holding good and above all that my anchor light was visible from any direction. I could hear my mate in the bottom bunk snoring up a fog. I climbed up onto my bunk, and just before drifting off to sleep I heard a roaring that put me on my feet in a hurry.

The roaring turned out to be the overdue yacht, headed directly into the side of my boat: a fifty-seven-foot fiberglass yacht loaded with marijuana and powered by two 12-cylinder turbo-diesels, and she rammed us broadside! The driver had fallen asleep at the wheel but woke up just before hitting me, and threw both his diesels in reverse—too late to prevent the accident, but soon enough to keep from cutting both sides of my boat completely in two. As it was, one side was cut from the top deck down to just below the waterline. Even though I was going to the bottom if something wasn't done in a hurry, I do believe the captain of that yacht was more scared than I. His problem was, he had a load of marijuana on board and didn't know if I was his man or not—but if I was or wasn't, he'd be stuck with it cause he had sure in hell put my boat out of business.

Somehow I didn't panic and fortunately I had a good, strong-minded mate with me and two good bilge pumps, plus plenty of plywood for patching the hole. I grabbed a four-by-eight sheet of plywood and stuck it over the main hole with a nail here and there, then stuffed clothing and blankets in the cracks. We were working like crazy, but the bilge pumps couldn't handle all the water coming into the boat. While my mate took over the patching job, I converted the intake of the big 2 ½-inch seawater pump on the diesel motor into the bilge. That saved us. With three pumps going now, the water slowly went down, giving us time to relax a little and figure out how to patch the hole enough to get us back across the Gulf Stream.

When the accident first happened, the captain on the yacht come up just close enough to ask if anybody was hurt and were we okay. I hollered back at the top of my voice, "We're all right. Just get to hell outta my sight!" He backed his boat off but stood by. After a bit I hollered out the password, "Jackfish," and the captain answered with "Mullet." I told him I wasn't about to take any pot with me; I'd be damn lucky to make it back across the Stream empty. All the same, he done his level best to put the load off on me, even knowing that chances were I'd sink with it. Under the circumstances, I didn't take so much as a joint from him.

By the time we got the boat patched enough to start back, it was broad open daylight. The weather was pretty much in our favor and we only had to stop one time, when the spray running down the deck come right on into the boat. We cut a few strips of plywood and nailed 'em over the hole, turning the water back out to sea.

I've often wondered who was the sickest that trip—that captain, stuck with a boat overloaded with pot and nothing he could do with it; or me, going back with nothing but a torn-up boat that would take months to repair.

*   *   *

Sonny and I next went down to the Keys to discuss an off-loading job that was to be brought in near Marathon. We hung around Lower Matecumbe for several days waiting on the dealer. When he finally showed up, Sonny for some reason didn't seem to think much of him. At the time, though, I had no reason not to trust the dealer. When he spoke to me later about handling all of his off-loading, I said okay, and Sonny and I split on friendly terms. The dealer told me that if I could get enough boats to do the job, we'd take a whole freighter load. I took every dime I'd made on the Fort Pierce trip and sunk it into boats to haul with. When we pulled out this time I had four shrimp boats of my own for the pickup, plus two good-size yachts and two large commercial boats to bring it in close to shore, and outboards with good men to carry it to the dock.

Somehow there was a misunderstanding on where the shrimp boats were to meet the freighter, and it took three days to finally make contact. While they were loading, the captain of the freighter tried to pass a kilo of cocaine along with the marijuana, to one of my captains. "No way," the captain says, and throws it back. "My boss says we don't handle drugs."

We unloaded one boat each night, until we got it all. We were working around the Keys, with everything going as smooth as silk, when one of the boys fell overboard while cleaning out his outboard and swam ashore, leaving the boat running out there by itself. Before he could get word to me, the Coast Guard picked up the boat. Afraid to unload there the second night, we unloaded 100 miles north in the Naples area instead of in the Keys.

Everything worked out fine on that run, except that the dealer only paid me for about two-thirds of the load, claiming that's all there was. Even so, I was so much better off by now that I called it quits with the intention of never going again. But then came "the big pot boom."

Many of the home boys got involved in off-loading and began to run it by my house in the broad open daylight, like hauling fish in the old days! To be honest with you, I just simply couldn't sit on my butt and watch 'em having all that excitement and fun, and me have none. So I declared myself back in the game.

23 / Crooks and problems . . . a trip to Colombia
/ . . . learning the game

I took a chance and went in business again with the same dealer I'd off-loaded for, only this time as partners on a fifty-fifty basis. I furnished the boats and done the hauling from Colombia to the coast of Florida; he made all the contacts and handled all sales.

On our first run I took one shrimp boat all the way to Santa Marta, Colombia. The trip went perfect both ways—until we came back here in the middle of the holidays, and then it turned into one hell of a mess! (On second thought, the way pot-hauling usually goes, I might say it was a typical run.) To start with, every clump of land high enough to crawl out on, in and around Naples and Chokoloskee Bay, had someone on it—tin-can tourists camping, sport-fishing, or just boat-riding night and day—leaving us no way to smuggle a bale in without being seen.

After three or four days with the boat laying out there with a load of "dynamite" and the crew thinking every minute it was gonna blow, we finally brought her in near Cape Romano, between Naples and Chokoloskee. The outboard crews got the pot off the boat okay, but nothing else went right. Some of the outboards got lost in the mangroves, trying to slip around the tin-canners, and just as day was breaking the crewmen threw the merchandise out anyplace they could get it ashore. Some bales were simply lost overboard and floated away. Other crewmen piled theirs in the mangroves and the tide rose over the bales before they could get to 'em again.

In the end it took ten days to do a one-night job, getting the merchandise on the road—with every pound of it wet and darn-nigh rotten. From start to finish I spent two months on it and never made a dime. In fact, I had to pay some of the helpers from my own pocket to keep 'em off my back and almost went broke doing it.

The dealer had me believing it was a total loss, but I found out later he ripped me off. He turned out to be what Sonny said he was from the start, a crook. We fussed and fought about that load for a month and then I'll be darned if I didn't let him talk me into *another* run.

This time, three shrimp boats went to Santa Marta and, from the beginning to the end, everything went perfect. All three boats unloaded in two nights, not a bale lost, stolen, or wet, and would you believe I never got enough out of The Crook to pay the fuel bill?

His first trick was to show me a newspaper article reporting that a trailer-load of pot had been busted, and he claimed it was ours. Next he claimed a crooked dealer had ripped us off for one whole boatload out of the three. There was enough pot there to retire on for good; instead, I lost my butt.

The Crook wasn't seen much around the unloading. His job, like I said, was on the setting-up end in Colombia and on the selling end here. It was my job to hire the help and the boats for the unloading. That, of course, turned out perfect for The Crook. The boys hardly knew him, and *I* was holding the bag. All the work hands involved held me responsible, and some got pretty unfriendly about it.

I probably could have walked away without giving 'em the first dime but that was never my way. Those boys had worked like dogs for me and I owed 'em—even though it's understood that if the pot gets caught or the dealer doesn't get his money, neither does the work crew. But this time was a little different. They knew the whole bunch of us was being ripped off. I took what little money I had left and split it amongst the crew. I had walked into that mess with plenty and came out with nothing but the shirt on my back and three run-down shrimp boats, besides owing the boys. I eventually paid 'em from what I made on other jobs, enough to clear my conscience.

When I came out of that mess, I made up my mind to make a go on my own. I still had my boats. By now I'd seen enough to feel sure that if I could only get up the money to push one small load through, I could then make a few good runs and retire again, for keeps. As for money, I'd lent out a lot and though I was never the kind to ask anyone for money they owed me, I stuck my pride behind me and did it. After dunning and borrowing what I could, I came up with just enough to make a little haul if I played my cards right.

I knew nothing about Colombia and had no contacts, but I'd picked up enough names and phone numbers to make a stab at it. One day I boarded a plane for Panama. I'd been referred to a man there that I talked into going to Colombia with me to look over the merchandise. One morning we took off from Panama City in a small plane and within thirty minutes were off the Caribbean coast of Panama at the north end of the San Blas Islands, near the Colombian border. There are several landing strips throughout the islands built by the U.S. in World War II—all short and scary, but the Panamanian pilots never seem to have any trouble making it in or out.

The San Blas Islands are one of the most beautiful pieces of nature I've ever looked down on from the air. There's at least 300 of 'em, all with snow-white sand and coconut trees. They're not very large, some less than an acre; the largest island isn't even a mile long. They're inhabited mostly by Cuna Indians, small and dark. The islands play out within a few miles of the Colombian border.

After we landed on a small strip on the Panamanian coast, we transferred to a big canoe with a seventy-five-horsepower motor on it, and headed out for Colombia. The Colombian captain was a very nice chap, only he seemed to think he was driving the *Queen Mary*.

As we passed the border into Colombia, there wasn't much difference in the coastline. It was getting late in the afternoon, with a slick calm on the water. It sure was a beautiful trip for a while—the pretty beaches, the trees, the mountains right down to the water in places, and the coastline villages. Later, I noticed a cloud I didn't like the looks of. When it caught up with us, the rain started, as well as rough seas. From then on, until we lay down that night with some dry bedding, it was nothing but hell.

The hard rain didn't let up until the next evening. It was rough for the canoe but somehow we managed, though we like to have froze to death. Finally, we came to big coves in the coastline and the captain cut across from point to point. It was raining so hard we couldn't see land, and we didn't have a compass. Sure enough, El Capitan got us lost!

Finally, we saw a blinking light and went in to check it out. El Capitan looks over the landmarks and says, "We are many miles too far south." Then and there I named him "Santa Marta" (the city of Santa Marta was farther down the coast, where we did *not* want to go). We then headed back up the coast, this time keeping the land in sight, and finally came to our destination—Puerto Turbo, Colombia. Going southeast from Panama, it was the first port on the coast, and did it

Colombian natives pretending to be farming bananas.

ever look good to my eyeballs. We got into an old shack for the bal-ance of the night. Next morning, it was still raining, and because his motor was acting up, we laid off Capitan Santa Marta and chartered another boat. It wasn't far from port, only a few miles across a big cove to the mouth of the river we were going to go up, the Rio Atrato.

Once we entered the river, it was smooth sailing in the rain; but there was dang-nigh as much water over us as there was under us. Late in the afternoon on the second day, the rain stopped. We were then at least 75, maybe 100 miles upriver. Hours later, we came to a large village with shacks on both banks of the river. Here we changed to a couple of small canoes and went farther upstream to the mari-juana farms.

A little before dark the natives started coming out of the river, their canoes loaded with bananas, pineapples, and other fruits and vege-tables like yucca, malanga, and nayme. The fruit and vegetables were only a blind; what they were really farming was marijuana. They really knew how to handle a canoe. There'd be only about three inches of freeboard showing, and in that fast-moving river, swollen

Colombian village on the
Panama border.

by all the rain, they were walking around in their canoes like they
were in a ship.

When we made it to the farming village that was our destination,
the water was extremely high—at least a foot deep over most of the
riverbank, where they were living in their shacks. Most of the merchandise we'd come to see was stacked in the shanties and some of
the people just flat refused to let us even poke our heads inside. (The
problem was that my buddy had a camera hanging around his neck,
one of the natives told us later.)

We looked over the "weed," and I picked out what I wanted. Then
it had to be graded and packed—a simple process, but it took a lot of
time. The natives were using hardware cloth, a big square piece of
galvanized-wire screen, set on a table about four foot high and
framed on all sides by a four-inch board. The weed was dumped on

Me and the donkeys,
loaded with the goods.

the screen for grading by men, women, and children. They stood and
scratched around in the marijuana with their hands like chickens in
the yard, picking out and discarding the long, hard stems. The screen
had square holes in it just large enough so the "shake" (weed that's
gotten too dry and lost its kick) would fall through.

The hand-packing was something else to see. They put a little of
the weed in a large wooden box that was standing upright with the
top end open and a bag inside. Then one of them stood inside the
box, patting the weed down with their feet, occasionally adding more
weed. It really hurt me to learn from my friend that these people, who
had practically nothing to live on and work with, got paid so little for
something that's worth a fortune. If they were real lucky, they might
get ten cents a pound for it!

We headed out, getting back a little after dark to the village where
we'd left our chartered boat. It had quit raining. We took advantage

of that and didn't wait for daylight. I don't speak Spanish so I didn't know what was going on half the time, but somehow Capitan Santa Marta showed up again and we ended up back in his seventy-five-horsepower canoe. Going downriver that night was a little scary because of the debris in the water from the rains, but we only hit one log.

Next morning, the wind was blowing a little and I knew it was gonna be a rough trip going back up the coast, even in a big canoe. I noticed a one-motor plane on a little airstrip and the thought came to me to go back in it, rather than take a beating on the water. The pilot said he wasn't allowed to fly across the border into Panama, but he could put us down in a cow pasture in a little village near it, and we decided to take the chance.

It was a rough looking plane but it run like a clock. When we reached the pasture, there were too many cows and burros on it for us to land. We tried to scare 'em off, but that didn't work. Next we flew over the village and circled it a time or two, and one of the natives came out on a donkey and cleared out the pasture for us.

But there was still another problem. The field was wet and the pilot was afraid that if he landed there he wouldn't be able to get back up again. We dropped down to see what it looked like closer up and the pilot shook his head. I pull out a couple big bills and says, "It looks to me like it's dry enough." He looks at the money and says, "It's getting drier all the time."

The natives walked my buddy and me into the village, a very beautiful place, with neat huts, snow-white beaches, and very large coconut trees leaning out over the water, with the little boys climbing 'em to get coconuts for us. My friend and I sat under the trees and had a can of sardines and some soda crackers for lunch while one of the natives got his canoe ready to take us back across the border to the village we'd left. I didn't eat much myself, most of my share going to the little *muchachos*. That little while I spent on their beach took me back fifty-some years to when I lived at Chatham Bend in the Glades. It too had coconut trees leaning over the water, for *me* to climb.

Three weeks after my expedition, I sent my most reliable shrimp boat down from Key West to pick up the "river grass" I'd ordered. Eight days later the boat was offshore a few miles from a little village

The Panama Coast Guard cutter, after towing my shrimp boat into the
village.

near the border when along came the Panamanian Coast Guard!
They towed my crew into the exact same village the grass was to be
picked up and locked 'em up in a dungeon.

One of the Panamanian men I was dealing with called me in
Chokoloskee and I met him in Panama City. But first I had to borrow
more money to operate. I rigged up some cock-and-bull story and got
it from a bank on a personal loan.

Señor (we'll call him) had spoken to the Coast Guard and there
really was no serious problem: the boys might or might not have
broken the law by coming in so close to shore, and the Guard wasn't
even sure what country's waters (Panama's or Colombia's) they had
been in. The Coast Guard cutter that busted 'em had had a bunch of
sightseeing commissioners on board, so the captain felt he had to
look like he was doing his job. After a couple of days, Señor talked
the Coast Guard into letting my boys back on the boat. Getting the
boat papers back took a little more doing, plus a little more cash.

That was just the beginning. Everything on that trip went wrong.
The minute the boys got back on board with their papers and were

ready to go again, their motor quit. After I asked around all over Panama City, I found a diesel mechanic who agreed to go down and have a look at it. But to get him there, I had to charter a plane at 500 bucks a trip! I went along with the mechanic and made notes of what parts and tools we needed. Coming back, we landed at Paitilla, a small airport in Panama City. The immigration people had themselves a ball with me for a while, but I talked my way out.

Early the next day, we left from a field in Colón, Panama (which *didn't* have immigration officers). It took about a week down there near Colombia, and several trips for parts, to get that shrimp-boat motor working again. While the work was going on I slipped back home and, unbeknowing to the mechanic and the pilot, borrowed enough money to pay 'em off.

One thing that makes it hard to do pot business most any place is, you can't expose yourself to the law by buying supplies. I was always afraid the people I bought tools and parts from might figure out what the goods were for and turn me in. Worst of all, there's simply no end to the smuggling. You not only have to hide your pot, you have to smuggle everything you put on board (including yourself), not to mention the boat. With everything in the world going wrong, it eventually gets to a man's nerves.

Somehow, though, just two weeks after I'd first met with Señor in Panama City, we were shipshape again. Now, thinking everything's all set at last, I'm waiting in the cheapest hotel in Panama City, cutting every corner I can get a knife to, because the only dang thing I got left is my used-up credit card and an airline ticket back home. I sit right there on my butt another two weeks, with the dealer telling me every day they're gonna load me *mañana,* and my boys laying to anchor off a village they can't go into for a good time. Then I get a phone call: "Come to Miami at once—urgent!"

I didn't know then, or for some time after, that I was dealing with two of the biggest crooks in the marijuana business. One of 'em lived in Miami, and when I got to his place he tells me there is no pot and never was any, that the bunch down there got drunk and gambled away every dime of our front money for the merchandise (*his* money, he says, *and* mine).

Back to Panama I go, fast. The crook there tells an altogether different story from his pal's in Miami. He says somebody didn't pay off the Colombian Coast Guard like they was supposed to, and when they got to the mouth of the river with most of the load, the Guard took it!

Now I don't know *which* crook to believe, or what the hell difference it'll make if I do. All I know now for certain is that I'm broke again and just as far down the creek as I can drift, without a paddle and with the tide running against me.

A couple of days later, when most of the shock had worn off, I had a serious talk with the crook in Panama City. He offered to get another load of pot together with what was left of the first, *if* I could give him $20,000! That, of course, put me to sweating. I not only didn't know where to get that much money but I was getting more'n a little leery of the whole situation. But I finally took him up on his offer. There just simply wasn't much else I could do, with my boat still anchored down there on the border of Panama and Colombia and the crew pulling their hair out. I wasn't about to quit now.

Before I started back to Chokoloskee to try and raise the cash, I made a little side deal in Panama City with a fellow I'd met in the little village we were working from near the Colombia-Panama border. He seemed like an all-right guy, and agreed to fly down there (at my expense) and look out for the boys and the boat until I returned.

Back home on Chokoloskee, walking around and kicking over the oyster shells, I tried to see a way to get up 20,000 bucks plus expenses (which wasn't a little). At that point I was just simply ashamed to hit up anyone else, especially with the Queen still begging me to give it up and settle back down with her and the kids before I had another heart attack. After walking the floor one night, I came up with the idea to borrow the money against one of my shrimp boats. It wasn't all that easy, but eventually I talked one of my old pals into letting me have the cash, provided he held the papers on the shrimper. At last, I boarded the plane back to Panama City.

My new Panama buddy came up from the village with good news and bad news. The good news was, he'd looked out for my boys on the shrimper as promised. The bad news was that the crook boy down there said it'd take two *more* weeks to get the load ready.

Meanwhile, my buddy introduced me to his Panamanian friend, a businessman. Knowing the officials as he did, he advised me to move my shrimp boat to Colón, about 200 miles northwest of the village, before the Coast Guard gave me any more trouble.

For another 500 bucks I chartered a plane back to the village. By the time we landed there it was late afternoon and the pilot didn't hesitate to tell me he was pulling out at 5:00 P.M. (In Panama they're afraid of the heavy rains in the evening.) A couple of natives and I went around the point in their dugout canoe to see my boys and bring the boat around. It was 5:00 before we got back and I heard the plane take off, so I crawled aboard that shrimper and we took her to Colón.

When we got to Colón the following evening, my Panamanian friend had his immigration friend clear us in. I took the boys to Panama City and set 'em up in the Conquistador Hotel. That first night, they took in the town (and probably a few of its houses) and I can't say as I blamed 'em, after what they'd been through.

While they were living it up, I was trying to live it down, in a beachfront hotel on Balboa Avenue facing the water, with curlews feeding along the shore. Right there's where I sat for *another* three weeks! How in the world I managed to hold myself together through all the problems that came my way on that run, I'll never know — maybe those curlews had much to do with it. I sat and looked at them and thought about Chatham Bend and Huston River.

Finally, the crook gave the signal and my boys loaded the shrimp boat with Panamanian beer and back they went, headin' for the village again. Just before they shoved off I says to the Captain, "Maybe you'd better check your fuel," and so help me, 5,000 gallons had been stolen! There went another day and over $6,000 for more fuel. Another two days and she was loaded with pot and homeward bound up the Caribbean. Nine days later, right on schedule, she made her rendezvous off the Florida coast.

This business hardly ever turns out like it's planned, and this being my first shot at buying and selling, it turned out *bad.* First off, those crooks only gave my crew about half a load and, like most always, at least half of that was junk. I do believe they packed in everything from dried banana leaves to seaweed with that marijuana. The first buyer I tried turned it down flat. The next buyer *stole* what he got—

never paid me a dime. The next truckload never even made it to the buyer; the boys in the warehouse ripped me off. Finally, though, before losing it all, I made a cash sale big enough to put me back on my feet and give me time to look around a little.

Then come the crooks, the Miami one and the Panama one, demanding money for the junk—for themselves and everyone involved in the deal, especially the farmers and graders and packers on the river (so they said). By this time I was so fed up, I got up enough nerve to turn the tables on those jokers. Instead of cash I started delivering to 'em in Miami the junkiest of the junk they'd unloaded on me, valuing it to 'em at top dollar, the price that good stuff was worth. Using a van, I delivered some of it every night, until they called me and said they'd pick up the last load themselves.

The two crooks come in a new-looking van, loaded up, and took off in the opposite direction from where they'd come. Later I learned they sold the junk somehow and left the country with every dime they got for it. Eventually one was seen in France and the other in Spain. As it often turns out, the poor native farmers and helpers never got a thin dime from them, though I did give 'em a good hunk from my own pocket.

By now I'd found out how the game was played and, by taking my time and with the help of a friend, I got enough out of that round to go for a swinging load of Colombian gold.

24 / The *Gambler* and the *Joker* . . . a perfect haul . . . Operation Everglades

I really didn't have to keep on pot-hauling. Even working with crooks, I'd made enough to get by. But I could never accept a failure; I just had to "do it right," regardless of what I was doing. But a perfect pot haul is so hard to make, and happens so seldom, most haulers never expect to do it. But before giving up the business, I was determined to make a perfect run from the Colombian mountains to the creeks back home. And that's not the half of it. If you have any success at all as a smuggler, there's something exciting about it that gets ahold of you and you can't shake it loose for hell. The challenge of getting by with something that big and worth that much had won me over.

For two reasons, not many dealers go to Colombia and examine the merchandise before buying it. First, you usually have to go up into the mountains in the far backcountry, and that can be a little on the dangerous side. Second, what you pick out you may never see. After you've turned your back, they'll pack what they want—like the crook boys done to me a while back—and you could get the sorriest thing they have, with no more kick to it than a blade of saw grass. The most practical way is to go there in your own boat, have a man stay there and watch the packing and pay cash. But that's one helluva risk. What if you get caught coming up the Caribbean? Then you haven't lost just your boat and crew, you've most likely lost your butt and every dime you own!

All by my lonesome, I boarded a plane for Panama City, where I picked up Señor, the man I'd learned to trust. He talked my language; in fact, he knew five different languages.

Next day, we boarded a plane for Barranquilla, Colombia. There we spent the night in the El Grande Hotel, rented a car next morning, picked up Señor's brother, and got an early start down the coast. We went through Santa Marta and on to Riohacha, near the mountains called the Sierra Nevada de Santa Marta, where the Indians grow Colombian gold like the Everglades grow saw grass! Señor had called ahead and the big wheeler-dealer down there was waiting when we pulled into Riohacha about one that afternoon.

From there we took a Jeep as far back into the mountains as we could go, until we came to a tiny village called Barranca: one old farmhouse and a couple of shacks with a few chickens, goats, and a cow or two in the yard. We stopped under a big shady tree and a nice-looking señorita brought us out a big pot of real Colombian coffee that was something worth drinking.

While we were having the coffee, a Spanish man came riding up on a little horse with a couple of burros and another horse in tow. The man was barefoot and bare-chested and wore a wide-brimmed straw hat. But what caught my eye was a Colt .38 revolver stuck in behind his belt right next to his dark, bare skin. When he stepped down from his horse and I looked into his eyes, I believed I could see what the old-timers probably saw in Ed Watson's eyes that day in 1910, when he snapped both barrels of his shotgun at the crowd on Ted Smallwood's dock on Chokoloskee.

I had no idea what the horses and burros were for, but I soon found out. Riohacha is one of the leading ports for shipping out Colombian marijuana. I'd come to buy a shrimp-boat load; to keep from getting ripped off again, I had in mind to examine every sample personally, leaving Señor's brother behind to see I got exactly what I bargained for. But to check out the samples, I'd have to ride a little horse up the side of a steep mountain, chock-full of boulders.

The man with the Watson eyes began to saddle up the burros and the extra horse. At that time I was at my heaviest, weighing 192, and I felt sorry for the little horse I was about to crawl on. It was so small I felt like a giant on a billy goat.

After the four of us got mounted, a tall, strange-looking man with a Colt automatic in his back pocket took the lead. Señor and his brother and I rode behind him, and the Watson-looking man took the rear—and I didn't ask why. How on earth those little animals stepped between those boulders and from one opening to another, while climbing almost straight up, is still a mystery to me.

When we finally made it to the top, it was so late in the day the packers had quit, but they opened several bales for me to check out. Never having smoked pot, I was no expert on picking out the best. Señor didn't smoke it, either, but he'd been around enough to know good from bad. It all looked good and I ordered from what was there. While I was digging around in it, I never saw the like of fleas in my life—they seem to hibernate in the stuff before it's sorted and packed. We left Señor's brother there to keep an eye on what they were packing. He done a good job, but later he told me the fleas and ticks like to have eaten him up.

On our way down we didn't have to guide the burros; they went right back on the same trail we came up. My little horse started under a large, overhanging limb and I let him go his way. As I bent over to avoid the limb, the saddle slipped and down I went, right into the big rocks. The first man to help me up was ol' Watson Eyes. His hand felt strong and firm, and I thought I could feel a callus on his trigger finger.

We made it back to the little farmhouse just at dark, had some more good coffee, and was soon on our way in the Jeep back to Riohacha. Before leaving that night, we agreed on a down payment in cash in the States, and the balance in full there one day after my shrimp boat was loaded in Riohacha and was on her way up the Caribbean on her final run. The loading date was set for twenty days from that day.

On our way back, Señor and I stopped at Santa Marta just before day for a nap and a shower, but the nap came up short. We both found ourselves chock full of ticks. We helped each other, trying to make sure we got 'em all, but Señor missed a couple on me. I found 'em later and the places I pulled 'em off was sore for two months or more. (If you pull 'em straight out, some parts stay in you; twist 'em counterclockwise as you pull, and there's no problem.)

That night we got stopped by some kind of banditos and if Señor hadn't been with me, I probably wouldn't have made it. They put up a road-block. When you stop, they come out from behind the bushes with automatic weapons and stick the barrel in your stomach. With Señor along there was no problem, but I've been told that if you don't have a Señor with you, they make you take everything you own out of your suitcase or whatever, and step inside a little room. When you get back, everything you left behind of any value will be gone, and nothing you can do about it.

Next day by noon, we were on our way back to Panama City.

*   *   *

Ten days before the loading date, the *Gambler*—a name I thought just perfectly fit that shrimp boat—left from Key West with a captain and crew of two, en route to Riohacha. Down the Caribbean lickety-split they went, with everything going their way for the first seven days. But then their long-range side band radio went out. They pulled into Barranquilla, a day or two short of Riohacha, for repairs. The captain soon contacted me in Panama City by telephone. I picked up my Spanish-speaking buddy and we got to Barranquilla the following day about noon. Within a few hours we had their problems ironed out and they were ready to go again.

Then came a problem nothing but time could solve. The same night the *Gambler* pulled into Barranquilla, there was a hijacking in the mountains, plus a couple of Americans were killed someplace in Colombia, and to cap that off some pot-haulers had a shoot-out with the Colombian Coast Guard and escaped. The Coast Guard put on extra boats, and marijuana smuggling came to a complete stop.

My crew moved into the most expensive hotel they could find, demanding money *pesos* so they could go out on the town. The truth is, they had me over a barrel with my britches down. If I didn't meet their demands, they threatened to catch the next plane for Miami, leaving me stranded. With nobody to watch her, the *Gambler* would've been stripped from stem to stern in five minutes.

Luckily, just when the boys were about to board that plane, the dealer gave the "let go," but he warned me there might still be a problem at the dock at Riohacha. I told the boys to keep their eyes peeled when they started loading, and to load like they'd never loaded before.

The *Gambler* got to Riohacha okay, and started loading about midnight. Just as they were finishing up, the fireworks started.

One of the most dangerous times in marijuana smuggling is while it's being loaded aboard the boat in Colombia, and it doesn't usually go very fast. It's first brought out from shore in dugout canoes and then loaded onto the boat, bale by bale; but you'd be surprised just how big those canoes are—forty foot long by four or more wide. When the natives are really organized, they can load a boat before you know it; but if they aren't, it's a long, drawn-out, dangerous job. If a hijacker happens by and opens fire with automatic weapons to scare the crew off while he steals a few bales, it can get pretty rough. And if lawmen that wasn't paid off from the start comes by, then business really picks up.

I'm not sure who it was, but somebody opened fire not only on my shrimp boat and the canoes but also on the burros bringing the pot down from the mountain to the beach. Luckily, the boat was about loaded, and the crew built a fire in that ol' diesel and got her moving. No one was hurt, but next day they noticed a few bullet holes in the cabin.

About 10:00 in the morning I called the *Gambler*. The crew seemed to be in good spirits and on their way back up the Caribbean but they reminded that me that the Gap was still ahead of 'em.

The Gap is a nickname for the Yucatán Channel, between Mexico's Yucatán peninsula and Cuba. It's about 100 miles across and is the main shipping lane for most boats coming out of the Caribbean, especially from Colombia. The pot-haulers were all scared to death of the Gap, because it's the one place on the whole route the U.S. Coast Guard can sit in the middle of with their radar and "see" every boat that goes through. If they see a shrimp boat coming from the south, they're most likely to stop her, for a shrimper coming that way is usually loaded with something besides shrimp.

To solve this problem I had sent out a second shrimp boat, with nothing on her, south through the Gap to meet the *Gambler*. The two boats were communicating with a radio frequency that no one, even the Coast Guard, would be apt to hear. I'd discussed all movements with both crews in advance. When the second boat first spotted the *Gambler* coming up the Caribbean from the south just before coming into radar range of the Gap, she made an about-face. (We called her the *Joker*.)

The *Gambler* held back while the *Joker* approached the west side of the Gap at 9:00 P.M. on a dark night, coming from the south as though she was en route from Colombia. After she got about halfway through the Gap, the blue U.S. Coast Guard lights commenced blinking. The *Joker* notified the *Gambler* (which ran back to safety), then stopped while the cutter pulled up alongside and the Guard officers came aboard. The captain walked up to the main hatch with a large flashlight and a big smile and says to his men, "Lift that hatch lid, boys, and we'll see what's below." When they raised the lid, the captain came darn near falling in the hole. All he found was a large empty hold with a few rotten shrimp in the bottom of it. The boat was shipshape and he had to let her go.

A light weather disturbance hit the Gap the following day with enough rain to knock out the Coast Guard's radar, and the boys took the *Gambler* with her swinging load right down through the middle of the Gap at high noon.

As planned, she didn't head straight for south Florida after clearing the Gap, because of the danger of being spotted off Key West. Instead, they headed up the west side of the Gulf, toward Texas, until they got so far that when they turned back for home, they were traveling in a more southerly direction as they approached south Florida. A shrimp boat coming from the south (the Yucatán or the Caribbean) sticks out like a sore thumb and is bound to be stopped. But coming from the north, especially if it's a shrimp boat, it looks like it's coming from Texas and really *is* shrimping.

I was in touch with the *Gambler* by ship radio. The last day about noon, I told the captain, "Betty wants you to call her at twelve A.M.," which he knew meant "twelve P.M.," the rendezvous time. Betty's telephone number was the loran reading for a spot on the coast between Chokoloskee and Naples, no larger than the size of that shrimp boat. About midnight that night, the *Gambler* was parked in that spot, unloaded, washed out by daybreak, then taken to Key West and docked, with her faithful crew in Sloppy Joe's Bar before noon.

That wound up my pot-hauling, with a perfect haul. And after all the marijuana I handled, sat on, and smelled, I've never smoked a joint, and never even seen cocaine. The home boys at Chokoloskee and Everglades City never hauled hard drugs. Nothing but marijuana.

✳   ✳   ✳

It wasn't an alligator in the Everglades that caught me, neither was it a Park Ranger, nor the Coast Guard, but the I.R.S.

One afternoon in August '82, long after I'd retired from all pot-hauling and was thinking I'd come out smelling like a rose, there came a knock on my door that somehow didn't sound good to me. Maybe it was the clothes the two men were wearing. (Here we don't wear a coat and tie, if we have one, except on special occasions.) After eyeballing them walking up my driveway, I wasn't surprised to see badges in their hands. They introduced themselves as special agents of the I.R.S., and their business was to examine my tax records. Since they were so darn hasty, I got a little hot under the collar and showed them their way out the same door they came in, without my tax records.

My lawyer spoke with the U.S. Attorney and found the government was running the biggest investigation ever on marijuana-smuggling in southwest Florida, particularly in the area of Chokoloskee and Everglades City. The U.S. Attorney said many would be indicted, and that I'd be included in the investigation. Right then I told my lawyer to start working on a plea bargain. The U.S. Attorney went along with the idea, but only if I would give information concerning Operation Everglades. I sent back word that trees didn't grow tall enough to hang me on that would get me to testify against my friends and neighbors. That stopped any action on the plea bargain for months.

Then the U.S. Attorney called my lawyer and agreed to try working out a deal. At that time, and during the making of my plea bargain, my testifying was never mentioned. After several months, we reached an agreement that was satisfactory to both parties. The first arrests in Operation Everglades began on July 7, 1983, about the same time I turned in my plea. I pleaded guilty to one three-year count of tax fraud and agreed to forfeit a large amount of cash and assets.

On January 20, 1984, I came up for sentencing. A few days before,

the *Miami Herald* had run an editorial that said: "How do you sentence a man like Totch Brown? A veteran of the Battle of the Bulge,
a Bronze Star winner, with near fifty years of close family ties, who
handed out thousands of dollars to his neighbors in need and was
never in serious trouble before." The judge said to me: "Mr. Brown,
you rendered your country—my country—*our* country a great service
in World War II, you've had a good life and you've been a credit to
your community; on the other hand, somewhere along the line you
got into a business that was a disservice to a lot of people."

Instead of sentencing me to three years, the judge made it fifteen
months. (About which I had no complaint; I had no right to break
the tax laws.) On April 3 I surrendered myself at the Federal Correc-
tional Institution in Lexington, Kentucky. Two weeks later they drug
me back to Miami before a federal grand jury and tried to get me to
testify against my friends (as the U.S. Attorney knew full well I never
would do). Because I refused, I was held in contempt and sentenced
to an additional eighteen months.

After serving eleven months, I went back into court with an extra-

Fun in the Everglades with my grandson Jesse (Loren's son) and Troubles.

ordinary attorney and thirty letters of recommendation. We proved to the judge "beyond a reasonable doubt" that I would never testify. The contempt charge was lifted and I served out the remainder of my original sentence in Kentucky. Right or wrong, I served my time as a model prisoner and walked out on November 25, 1985 and went back to Chokoloskee with the Queen.

* * *

Looking back on my life, I can tell you that living in the heart of yesterday's Everglades seems almost unbelievable to me now. There were times when I couldn't see how I could possibly make it, but

somehow everything from boyhood up eventually fell right into place for me. I walked out on the Everglades a time or two, but they never really let me down. Now and then they put me through hell, but there were other times when it was smooth sailing, with a place to lay my tired body down and a little something to eat by a campfire. If I had it to do all over again, I still wouldn't take the city way of life. I'd go back down the same old mosquito road across the Everglades, with the same Queen of the Everglades at my side.

Appendix 1 / What's happening to the Everglades?

When the Everglades National Park was established in 1947, most hunting and commercial fishing—our main source of livelihood in the Ten Thousand Islands—gradually came to a stop in park waters. Taking in all oyster beds, sandbars, and mud flats, the park includes most of our main fishing and hunting grounds. Chokoloskee and Everglades City were just barely left out of the park, so close that the boundary line touches the island in two places. Since the early days Chokoloskee and Everglades City have been the headquarters for the native fishermen, including those who lived on Lostmans Beach and other beaches along the coast. A few of us, like my brother Peg and myself, kept right on hunting through the '60s until alligators were declared endangered. Stopping the hunting was much harder on some than others, since they got most of their fresh meat from the wildlife.

This was one helluva blow to the people of the Everglades, especially along the southwest coast. There were (and still are) many that knew no other trade than the fisherman's and no other country than this one. The only fishing grounds left for them were the open Gulf and Florida Bay, which are outside park limits. Gulf fishing is mainly for pompano and mackerel (in the winter months only) and for crawfishing and stone-crabbing. Many fishermen in the Chokoloskee Bay area and in the Keys couldn't afford the expenses involved in Gulf fishing, and gave up the one trade they knew. Some left the bay and went other places to fish, but only to their sorrow. Some hung on here, doing anything they could to exist.

The first commercial fishermen to really feel the effect of the park's establishment lived in Flamingo, on the north shore of Florida Bay. I was living there myself in 1951, fishing for mullet and pompano, when the park rangers closed off the one and only road connecting Flamingo to the rest of Florida. The villagers felt like they'd been deliberately cut off from the world, just so tourists could sightsee in their homeland. Then the park threw them out and burned what they'd left behind (and what it had taken a lifetime to get). Then the politicians dammed off the water to drain the land in the northern Everglades to be used for cattle ranches and farmlands. This land was not part of the park; but the damming also dried up the southern Everglades, and it had a terrible effect on the whole Everglades environment.

Today no one is allowed to live either on the land or on any type of boat in park waters. The people who had deeds to their properties within park boundaries were paid a little bit of nothing and told to clear out. The old squatters who lived on the shell mounds throughout the Islands without deeds were kicked out with no compensation.

The park people could have left us a narrow strip along the coastline—say, four miles wide and twenty miles long, from Chokoloskee down to Lostmans River—to give us time to adjust to the changes, and maybe keep on earning a living the way we'd been doing for so long. But it seems they just simply had it in mind to run us to hell out of the Everglades (and they darn nigh succeeded).

Most of the park rangers from the very start have treated us natives like we're a bunch of intruders who don't have any rights here. They give the impression that we're no longer welcome here—that we should get out and leave it with them and the outsiders to play with. I often wonder who they think settled and looked after this place before they ever even saw it. One thing's for certain, it sure wasn't a tourist or a park ranger.

One park ranger, Barney Parker, did meet us halfway. Unlike most rangers, there were times Barney threw down his rule book and used a lot of good common sense. I met up with him late one afternoon, when I was riding along Lostmans Beach in my gator boat. Barney could plainly see I was on a gator hunt, but he didn't search my boat. Instead, he said, "Totch, I could take you in for this, but I'm not going to because I know how you feel—that you're only taking something that belongs to you and, in a way, you're probably right. On the other hand, though, it's no longer a hunting ground. Today, it's a national park, and sooner or later you're gonna have to accept that." Before we parted that afternoon, Barney said to me, "Totch, try to find something else to do. Someday I may be forced to tow you in and that'd be hard on both of us."

On the other hand, if they had let us stay in Flamingo and the little settlements along the southwest coast, that might not have worked either. Maybe the park people saw better than I did, that the developers, the retirees, and the sport fishermen might have soon gobbled up most of the mangrove swamps and mud flats, plus every darn piece of shell land high enough to stand on without getting your feet wet.

Today this country probably would've been covered with everything from shacky sport-fishing camps to the tallest of high-rises and condos. Most likely, their laws and regulations would've been harder on us natives than the rules of the park. To cap it off, the taxis would be boats, and the way they'd race around would make it too dangerous to run our own. In fact, those of us who stayed would probably have ended up working as bellhops in a hotel.

Maybe the time for us had simply run out. We'd had it long enough—some might say that we'd abused it long enough. But to my way of thinking, it was just the opposite: we *cultivated* the country, and, with the help of the Seminoles, kept it alive. We never threw up the first dike or cut the first canal to drain away the rainwater the good Lord sent down to the Everglades. Neither did we take away the brackish water from all the creatures that live in brackish water only. Instead, others—and it wasn't Seminoles or fishermen—cut canals across the Glades, drained the rainwater into the salty Atlantic Ocean, and played hell with my backyard.

*   *   *

Most people are under the impression that the park includes only the prairie grasslands of the Everglades, but that's not the case by a long shot. Covering much of Florida's southwest coast and almost all of the Ten Thousand Islands, the park reaches from just south of Marco Island near Naples all the way down to the Florida Keys near Long Key, plus two miles out from the coastline into the open Gulf of Mexico.

Most people other than the natives call it all the Everglades. To me there are two different countries here: the mangroves and the Glades themselves. Florida's southwest coast is made up of a group of low mangrove keys known as the Ten Thousand Islands. The immediate coastline has high white sand beaches that the natives lived on before the park was established. The second part of the mangroves is the narrow strip of low mangrove mainland swamp, maybe five miles wide, that separates the Everglades proper from the Islands.

The Everglades proper is the mainland, about 4,000 square miles of flat prairie grass that slopes southward at one-fifth of a foot per mile. The rainfall averages fifty-five inches, June through October. In rainy season, the most southwest part near the mangroves gets anywhere from a few inches up to two or three feet under water. When there's water on the Glades it is fresh; I've drunk it by the barrels. In dry season it's as dry as a powder house, but you can still dig down a couple of feet to fresh water.

The strip of mangrove mainland has many little rivers not much wider in the narrows than a rowboat, running all the way to the grass-lands of the Glades. In rainy season these rivers slowly drain the rain-water off the Glades into the Islands. As the rainwater from the Glades mixes with the salt water coming in from the Gulf, it becomes brackish. Most all the fish and a big portion of the wildlife, especially the saltwater birds, do most of their breeding and feeding in the brackish water here.

The fish and the wildlife all follow the brackish water line. In the driest of the season, April and May, the brackish line is at the very head of the rivers near the Glades, and so are the fish and game. As the rains come on, the brackish line slowly drifts down the rivers into the Islands and eventually to the coast.

The smallest of the creatures comes to life in the brackish water and right then and there is where it all begins: from the tiniest little shrimp, crab, bird, and fish on up to the largest of the animals, one eats the other, with the alligator eating on them all.

Most of the fish and wildlife will not breed good in fresh or salt water. In fact, most of the food chain for the entire Everglades comes from the brackish water country. The dams have cut off the fresh water from the southwest Everglades, cut down on the brackish water in the mangroves, and played hell with the creatures that breed in it.

Back in the mangroves there were many brackish water marshes with lakes, ponds, and low places the wildlife simply thrived on; you can't even see these marshes from the shoreline in a boat. With the help of the Seminoles, we used to keep the little rivers running through the mangroves to the Glades open. The gushing flow of rainwater draining off the Glades in the Islands helped too. We traveled the little rivers regularly in rowboats, usually hunting for deer.

Paddling up the rivers of an afternoon in the drying-up season, with the water brackish near the Glades, the activity was something to see. Along the riverbanks most every log had someone on it. Turtles everywhere: alligator turtles, streaked heads, snappers, soft shell, mud, diamond-backs, you name it. There were plenty of otters all over the place. Snakes by the dozens: black snakes, green, grass, occasionally a cottonmouth moccasin, and, out in the Glades, a rattler now and then. At times, when gator hides weren't selling, there'd be alligators laying across one another. There were birds and ducks by the thousands, from the big storks (as we call iron heads) and the snowy egrets right on down to the little kingfisher. In the narrows, with the mangroves entangled overhead, it was like paddling up a long narrow tunnel. Wasp nests the size of a man's cap were hanging down. Fish were so plentiful in some of the rivers you wouldn't throw a trolling spoon (lure) over the side without a fish of some kind grabbing it. Using a hand line, we could throw a spoon and pull in fish by the dozens.

Today it's an altogether different story. The brackish water in the Islands is very skimpy, and so are the fish and wildlife. Back when the rainwater was waist-deep in the Glades, it was fresh enough to drink in October in Chokoloskee Bay—but no more. Today what wildlife there is left can barely exist. The truth of it is, there are times you've really got to know your stuff to even catch enough fish to grease the pan.

A big part of the problem has to do with the burning of the marshes. Before the park was established, we burned off the wet marshes once a year with the help of the Seminoles. This did not hurt the wetland and kept the mangroves, shrubs, and sawgrass from taking over. Shortly after the Everglades became a park in 1947, the authorities stopped all burning. Today, the marshes that were so filled with wildlife have grown up to nothing but a mangrove swamp, and the ponds and the game are no more. It has grown up so thick that even a Glades rabbit would be forced to turn it down.

Another serious problem developed when the road to Choko-loskee and the western gateway to the national park in Everglades City both opened in 1956. This drew people into this country by the thousands. Right then is when the Everglades and everything in it began to catch living hell! Outboard motors became dependable around the same time. Channel markers were put up and charts of the islands became available. Marinas and trailer parks were set up, and boats began to roar through here like cars on a race track. Outside of the park, when the hunting season opens, the airboats roar across the prairies, doing fifty or more miles an hour, with the swamp buggies right behind 'em; the hound dogs begin to bark, and it's enough to scare every living creature in the Everglades half to death including me!

When it started, there was no limit or size on the fish they could catch. The tourists, or the tin-canners, as we call 'em, came in their tin trailers with their tin boats, tin cans of food they canned themselves, and a ten-dollar bill. Day in and day out they filled up their tin cans with fiddler crabs they caught on the beach for bait and fished this country to death. They caught and sold enough fish to pay their expenses and take home extra cash. If a tin-canner saw a charter boat on a fishing hole, the next day there'd be a tin-canner on the hole or a white rag tied on the spot. Unlike the natives, they sold everything large enough to swim.

While the tin-canners were doing their best to fish the country to death, so were the sport fishermen. They even took to graining, or harpooning, the fish at night with a bright gas lantern. We tried dropping rifle balls near 'em, but we didn't really stop them till our county sheriff helped us get a new law passed. And then there were the charter boats and commercial fishermen, including myself. There was a time when thirty-five or forty charter boats were here daily, laying it on the fish just like everyone else. There were so many fish from the charter boats that the wholesale fish company would back up a big truck to the charter dock at the end of the day with platform scales and hundred-pound fish baskets. Day after day, they carried off fish by the thousands. And God knows how many hundred-pound tarpon were left hanging on the picture rack to rot during the spawning season when they were trying to multiply.

The mullet net fishermen were right there doing their part and more. In the '60s, the mullet fishermen in the Chokoloskee Bay country—including the Everglades National Park—fished in rowboats, mostly at night. At night, most all fish gather around the oyster beds and mangrove shore lines, and that's where the fishermen would put their nets. Even though they were only after mullet, they caught both game and bottom fish by the thousands. But back when there were still gobs of game and bottom fish, the mullet fishermen changed their way of fishing. They went from rowboats to well boats (power boats), started to fish on the mud flats where there are very few game or bottom fish, and quit fishing at night around the oyster beds and mangroves and went to daytime fishing. (They do still fish a little at night when the mullet are in schools during the three weeks of spawning season, but not in a way to catch many other fish.)

The truth is, today the mullet fishermen in this part of the country do not catch as many game or bottom fish as the pleasure boats. If you check the amount of game and bottom fish that go over a pleasure dock through the run of a day, and compare it with the wholesale fish dock where the commercial fishermen sell their mullet, you'll get the surprise of your life. Many people have the wrong idea about the commercial fishermen. A lady in Fort Myers told me a few days ago that she purely hated them. She said a fisherman put his net out in front of her house and the next day a dead snook drifted up on her beach, and she said God knew how many more he carried away. She didn't realize that the fisherman couldn't legally sell the fish, and that's why he had thrown it back. It's even illegal for a fisherman to catch a snook from his commercial boat with a casting rod. Now and then a fisherman will catch a game fish, but they throw them back, usually unharmed. However, one will occasionally drown, as we call it, from a tight net around its gills, like the snook she saw.

Snook are a good example of what's wrong with the fishing laws in the Everglades. They were never really commercialed that much on the southwest coast of Florida and the Chokoloskee Bay country, including the Everglades National Park. There were a very few fishermen that put in a special, extremely expensive net only for snook, mainly around Naples. A few thousand pounds at a few different times were caught.

When snook were declared a game fish, and commercialing and even casting for snook on a commercial boat was banned, they were still very plentiful. No more snook were caught by the commercial fishermen. Today, there's not a professional guide that can guarantee even one snook a day, because the pleasure boats have fished them to death. (The exact same thing happened with the speckled trout, which were only commercialed here by hook. There's very few left, but there were plenty when they stopped them from being commercialed.)

Snook—the top game fish in this part of the country—spawn in May, June, and July. Some of the sport fishermen found that while the snook were spawning, they'd take live bait like they were starving to death. The sport fishermen used little pinfish and other small fish for bait and caught the big ten- to twenty-five-pound spawning snook by the hundreds. Plenty of 'em went to restaurants. This went on for years, and we've darn nigh wiped them out. While they were trying to multiply it should have been a closed season. Today part of it is, although fishing for snook is still allowed until the end of May, the first month of their peak breeding season. Also, live bait should *not* be used on spawning snook—only artificial lures. It's so easy to catch them then with bait, natives never do it; it's like taking an unfair advantage, and downright unsportsmanlike.

Forty-five miles south around the Shark and Harney Rivers, there's an area of many miles that once had some of the best game and bottom fishing. In '65 I was charter-boating and occasionally went down there on an overnight trip. The little rivers there had solid schools of tarpon in them. Today, you'd be lucky to find a dozen in the whole country. What happened? Well, tarpon are a very scary fish—I believe too many pleasure boats running through 'em doing thirty or forty miles an hour ran them out of here.

How can we bring the Everglades back? Although in my opinion we'll never see the Everglades again as I saw it in the '30s, there may be ways to bring some of it back.

One of my very first moves to bring back the wildlife would be to set fire to every marsh and lowland in southwest Florida. They must be burned yearly, in April and May. A simple way to do this would be to let the Seminoles come back into the park, and they'd take care of that in a hurry. To me, the Seminoles were a natural part of the Everglades. While the government was doing their best to do away with the Seminoles, they came darn nigh to doing away with the Everglades.

Damming off the rainwater from the Everglades has hurt the Glades and, in turn, cut down on the brackish water in the mangroves. They dammed away the clean rainwater from the Glades and filled it full of cow dump and poison. The water problem has much to do with politics—drying up land for large cattle ranches, cane fields, you name it—so I seriously doubt that it'll ever be brought back up to snuff.

As for the Florida panther, in my opinion the same thing that happened to all the rest of the wildlife around here is what's happened to them: people have played hell with their habitat. When I was young there were so many panthers around, you had to take your pigs and calves to bed with you at night to keep the cats from eating 'em up. Now the experts claim there's only twenty-eight left in Florida. Well, if that count's even close, something needs to be done and fast, but not the way I've been hearing about it. To keep the cats from getting killed by cars (which is mighty seldom), the authorities have just had a special fence built across the Everglades from coast to coast on both sides of Alligator Alley (I-75 from Fort Lauderdale to Naples). I doubt the panther deaths on the highway average one in ten years.

They also cut tunnels under the highway for the cats to travel to and fro. The fence and the tunnels cost many millions of dollars and that's not the half of it. The fence disturbs the wildlife habitat. The animals move with the seasons and follow the waterline, and they can't get across that fence. Come rainy season the tunnels are completely underwater—even an alligator wouldn't swim down there through 'em.

Parks and preservation are definitely a must, or there won't be anything left on the face of the earth but a hunk of plastic. All the same, spending millions of dollars on a useless, harmful fence and tunnels is not the answer. For a thousand dollars apiece we can buy panther kittens from someone who'd raise 'em like house cats right here in the Everglades and turn 'em loose to start restocking the country—and that wouldn't cost much at all. Then we could take the millions they're spending on guesswork and help all the wildlife in the Glades.

I notice that in the main passes throughout the Islands, the wake from the boats are washing the live oysters and shells out into the mangroves, forming high shell land. I know I done my part of this. I also know it'd be a crying shame to slow people down to a crawl while they're out trying to get away from it all. All the same, though, if the wake of so many boats is enough to actually build up high shell land, I wonder what it's doing to the habitat of the fish and wildlife. Especially with most of 'em being outboard motors and leaving oil on the water that probably kills the small minnows and bugs that fish feed on. Maybe five-mile-an-hour limits in active areas should be set up, with higher speeds allowed in the less active areas to let 'em dig off. They should definitely keep everyone out of the heavy breeding and feeding areas.

Though I've been a hunter and fisherman all my life, today I want to help the animals as much as I can, especially the cat family, my favorites. But Florida panthers aren't the only animals getting scarce. All the rest are also going downhill. From one who's lived a lifetime in the Everglades and survived on what it had to offer, believe me: if we don't do something toward saving 'em, they might all be gone soon, like the dinosaurs.

Appendix 2 / The life and times of Grandfather McKinney

In 1926 Charles G. McKinney prepared the following brief autobiography at the request of the weekly *American Eagle,* for which he wrote a regular column under the name "Progress."

The Man Who Put the "Chuckle" in Chokoloskee
C.G. McKinney (Progress) Who for Nearly Twenty Years Was
Correspondent for the American Eagle, Estero, Fla.

The northern newspaper syndicates have had their Abe Martin, their Mr. Dooley and their *Bingville Bugle* items, but it remained for the *American Eagle* to discover C.G. McKinney, a rustic genius, quite an original, for over forty years a resident of Chokoloskee Island, and who for nearly twenty years past has been regaling our readers with his quaint comment about the boot-leggers, backsliders and unregenerates, the preachers, teachers, Indians, old hens and the social doings of that far-flung outpost of civilization in the Ten Thousand Islands. His items have been widely quoted in the Tampa and other state papers and we thought it only fitting that on his seventy-ninth anniversary he should give us a sketch of his eventful life, the first installment of which will be found herewith.

Autobiography of C.G. McKinney

Part 1

Some of the readers of the *American Eagle* want some of our biography. Now as to that, we will give them some briefs beginning on the ground floor with biography and reminiscences.

First to begin with I was born in Sumter County, Georgia, one Sunday morning about 5 A.M. and it was just 79 years ago tomorrow (8th day of August 1847), and I was the possessor of one fully developed jaw tooth, which my mother gave to the family doctor (Dr.

Bagley). This was 16 miles from Americus, Ga., about 14 miles from Oglethorpe, four and a half miles from a village called Danville.

My father and family moved to Columbia County, Florida, in 1854. He was a blacksmith, wheelwright, carpenter and shoemaker, and I was taught some of these, besides tanning leather with red oak bark. I made shoes during the Civil War for the neighbors, but when I came to the age of 17 the officers were conscripting all the boys and everything that looked like they were able to shoulder a gun. We had a neighbor (Mr. Bill Wingate) who was home on furlough from his command, Fort Meade, Fla., and he advised my parents to let me go back with him and join Captain Hendry's company under command of Major Mornilim; so I went and joined Captain Hendry's company.

I often think of a trip the company took down near Fort Myers. Captain Hendry and Lieutenant Boggess and some others on horseback were far in advance of us infantry and they came in haste to meet us and reported that the blue coats were coming for us. The command was for us to get harbor under palmettoes or brush and be prepared for an attack, but it was a false alarm. I got close up to a pine tree with palmettoes round it, and all of us hid out. The cavalry went away ahead again and came back again, driving a beef or two along for our supper. We ate our supper and had orders to sleep with our rifles by our sides. Picket was posted and we lay down for rest, and were not molested all night. The next day, farther down toward Fort Myers, and about 2 or 3 p.m., we came to an old deserted cow ranchman's house where the blue coats had just left. Their fires were still burning where they

had cooked a lot of beef, it appeared. I think many times how glad I was to pick up some old beef bones around the blue coats' camps which contained some gristle and meat. I and some of the other boys feasted on those bones until we could get another beef or two butchered for supper. In the meantime the horsemen learned that the blue coats had gathered a herd of cattle and swam them across the river near Fort Myers and were gone. Then how proud we felt that we were not likely to be butchered by the blue coats. Now we turned homeward to Fort Meade. When we got back all was quiet.

The officials were hunting out some good-looking, strong boys to handle the artillery; so they caught me in that little bunch, as I was about as good-looking as any common scrub, was not quite 18 and weight 181 pounds. So we were transferred to Lieut. John Craton's artillery squad and stationed at Brooksville, practicing shooting every Friday at an oak tree about a mile away across Mrs. Eubank's farm. We took a little trip to Crystal River near Bay Port, but found nothing to shoot at, so we hauled our old .36 guns back and began practice at the oak tree.

Then it was not long until we got news that the war had closed, that someone was defeated and had lost out, and the colored folks were all free, just as my father told them that when the war was over they would all be free. He talked to the colored folks that way and of course the owners of them took him up and fined and jailed him. But nevertheless his words came true.

Well, I got back home alive after the Civil War (or the little scrap they had over here), and it was in Columbia County, Florida. Then I went down into Alachua County and Mr. John Grimes, an elderly gentleman, got me to moonshine for him. He had an ideal place for it down in a sink hole, 40 feet below the top, with a nice spring of water there and plenty of clear water. There were some small fish there also. It was on a public road which ran above the still 45 to 50 feet. There was perpendicular wall on the west side of this sink hole, solid rock, and a few logs had been thrown across the top of this wall with a windlass and rope for the traveling folks to draw water. The still and barrels of beer, etc., were just back a few feet, and the only way to get down there was to go a circuitous route for about 150 to 200 yards over a bad scrub road or trail. Mr. Grimes had an 80 gallon still and I managed to make all the moonshine that the officers and some others of the devil's disciples could use. I found that the officers were the best customers that we had.

But I had to leave and go home to stay with my parents and work on the cotton farm. Mr. Grimes kept on running the moonshine business for a year or two, but he was taken to court about the thing and it just simply ruined him. He had a nice little farm, peach orchard and some hogs and cattle, but the courts, lawyers and the opposite gang took everything he had. It caused him to take a bad backset otherwise and he did not live long. This was in 1867.

I stayed at home until 1869 which brought me to the whisker age, and like nearly all other he-ones at that age, I decided that I was born in the wrong place and would have to travel some; so in 1869 I went to Texas and hired my time to a boss carpenter named Mr. L. G. Moses for $30 per month in gold. But I decided to go back to my dear old Florida home and mother and father.

Then I took up a homestead of 160 acres of land and sold 120 acres of it to Mr. Mike Whetstone, reserving one 40-acre tract that ran across the Santa Fe River, on which I decided to put up a water mill. The river was 112 yards wide at the point where I located my mill site and it was running swiftly. Nevertheless I went to work by my lone self, getting out timbers 10 × 10 and 30 feet long to frame together to span the width of the river, while all the folks in the county laughed at me for being such a fool as to think I could put a dam across the river and raise a head of water to grind corn. I worked at it nearly one year by myself and then I hired a colored preacher, named Joe Kellen, to help me. He and I got the timbers ready to frame, framed them and put them in the water, weighing them down with rocks, setting the posts four feet high on the lower timbers (down stream), and then split out timber 14 feet long to put on the upper and lower sills. When they were adjusted the water began to rise and with the accumulation of drifting grass and moss I soon had a four-foot head of water. Then I bought a set of mill stones from Livingston's factory,—good French burr stones. So I went to work grinding corn.

Pretty soon I put in another water wheel and some gins and ginned cotton for the folks; soon I bought another water wheel and put in a sawmill, while the folks in that country talked and called me such a fool, one of them, Mr. Joe Smith, saying he could eat all the lumber I would saw there. But I never was of the kind that would be cast down by idle talk. It has always been my plan to believe that I had a head of my own and that it was good for something,—not just a knot tied in the top of my backbone to keep it from raveling out, like a good many of this world's cattle have. I sawed many thousands of feet of good pine lumber there and sold the best yellow pine rough heart lumber at $8 per thousand. I sawed quite a lot of lumber for the S.F. and W.R.R., when it was building the line through Columbia and Alachua Counties. This railroad then was the H.B. Plant System Railroad.

I have thought many a time of Dr. Smith who lived about 30 miles from my mill. He had no acquaintance with me whatever, but he drove up to my mill about noon one day, got out of his buggy, walked down in the mill yard, saluted me and said, "I hear that you are the only man in this country that has a d__ bit of sense." I thought that was a little abrupt, but I suppose he had possibly heard something in some place.

I was always a man to stir around early in the morning while I had hands working for me on the farm and in the mill. The colored folks called me the man that gave them two suppers. I would get up at 4 o'clock and get breakfast for a bunch of colored folks. I had a big baking pan that held 56 biscuits and I would fill it each morning. We would eat by lamplight, get out to work before sunrise, and weigh by lamplight the cotton that the hands would bring in from the cotton farm. I hired them to pick the Sea Island cotton by the pound and they stuck to it late.

Part 2

Well, boys and girls, I am here to tell you more of my little efforts. I neglected to tell you about the mill dam work I did. I was so determined to disappoint my neighbors and come out victorious. The Santa Fe River has a solid rock bottom and I got in my framing for my dam; then I took a crowbar with a steel point and chiseled out a groove all the way across the river,—112 yards. This groove was on the upper side of my framework beside the upper still. I grooved it 12 to 15 inches deep all by my lone self. Then when I finished this I got a colored man by the name of Ned Bradshaw to help me put the piling down the groove which consisted of a double line of inch boards. We drove them down one at a time, then took it up to see where it struck the rock and chopped out a gap in it to make it fit in the bottom so water could not go under it. There was one place that was about three or three and a half feet deep and I could not stoop down and drive a nail,—I would float up. So I took a 3-pound hammer in one hand and a 40-penny nail in the other, and my good man Friday then put his hands on my back and held me down until I drove the nail. That was pretty tough work, but it had to be done to accomplish my desires. I finally piled it across the river then; I put my timbers on and soon raised four feet of water.

With all this mill work and farming cotton, corn, oats, peanuts, etc., I ran a grocery and dry goods store, bought cotton, chickens, eggs, etc. I had a good trade. Some of my customers would come 30 miles away from other stores and bring their cotton, chickens, eggs and anything they had to sell just because I paid them more for their products than anybody else and sold them goods cheaper than anybody else, on the same principle that I am doing today. Some of the folks here today will say, "That old thing gets a pension; he don't care whether he makes any money or not." Fifty years ago I did not get a pension. I never have aspired for riches; it looks like a foolish thing for a man to get all of this world's goods he can and lie down and die, and his children fight over it.

I dammed up a spring,—only a narrow creek,—where it emptied into the river just below my mill and raised two feet of water and put in 12 pestles to beat rice in the old style. I could put those 12 pestles to work and they would run night and day without any attention. I would let them hammer all night and go the next morning and the rice was clean of husk. But the planters would not grow the rice to keep the work up as they had promised me they would.

In the meantime we got to where we had to have a post office as our office was ten miles away at Newnansville. So I got up a petition and sent it in to Washington. Soon the folks there gave me a post office and Judge Bradford of Newnansville asked me to let him name the office for me. I told him, "Good! Go ahead." He was sparking old Brother Cowen's daughter and her name was Joella; so he wrote the name and Postal Department took his "J" for an "I" and that made it Ioella. The judge said that must be changed by all means; so I sent the stamp back and had it changed to Joella. After all that his dear, sweet Joella kicked him out. I think that was real trying on his nerves for a man of his age and social standing, but nevertheless he had to endure the torture and make the best of life he could.

I was postmaster at Joella for a few months until the S.F. & W.R.R. was finished up to High Springs. They had no post office there and the Postal Department suggested that I move Joella to High Springs. I had bought some realty there and had a dwelling house there; so I moved the office to High Springs and it was called High Springs then.

I had a brother that ran a merchandise business at Fort White, and he ran a booze shop with it. He died and his wife did not keep up the booze shop, so my friends persuaded me to go over there and run a booze camp. So I bought a small lot from my brother's widow and hitched in with my booze and did so much business until I found that I had too many friends. Old Brother Mooreland, a friend of mine, wore the knees of his pants out praying for me to change my pursuit of living. So I thought, inasmuch as I had so many friends, white and black, Christians and sinners, that I would just close out my booze ranch. In those days it cost $750 each year for license to run the thing after getting signers to a petition. That article was a scrap of paper that the Christians, rich and poor, would all sign nearly.

I fooled around in Alachua and Columbia Counties on the Santa Fe River, having the chills and fever every fall and I had pneumonia twice; my friends and the doctors told me if I ever had pneumonia again I would sure have to move to another planet from whence no traveler ever comes back again. So I decided, rather than take my chances among a lot of strangers and possibly heathen, dagoes and all kinds of things that I had no acquaintance with, I would just come down to Chokoloskee, and I never had any more chills and fever or pneumonia either, and I am doing as well as might be expected for a spring bird.

Well, now, good folks, I came down to Chokoloskee from High

Springs, where I was getting my mail twice a day and handling Uncle Sam's mailbags, hanging them out on the catcher. The morning and evening mail train came along at a speed of 40 to 50 miles an hour and grabbed the bag from the post and made no halt,—just pitched out one or two bags for me to pick up off the ground. I came here to Chokoloskee about the middle of March, 1886, and evaded the long trip that the doctors and the best friends that I had told me I would take if I ever had pneumonia again. So I have had no more pneumonia nor any other sickness to speak of since I came here.

I came to Captain Turner's home on Turner's Creek. His name was Richard Bushrod Turner; an old Indian warrior, he was with Captain Parkhill when the Indians shot and killed him. Captain Turner said they took Captain Parkhill's body to the mainland and buried it; then burned a big lot of timber over his grave to keep the Indians from finding it and digging it up. Captain Turner was a good man and lived on his place on the river I think about two years after I came here.

He and I worked at farming, growing cabbage, eggplants and cucumbers, bananas, etc., and I tried to clear up a small island up Turner's River, which is called now and known as McKinney's Island. I cleared up about half of it and grew some fine bananas and some fine cabbage and some fine cauliflower and tomatoes. I had one tomato plant on the island that grew 15 feet across and I often picked a 10-quart bucketful of good tomatoes at one picking. They were a small variety of tomatoes but an unusually heavy bearer. The strange part of the thing was I thought I would make some forward cabbage plants for next year to set and the rainy season and hot sun on the land killed it dead; it would not grow a cabbage plant or tomato big enough to transplant at all. They turned white and would not grow so I quit the thing.

I chopped wood, caught a few fish and oysters all for the Key West market. We had a chance to ship those products about once a month and we could get our mail from Key West once a month; sometimes it would be six weeks. That looked kind of tough for a gentleman of my caliber that had been used to mail twice a day. So it put me to studying some and I stirred up my think tank. There were only Cap-

tain Turner, myself and wife and two Catholic families on Chokoloskee Island; so I kept on stirring up my think tank and wanted to
see if there was not some way to get out of this trouble or make conditions a little better.

By and by a family or two more came down from up coast,—Mr.
G. Lopez and Mr. George Howell,—and we began to talk about
school. Eventually we got Monroe County to furnish a school for the
seven or eight pupils. Mr. Lions, an elderly Irishman, was in the community and he taught the school in an old house. After that Mr.
George Howell and I built a palmetto shack to use for school pur-
poses and Miss Annie Metcalf taught in the palmetto shack. It was so
hard to get Monroe County to do anything for us in that line, but we
hung on until it was declared that this neck of the woods belonged to
Lee County and they did a better part for us.

All this time I was working at vegetables and catching some red
birds to send to the Key West market; they were worth from 50 cents
to $1.25. I chopped wood and got $3 per cord for it. I hunted alligators and sold the skins for 50 to 60 cents each for 7-foot lengths; now
they are $3.50 each.

In all this working for a living Mr. G. Lopez and I went plume bird
hunting and killed a lot of egrets and alligators. I often think of one
morning; we had just finished skinning 15 or 20 alligators and had
dropped the carcasses in the water alongside the boat. Mr. Lopez
told me to go and get some water to make coffee. The 'gators were
thickly drifted against the boat, and I told him about it, that I did not
think the water very desirable for coffee. He said, "Push them out of
the way." So I pushed the 'gators out of the way a little so I could get
the bucket down between them. I got a bucket of clear water and we
had some very good coffee. I thought if he could stand it I could also.
We ate our lunch and went to the birds' nests a few hundred yards
away and began to shoot the mother birds and kill them from their
young; then the crows would go and take the eggs and the young
birds and carry them away to eat them. It looked too hard for me. I
decided that I did not think it was doing God's service, and I never
went on that kind of a hunt any more.

A long while after this I went up Turner's River and cleared up a lot of land not far from where the Tamiami Road is now. It was an old place that an Indian had deserted. I cleared 5 or 6 acres there and planted a lot of pumpkins and some sugar cane, rice and cabbage. But it was a failure,—too wet and too hot in the summer and it killed my stuff. So I called the place Needhelp. I suppose Mr. Barron Collier will help it some time or other in the distant future.

We got so far along that we needed a post office so badly that I got to thinking about it and talked it to what few settlers there were. They laughed at me, and called me a fool to think that I could do a thing like that. They said that Captain Phister tried to get a post office when he was living here part of his time, and he was a moneyed man and had a whole lot of sense, but he failed to get a post office for this neck of the woods. Nevertheless that did not cut any ice with me if I was the biggest fool in the Ten Thousand Islands. I drew up a petition, carried it around to all the folks that I could hunt up and by hard pleading and coaxing I succeeded in getting nearly a dozen signers. I sent it in to the postal department and they would not establish an office for me or give us a mail route to any place unless I would work at the thing a year and try to get the mail off to Key West every chance and chances were very scarce. I was of the kind that do not know much about that word fail; it had been torn out of the book I was studying in those days. So I put my shoulder to the wheel and the department sent me a mail pouch and stamping outfit after I had named the office. I called it Comfort and I was commissioned as postmaster of the post office Comfort on the 13th day of February, 1891, by Postmaster General J. M. Wanamaker. So I began hunting up someone to carry the mail, and I found from time to time some boat going to Key West. I would take my little skiff boat and my mail bag key and dating stamp along and if I found anybody that wanted to have a letter mailed under the Comfort stamp I just got out my dating material, unlocked my mail bag, put his letter in and went on my way. It was sometimes three weeks before I got a boat that was going over to Key West with a load of wood or vegetables, and I had to row my boat up to Allen's River [now the Barron] two or three times, sometimes, before I found when the boat was going to sail with my mail.

I began this about the 13th day of February, 1891, and in 1892 the department let a contract for a route to Key West. I think Capt. Will Gardner got the contract. So we had accomplished something anyway while the cancellations amounted to from $5 to $8 per quarter. I felt that I had disappointed those folks that called me such a fool.

The office was called Comfort for about eight months when some smart Aleck came along and one of those swamp angels [mosquitoes] lit on his topknot. He just declared that Comfort was not a proper name for the office when a gentleman of his caliber was annoyed by the swamp angels like that. So we decided to have the name changed to Chokoloskee. I spelled it for the department and asked them to spell it; they wrote me to spell it myself like I wanted it and I had to spell it myself. It is, of course, an Indian name and means in the American language "Old Home."

I feel like I am the daddy of Chokoloskee. There was a gentleman from New York a few years ago here and he asked me about this name. I told him why it was called "Chokoloskee," and I told him I was the daddy of that name. He had his kodak along and wanted me to stand for a snapshot, so that he could say that he had a picture of the daddy of Chokoloskee. I told him to send me a copy; when he went back to New York he mailed me a copy marked to "The Daddy of Chokoloskee, Fla."

Some of our best friends said that it was spelled wrong, but it has stood the test for a long time. So I received another commission as postmaster at Chokoloskee, issued by J.M. Wanamaker, dated the 14th day of October, 1892.

Mr. G.W. Storter tried to get me to throw up Chokoloskee and move the thing to Everglades. I told him, "No, we can get you an office up there at Everglades." So he drew up a petition and with my official recommendation and signature at the top, we soon got him a post office at Everglades. So I felt that I was helping someone all along the line.

I find that I was reappointed postmaster at Chokoloskee on the 15th day of August, 1900, by W.S. Haumberger, assistant postmaster general. I have served as postmaster nearly 20 years, first and last.

Part 3

You know last trip I only got the post office to working on time. Now I got busy on the school.

I owned or called a little scrap of this island on the southeast side mine, and it joined my Catholic neighbor. I tried to get him to agree to "Let's give a lot to the school folks," but he just bluntly refused and told me he did not want any school, because it made grand rascals out of the people. Of course that put a quietus on that special spot of land for that time, but it did not put a quietus on my efforts.

In the course of time and human events, I got in correspondence with a friend up in Bradford County, Florida (Mr. Garland Shealy). He had married a niece of mine and I got them to buy out my Catholic friend and me, and Mr. Shealy gave a school lot at the place where it is now, which is a very desirable one. We have been lucky enough to have a school there every year.

While working at this thing I was working on my little house and after a few months more I bought the home where I am now living from Mr. John Howard and went to work getting out timbers in the cypress swamp near Needhelp. I worked many days and weeks there, standing in water from six to twelve inches deep, splitting out boards from cypress logs and hewing out square timbers; then rafted them down Turner's River to Chokoloskee Bay and across to my home place on the northwest side of the island.

I remember quite well one morning, when I was standing in the water trying to make a cup of coffee, on the 26th day of June, 1900, I heard some noise that appeared to be some person knocking on a log. I learned later that it was a black bear pounding on an old rotten log with his fist, tearing it up to get some grubs out of it. By and by I heard some splashing in the water, similar to a person wading. There were high ferns all through the swamp and I took up my ax and stood perfectly still. In a moment or two more I saw the ferns begin to shake and a big black bear stuck his head out, coming nearly direct for me. He got up within about 20 feet of me where a palmetto log was lying, and he put both of his front feet on it and began to look at the surroundings. I caught his eye look off from me and I cast my ax at him with all my might. It passed just under his head and dropped into the water just beyond.

He thought that he might not be welcome, so he humped over the log and went in a bear trot towards the river. Thus I escaped having a bear fight. If my ax had struck him in the side of the head and stopped him just a little, I would have jumped on him with my ax and we would have had a racket right there by our own selves in that swamp.

Well, some old boys say, "Why did you not shoot him?" Bless your life, boys, I had no gun at all. I just worked all day in that water, and tied up a little boat sail I had in a tree, coiled up in it wet at night and slept well; got up before sunrise, made me a little fire on top of a stump to make some coffee, fry some meat and cook some grits. Then I ate my breakfast and went to work on those old cypress logs, sawing, chopping, hewing and riving out [splitting] boards to cover the house I am now living in and under those same boards. I nailed them on myself, about 1901.

During all this time I was running a little merchandise business in a very small way, and a little vegetable farming also.

When I was trying to sleep in that thick swamp I would often hear strange noises of birds and some coons, and other screams which might have been panthers, but I had no gun and felt perfectly safe as at home. The hoot owl was great company; he would scream out in the dead, silent hours and almost make one shiver to think about what fine, agreeable neighbors he had. I very rarely saw a rattlesnake. I killed a few, just for meanness, when I was about the age of 20 and used to carry one or two of those rattlers' fangs in my pocket to pick my teeth with; but, thank the Lord, I have no teeth now.

When I was about 18 I took a notion that I wanted to study some on obstetrics and studied on that line a whole lot. I bought some books and lined up on that profession and medicine also. I suppose, if I had gone to medical college I would have made a quack doctor or something else, but I did not get the chance. When I went to Texas I fell in company and roomed with an English doctor who gave me permission to overhaul all his books, recipes, etc. I picked up a lot from them and when I came home I did quite a lot of pill making for the neighbors with fine results. I did not have to make any bread pills as the English doctor told me he used to do when he was practicing in London. He said when he ran out of pills sometimes he would make some bread pills, go to his patient, administer a dose and tell the patient they would act in a few hours. When he called again and asked about his pills, the patient told him they acted fine and that he was improving fast. That showed him that it was all in the mind and suggestion which is right at this day and time. If the patient has confidence in the doctor he can use bread pills and suggestions that will do the work.

When I was 23 years old I had my first experience and practice in midwifery on Feb. 6, 1873, and have been practicing every now and then since. I have been here in this neck of the woods over forty years and have had quite a lot of calls far and near and have had good success,—never lost a case, but had some very hard cases and had to work hard, but had only one difficult case where I had to do some surgical work and I came out successful to the finish.

I always made it a point to be of some use in the settlement wherever I located. I extracted a lot of teeth for black and white and Indians since I lived here. I have had over fifty years' practice in midwifery. My name was registered in the Board of Health office in Jacksonville many years ago, and is still there, but since we have some doctors not far away I have but few calls, while at the same time I am just as competent and just as able as formerly to do the work.

In 1910 we had a fearful storm in October with high water. There was not more than one-tenth of this island out of water. Things looked real scary; the folks all bunched up on the highest places, some went to the high mounds and a lot went to the school house, but the water ran over the schoolhouse floor ten or more inches and Mr. C.T. Boggess was lifted off of his feet and dropped down in such a manner that the fall knocked one of his ankles out of joint. The folks carried him to an old house, laid him down in the floor and sent over for me to see if I could do him any good. There were three or four men there, but they had tried no plans to get him out of his trouble. After a hard tussle breasting the stiff wind I reached the old house, told one of the men to hold Mr. Boggess' knee down with his hands, while I grabbed hold of his ankle and jerked it back into position instantly. I gave them some advice and he soon got able to get along on both feet again.

If there were to come a storm like the 1910 storm again, the little city of Everglades would look like a last year's eagle nest that had been wrecked. But such things happen very seldom here, while we expect it each full moon in August, September and October. We always pray for it to be vetoed if it is scheduled; we always hope and pray for the best whether we get it or not.

We come up to the point now where we thought we needed a church and a lot of preaching; so we went to work, got signers to a petition, bought lumber and I gave part of my domain for a church lot. I bought a bell for it and furnished nails to build it. The folks soon put up the house and we have had a lot of preaching done since, but it seems that it has not done as much good as it might have done. Lots of folks do not care whether they go to heaven or not; they think here is good enough for them. I once had an old friend who said he always praised God and the devil, too, because he did not know in which hands he would fall into. It might be a good idea.

Now, ladies and others and gentlemen and others, I think I will wind up this chapter. See if you can't chip it out and make you a pocket piece of it. But don't forget that I will let you hear of me once a week right on for a long time yet. I feel that I have not been in anyone's way and hope to hear from some of you folks and see some of you in the sweet by and by. Be good now, all of you; if you can't be good, be as good as you can. Call when you can and see how I look and do at home.

I received a nice letter from a lady in Illinois ten days ago and a nice letter from a gentleman in Rock Island, Ill., this week. I am glad to hear from these good folks. It has a boosting tendency anyway.

Thank you for your attention, and goodbye.

C. G. McKinney.

Sage of Chokoloskee Dies Suddenly

It came as a great shock when we learned on Monday of this week of the death of C.G. McKinney which occurred Saturday morning, Oct. 16, 1926, on the dock at Everglades where he had gone with his motor boat for a load of freight for his store at Chokoloskee. Under the nom de plume of "Progress" Mr. McKinney had served faithfully as correspondent for the *Eagle* for nearly twenty years, rarely ever missing an issue, and by his optimism, quaint philosophy and dry humor had become widely known, his Chokoloskee notes being often quoted by other papers. His life as a pioneer had been an eventful one and several months ago we suggested that he write his biography for the *Eagle*, which he accordingly did, little thinking that publication of its last chapter would be almost coincident with the close of his earthly career.

Mr. McKinney was hard hit by the hurricane, his little store being demolished with considerable loss of stock. The real cause of his death is not known at this writing, but it is believed that he had over exerted himself in endeavoring to set things to rights after the storm. He is survived by a widow, a son and daughter living at Chokoloskee who have our heartfelt sympathy in their hour of bereavement.— Editor's Note, *American Eagle*, Estero, Fla., October 20, 1926.

Chokoloskee Mourns

"Progress" has departed. The correspondent of Chokoloskee has written his last news items. He was only an aged and obscure store-keeper of an unknown village on the edge of the Everglades, yet thousands who have read his unique reports and observations will feel a pant of sorrow at his death.

C.G. McKinney was born in Sumter County, Georgia, 79 years ago, August 8, 1847. He served in Florida in the Civil War. He lived some time in Columbia and Alachua Counties, and first opened the High Springs Post Office. He moved to Chokoloskee, in the Ten Thousand Islands of the lower Gulf Coast, 40 years ago, and was later its first postmaster.

For many years he has been sending in all the local news to the Estero *American Eagle* every week except some weeks when he did not have a postage stamp. Writing for the *Eagle* under the name of "Progress," he has also corresponded for some younger papers in that section as "Optimist." This year he wrote his interesting autobiography for the *Eagle*.

He had his general store and warehouse on the bayfront at the foot of Easy Street, the main street of the island settlement, and despite his age he made frequent trips to Everglades, five or six miles up the bay, alone in his rowboat to get his freight. A few months ago he got an "off and on" motorboat. It was at Everglades last Saturday that "Progress" dropped dead on the dock. His body was taken back to his island home for burial. His wife, his son, his daughter, and many readers mourn him.

"Progress" has moved at least to a more Elysian Isle than Choko-loskee, one where no school teachers are needed, where there is no lack of preachers, where there are no disciples or Indians drinking low bush lightning, where there are no swamp angels buzzing and biting.

After the September hurricane he wrote, "Our warehouse was washed away and we sustained a heavy loss for a poor creature who had nothing much to lose. The Good Book tells us that he that has must lose, while he that has not cannot lose, so we are feeling good over having little." But in his last news letter he admitted, "We are feeling kind of blue in spots from overheat in working at the wreckage and other troubles."—*Collier County News,* Naples, Fla.

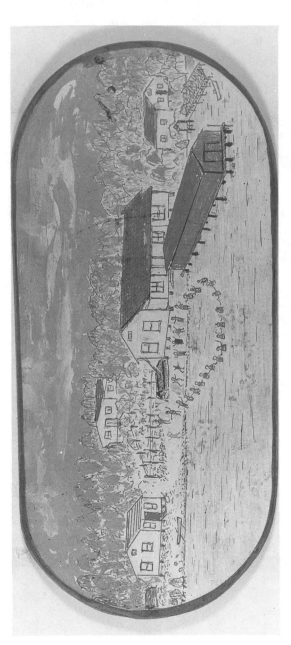

Written on the back of this drawing: "This is the first church and first baptising on Chokoloskee Island, 1913, at Mr. McKinney's landing—his store and home. About 40 or more was baptised this day. It was a great day I will never forget. I was in this group, my mother, one sister, and one brother. Most of the ones that was in this group is gone now. 69 years have so quickly gone but these precious memories still live on. This picture is still fresh in my mind. This was the greatest revival that ever swept through the 10 Thousand Islands. Everybody was stirred and concerned, even Infidels . . . Brother Tom Crews was the minister that baptised us that day. . . . Mrs. McKinney was the first convert. Mr. McKinney didn't take any part in this affair, but he would go to church now and then, especially when a new preacher would come, so he could have some news for the paper. He would listen and fan with his turkey wing while he was in the church. As soon as the altar call was given he was ready to go. He was a nice old man, everybody liked him. I REMEMBER.—ROB STORTER."

Appendix 3 / Captain Totch's recipe for Chokoloskee Chowder

This recipe is something like Manhattan clam chowder, made with tomatoes instead of milk. My chowder can be made either with fish (grouper, red snapper, redfish, snook, and pompano are especially delicious), clams (fresh or canned), shrimp, or crawfish ("Florida lobster"), or with fish and shellfish mixed together. This recipe comes from over 100 years of research in Chokoloskee Bay, so please follow it carefully.

To "do it right," start by putting on 3 large-size potatoes, peeled and diced—in a 4-quart pot with plenty of water. While the potatoes are boiling, dice a 3 × 3-inch piece of thin, lean salt pork into half-inch squares. (Lean is usually hard to find; if you can't come up with it, cut what you need from the lean part of a larger piece of fatback—the fatter it is, the more it should be fried out.) If you don't like or can't eat pork, try a little butter.

With a heavy fry-pan, start frying out the salt pork. Soon there'll be a little oil from it; then add 2 orange-size onions (sliced or diced), and immediately add a more than normal amount of black pepper (the hot oil kills the burning in the pepper, leaving a good flavor). Also, if garlic is desired, add several chopped cloves with the onions (or add later with the tomatoes).

Stirring often, fry both the onions and pork down to about half-size or less. (Scorching 'em a little won't hurt; in fact, it'll color the chowder a bit.)

With the potatoes about half-done, add one 28-ounce can of whole tomatoes, chopping them a bit and taking out the hard core. Also, add the fried pork and onions (including the oil from the pork) in with the potatoes.

When the potatoes are done as I like them, the square corners will begin to become round, making a thicker soup. Skim off the foam floating on top and add the fish (or whatever), but only for about 5 minutes' good boiling time (or maybe a little more).

Some like a lot of fish in the chowder, while others like myself like less (maybe 1½ pounds). I prepare fillets small, about hand-size (some like 'em diced). (The next time you warm up the chowder, which to me is when it tastes best, the fish will fall apart anyway.)

The kind of fish really doesn't matter that much. Try for a more solid fillet, like grouper or red snapper. (A large pompano makes a wonderful chowder if you can afford it or find one.)

Cooking time after you add the fish (or the shellfish, or the two together) is about 5 minutes, maybe a little more, but watch it: The fish will fall apart right away after getting done; the clams, shrimp, or crawfish will get tougher the longer you cook 'em.

For clam chowder with canned clams, 1 6½-ounce can of minced or whole clams will do, but I like 2 cans. Using fresh clams, chop 'em up a bit—the same for crawfish or large shrimp.

Appendix 4 / Citation for a Bronze Star

Headquarters 87th Infantry Division
APO 448, U.S. Army
25 June 1945

I. *AWARD OF THE BRONZE STAR MEDAL. Pursuant to authority contained in AR 600-45, dated 22 September 1943, as amended, a Bronze Star Medal is awarded to the following:*

Loren G Brown, 34838476, Sergeant, Company L, 347th Infantry Regiment, for heroic achievement in action against an armed enemy of the United States near Saalfield, Germany, on 18 April 1945. Sergeant Brown's machine gun squad was supporting the advance of the riflemen in the platoon when they were pinned down by exceptionally heavy machine gun fire. Realizing that the enemy machine guns would have to be silenced if the company was to take its objective, Sergeant Brown crawled forward, reaching a position from which he could throw hand grenades into the enemy emplacement. He succeeded in killing four of the gun crew and thus made it possible for the platoon to proceed with the attack. His courageous action typifies the highest standards of the armed forces of the United States. Entered military service from Florida.

BY COMMAND OF MAJOR GENERAL CULIN:
Grant Layng
Colonel, G.S.C.,
Chief of Staff